The Making of the Diplomatic Mind

THE

Making

OF THE

Diplomatic Mind,

The Training, Outlook, and Style
of United States Foreign Service Officers,

1908-1931

———

BY ROBERT D. SCHULZINGER

Wesleyan University Press

MIDDLETOWN, CONNECTICUT

The publisher gratefully acknowledges the support of the publication
of this book by The Andrew W. Mellon Foundation.

Library of Congress Cataloging in Publication Data

Schulzinger, Robert D., 1945-
    The making of the diplomatic mind.

    Bibliography: p.
    1.   United States. Department of State. Foreign Service.
I. Title.
JX1706.Z5S38   353.008'92   75-15790
ISBN 0-8195-4086-2

Manufactured in the United States of America
First edition

To my parents

Contents

Acknowledgements

SINCE the time I first conceived this study of the professional outlook of a dedicated, troubled, and amusing group—the first generation of American career diplomats—I have accumulated large intellectual debts. My friends Henry Abelove, Elizabeth Bazell, Frederick Cooper, Leonard Dinnerstein, Bruce Kuklick, Craig Liske, and Leo Ribuffo spent long hours listening to me talk about professional diplomacy and reading drafts of the book. Gaddis Smith, who supervised my doctoral dissertation at Yale University, encouraged me to begin this study and criticized the earliest, roughest versions. Walter LaFeber read the book manuscript and showed how to improve its readability.

Yale University and the Graduate School of International Studies of the University of Denver provided an atmosphere conducive to work and, more tangibly, generous financial support. The G. S. I. S. also supplied me with a student research assistant, Louis Ortmayer, who compiled many of the statistics in the book.

The staffs of the libraries of Columbia University, Harvard University, Yale University, the University of Wyoming, and the Hoover Institution on War, Revolution, and Peace and those of the Library of Congress and the National Archives often went beyond the call of duty to help.

Denver, Colorado   ROBERT D. SCHULZINGER
May, 1975

The Making of the Diplomatic Mind

Introduction

AMERICAN career diplomats led frivolous lives in the nineteenth century. Senior diplomatic posts went to a president's political friends, few of whom knew or cared about diplomacy. Occasionally, effective and respected representatives like George Bancroft, John Lothrop Motley, or James Russell Lowell came along to redeem the honor of American diplomacy, but these luminaries did not regard their political mission as their lifework. Indeed, they found abundant leisure to pursue their literary careers while serving the government abroad.[1]

In the junior ranks, salaries for diplomatic secretaries were so low (or even nonexistent) that only rich men could afford to enter the Foreign Service. Many well-to-do youths drifted into diplomacy for want of something better to do, but their workday in the Service hardly excited them. American missions and consulates overseas were open from 10 A.M. until noon, and then, following a two-hour lunch break, from two until four in the afternoon. Even during such abbreviated hours, junior secretaries had to struggle to keep busy. They copied dispatches into large volumes for their chancery's archives, while dreaming of doing important political work. But unfortunately, politicians seldom asked diplomats for advice on foreign policy, and career diplomats almost never found themselves appointed to ambassadorships, ministries, or high posts in the Department of State.

Henry James once complained that America's lack of a professional Foreign Service was part of her cultural barrenness. In James's beloved England the Diplomatic Corps, the Church, the Navy, the Army, and the National Universities formed an establishment which gave calm direction to national affairs. Without those traditional institutions, Americans, according to James, were naïvely optimistic about culture and politics, and the

United States experienced more social turbulence than did England.[2] When American diplomats compared their own insignificance to the wide authority European governments granted their diplomats, they became profoundly jealous and depressed. Few of the young men who entered American Foreign Service work in the late nineteenth century remained diplomats for long. Those who stuck it out vowed to improve the prestige and effectiveness of their Service.

In the first quarter of the twentieth century, through the efforts of an ambitious group of diplomats, consuls, and businessmen, the United States acquired a professional Foreign Service. The founders of the new organization hoped it would bring Jamesian stability to American foreign policy. The Foreign Service reformers wanted to place diplomacy under the guidance of serene and imperturbable professionals. But the diplomats' hopes to dominate the formation of foreign policy failed. Their lack of success was due partly to the unrealistic nature of their goal. Career diplomats were by no means the only people interested in foreign policy: nongovernment officials, politicians, and other civil servants contended with the career diplomats for a say in the conduct of foreign affairs. Competition by itself, however, does not explain the diplomats' inability to achieve prominence in the making of foreign policy. Their political failure also resulted from the contradictory attitudes they developed toward their own service, American society and politics, and the international system as a whole.

Foreign Service officers developed their inconsistent beliefs about their profession over the course of twenty-five years. Like most collective outlooks, the diplomatic mind was the product of compromises and accommodations. The diversity within the diplomats' outlook appealed to a variety of outside interests—those of the educators, businessmen, and politicians who controlled the destiny of the Foreign Service. Moreover, their inconsistencies represented an attempt on the part of the two branches of the service, the diplomatic and the consular, to resolve, or at least reduce, their fundamental differences over the nature of Foreign Service work. In sum, the basic incoherence of the Foreign Service outlook left its diplomats and consuls intellectually uneasy. Their troubled spirit, in turn, prevented political leaders from granting Foreign Service officers complete independence in foreign policy work, because the politicians never knew precisely where the Foreign Service officers stood.

A Nonprofessional Career

Ambiguous definitions of professionalism lay at the root of the intellectual difficulty of the career Foreign Service officers. At the turn of the century the two branches of the Foreign Service of the United States, the diplomatic and the consular, were burdened with two distinct and unfavorable public images: diplomats were regarded as effete, ineffectual, and snobbish, whereas consuls had a reputation for uninspired drudgery. In the nineteenth century the various duties of the two branches had contributed to the difference in their public reputations. Americans followed European practices in separating diplomats and consuls. Traditionally European foreign offices had carefully divided the political work of high policy—the job of diplomats—from the economic and social activities of consuls. In European practice, diplomats were accredited to heads of state or government in foreign countries, while consuls presented their credentials to foreign offices. Also, diplomats were stationed in capitals and did the work of their *governments,* whereas consuls resided in other cities as well, and attended to the needs of their country's *private citizens,* offering them advice on local business conditions, protecting their interests and property, standing by them when they ran foul of the local law, and handling immigration. In Europe and America diplomatic work came to be considered grand but a trifle melodramatic, consular duties useful but dull. Since Americans in the late nineteenth century thought their overseas interests to be predominantly economic and social, the consular corps received higher salaries than the diplomats. Money yes, but prestige came harder. Some Americans had the scornful European attitude that consuls were grubbily middle class. However, as American political interests developed in the late nineteenth century, men wanted to join the diplomatic branch and present America's political aims to the sophisticated dynastic diplomats in Europe.[3]

In the decades after 1900, both groups wanted not only to reverse the unfavorable judgment of the public, but to secure job tenure, and each longed for something the other possessed. Diplomats wanted the higher salaries of the consuls, while consuls coveted the easy social grace of the diplomats. Both groups realized that the professions, with their aura of rigorous standards of entry, of a hard intellectual core, and of tight self-government, had gained strength in the United States since the Civil War;[4] they also noted that trained professionals had reaped many of the social rewards of the progressive movement's cult of expertise.[5] In other words, both diplomats and consuls naturally wanted a share of the respect which accrued to the professionals.

Both groups used a type of professionalizing rhetoric when they agitated for a new Foreign Service during and after the First World War. They purposely kept their definitions of professionalism vague, for they realized early in their movement for reform that the adoption of a too-strict definition could entangle them in conflicts with other groups and with each other. Both diplomats and consuls believed that if they defined Foreign Service skills narrowly, as the acquisition of technical knowledge, then foreign affairs specialists of the universities and other government agencies could assert their own claims to conduct foreign policy.[6] For the diplomats the problem of technical knowledge was easily solved. Their general skills gave them whatever rights they possessed to direct high policy, but once technical knowledge was elevated over general ability, the public would regard Foreign Service officers as mere clerks. The problem was more complicated for the consuls. While they had a public reputation for greater technical skill than did the diplomats, that very skill could prove to be their political undoing. If the consuls relied exclusively on technical prowess, they feared they would never rise to positions where they could give general political advice.[7]

Foreign Service reformers, men like Wilbur J. Carr, Tracy H. Lay, Joseph C. Grew, Hugh Gibson, Leland Harrison, Jr., and William Phillips, insisted that politics among nations were so complicated that only a certain type of "expert" could understand them—one who displayed not so much a technical knowledge as *une certaine habitude du monde,* a phrase the Americans borrowed from French Ambassador Jules Jusserand.[8] A successful Foreign Service officer was a self-confident man of the world, a generalist who greeted difficult new situations with unflustered deliberation. And diplomats considered that vague breadth of vision as the essence of democratic professionalism.

Characteristic of the Foreign Service outlook, was a combination of admiration and revulsion for other groups and ideas. American diplomats and consuls both admired and resented European diplomats. The Americans loved the Europeans' smooth practice of diplomacy and longed for the public respect the Europeans enjoyed, but they also believed that the aims of their European counterparts were inferior to American foreign policy goals. The Foreign Service reformers, who had absorbed the notions of the uniqueness of American history and institutions from progressive reformers,[9] argued that the peculiar history of the United States, its lack of a plutocracy and a proletariat, its preoccupation with commerce instead of national glory, made its foreign policy more pacific than that of any European power.

Moreover, Foreign Service officers extended their ambivalent attitudes to other groups of Americans. Diplomats gave lip service to the idea of a democratic foreign policy having popular support. They recognized the need to please the American Congress and courted individual congressmen and senators, but, like many flatterers, they sneered at congressmen among themselves, and were easily alarmed by popular participation in foreign policy. Such attitudes had a bureaucratic logic behind them. In order to convince the Congress to make their jobs secure, the diplomats argued that their aim was to shape a democratic foreign policy that served the interests of the American people, but that only Foreign Service officers, devoting themselves full-time to foreign policy, could define American interests in a complicated, competitive world.

Although diplomats needed assistance in setting up a new Foreign Service, they feared that outsiders wanted to restrict their exclusive control of the new corps. Their touchiness about amateur control took an ironic form in their relations with elected officials. Politicians who presented independent ideas, however well-reasoned, provoked the resentment of the Foreign Service officers, who considered them amateur meddlers; but congressmen, senators, political appointees, and presidents who deferred to the diplomats' superior grasp of foreign affairs won the friendship of the Foreign Service.

The diplomats' attitude toward the constituents of their own Service followed the pattern of obedience to the democratic ideal and contempt for diversity. The reformers argued for higher Foreign Service salaries in order to open the diplomatic field to all qualified Americans, regardless of their economic position. After the reform movement's success in 1924 with the passage of the Rogers Act, the service recruited new members from wider economic and educational backgrounds.[10] At the same time, however, the reformers dedicated themselves to the ideal of a foreign service as a narrow guild, deliberately isolated from the larger American society. Both the democratic and elitist notions were held sincerely by the diplomats, who, aside from important exceptions in the cases of women and blacks, cared little about the source of their recruits. They wanted to recruit men of various backgrounds whom they would train to absorb their own exclusive, aloof attitude regarding the world.

The Foreign Service reformers gained their greatest victory in 1924, when Congress passed the Foreign Service Reorganization Act introduced by Representative John Jacob Rogers of Massachusetts. The law amalgamated the diplomatic and consular branches into a single Foreign Service which assumed the diplomats' vague definition of professionalism. Outwardly, the new Service resembled other professions. Like them, it selected recruits on the basis of their promise for the future rather than their ability to fill a specific job. It required that recruits serve a probationary apprenticeship, resisted lateral entry into the Service, developed a high *esprit de corps*, and insisted on regulating itself.[11] Yet for all its formal professional characteristics, diplomacy did not become a profession in the sense that medicine or law had in the progressive period.

Why is it wrong to think of the Foreign Service created by the Rogers Act as a rigorous profession? The boundaries which distinguish professions from other occupations are not distinct, but there are certain "core criteria" which define an occupation's professional status.[12] Most important among such criteria are a rigorous intellectual formation, some procedure for making certain that staff workers live up to it, and evidence that they have some socially useful goals in mind which can be fulfilled by no other occupation. When these requirements are not met, the professional status of an occupation becomes equivocal.

The Foreign Service that emerged as a result of the Rogers Act was a soft, or equivocal, profession. It differed from other, more rigorous professions in its lack of a persuasive social and intellectual domain which excluded outsiders from Foreign Service work. More rigorous professions like medicine, architecture, the law, or engineering had established distinct objectives and explicit methods of procedure.[13] The competence of the followers of such professions could be publicy assessed by the results of their work in terms of their stated goals and standards. The Foreign Service, unfortunately, lacked that type of solid intellectual core. Its successes and failures were less easily judged by the public, because Foreign Service officers never made clear the precise functions, methods, and goals of their Service, a fact that deliberately kept its function vague so that its officers could play a gentlemanly, generalist role. The professional diplomatic service they sought was not a true profession but a job with secure tenure.

The Convergence of Ideals and Self-Interest

The complex and inconsistent view of diplomatic work extended beyond definitions of a foreign service career to statements about politics. Diplomatic political thought shared many premises with that of other Americans during the progressive era.[14] Several early career diplomats—William Phillips, Lewis Einstein, F. W. Huntington-Wilson, and Henry Fletcher—were personal friends of Theodore Roosevelt and supported his attempts to fashion an active and firm American foreign policy. The professional diplomats detected a convergence of American "ideals" and American "self-interest" that was compatible with Roosevelt's progressive doctrine. They saw the world as a competitive arena in which each state pursued its own self-interest; but while the United States resembled other countries in its self-interest, it differed from them in that its national interest was "unselfish." The peculiar, nonfeudal history of the United States made it the logical candidate to act as the balance wheel of the contentious world system, as America was immune to old dynastic rivalry. Its democratic political development and commercial strength made it the one world power whose interests complemented rather than clashed with those of other states.

Before the First World War, diplomats and the professors of international relations close to them elaborated a theory of world politics which held that some conflict among states was inevitable. Total war, however, could be avoided. The outbreak of hostilities in 1914 surprised the diplomats, but they quickly recovered their self-confidence and, for the next two years, insisted that the United States enter the war on the Allied side. They believed that American intervention demonstrated the unselfish nature of American self-interest, for the nation entered the war as the regulator of the international system. The coming of the war convinced diplomats that the United States needed more than ever the skills of a career Foreign Service of political reporters to predict the next resort to arms.[15]

In the decade after the First World War, Foreign Service officers insisted that the United States pursue a vigorous, independent policy of which they would be the principal directors. In the twenties, diplomats took over the rhetoric of American businessmen, who wished to expand American commerce. The diplomats' advocacy of commercial expansion combined sincere commercial fervor with career self-interest. They argued along the traditional liberal line that the United States, a commercial nation, was more modern than the dynasties of Europe, and insisted that world-wide adoption of American trade principles would diminish international strife and preserve American commercial advantage over other great powers.[16] Moreover, they sincerely believed that a professional Foreign Service helped the United States maintain its world advantage, but their rhetoric regarding trade expansion had another and more selfish motive. They realized how deeply the desire to expand commerce was rooted in the

American people, and they played upon it by advocating a career Foreign Service. Privately, among themselves, diplomats rejected the notion that foreign commerce was the sole purpose of foreign policy, but they were worried by the fact that a portion of the American public maintained this principle. Thus their advocacy of trade expansion helped them to gain popular respect for their profession. Yet diplomats wanted to use their secure rank to regulate great power rivalry as well as advance American commerce. Their lobbying to gain a political end in an era of commercial expansion sharpened their contempt for public opinion.

Career officers of the twenties accepted many of Woodrow Wilson's assumptions about world politics but rejected his political methods. They did not believe that an aroused world public opinion, acting as a moral force, regulated the international system. Indeed, their struggle for career prestige had convinced them that popular opinion was a dangerous source of foreign policy wisdom. Their experience also convinced them that military power was incapable of deterring armed conflict. Instead, they believed that the career Foreign Service was the "first line of defense" against international strife.[17]

The foreign policies that diplomats wanted the United States government to pursue combined contempt for idealists and amateurs with a Wilsonian belief in an American mission to regenerate the world. Far from being moralistic lawyers, the diplomats advanced a theory of international law rooted in the hard facts of world politics. They considered the law of nations the means by which powerful states arranged the world for their own good. Strong nations enjoyed the benefits of regulated international competition from international law. Weak states acquiesced in the law of nations because it made the world predictable. While in the last instance, international law made the world more peaceful, diplomats believed that the road to peace was long and difficult. The career Foreign Service guided the United States along that road.

The professionalization of the United States Foreign Service occurred in the era of the open New Diplomacy, when the old dynastic diplomats were in disarray. The 1920s was a decade of great self-doubt for the European diplomats and of great self-confidence for the Americans.[18] Ironically, the American understanding of diplomatic methods derived from the Europeans. Americans displayed a fondness for the intuitive approach of the world-wise European diplomats. On the other hand, their notion of foreign policy was distinctly American. United States diplomats accepted the European description of their jobs as "the application of intelligence and tact to the conduct of official relations between governments of independent states,''[19] but they claimed that their aims were distinctly American.

American Foreign Service officers divided their loyalties between the international guild of diplomats and their own conception of the United States' national interest. At home they were spokemen for the methods of the Old Diplomacy; abroad, they explained the goals of the commercial, democratic United States. While they considered themselves obliged to teach their countrymen a healthy skepticism about world politics, their mission overseas was to persuade other governments to subscribe to a meliorist vision of world politics.

The career diplomats' outlook was a set of complex, interrelated, and often unrecognized contradictions. But for all its logical flaws, it was professionally satisfying. Their outlook deliberately isolated them from the public at large, but they hoped that such isolation would gain them the public respect necessary to fulfill popular foreign-policy aims. These intellectual inconsistencies were the result of bureacratic developments, political events, and personal clashes. From an explanation of the relations among the structural, political, personal, and intellectual histories of the early years of the American career Foreign Service, an understanding of the diplomatic mind emerges. Such an understanding helps explain the behavior of men who participated in designing American foreign policy during the middle third of the twentieth century.

PART ONE

Pioneering Days

I

Diplomats and Professors
Look at the World, 1900-1931

Diplomatic Life in the Late Nineteenth Century

CRITICS of the Foreign Service of the United States often accused it of being a system of overseas relief for the unemployed sons of the moneyed men of the eastern seaboard. One historian, Arthur M. Schlesinger, Jr., condemned the career service of the years before the Second World War as a "refuge for effete and conventional men who adored countesses, pushed cookies and wore handkerchiefs in their sleeves."[1] Professional diplomats themselves reminisced that in the early years of the twentieth century the Foreign Service was a haven for playboys.[2] This criticism magnified the accomplishments of the reformers, who had to overcome the inertia of the "cookie pushers." Many of the reformers inside the Department of State entered diplomacy with only the foggiest notion of the idea of "career" or "civil service," but they slowly developed an appreciation of the career concept. They learned the diplomatic craft haphazardly, on their own initiative, without guidance from their superiors. They tried to recruit new officers with a serious commitment to a lifetime career, and sought to create orderly ways to train entrants. The professionalization of the Foreign Service became the story of men who had become diplomats in order to escape from boredom, changing themselves and their successors from indolent joy-seekers to serious career officers.

As for their backgrounds these men were invariably from wealthy families, with a disproportionate number of them coming from the East coast, and most of whom were educated at private schools and universities in the United States or Europe.[3] What these bare facts do not disclose was precisely why such men chose to enter the Foreign Service rather than some other profession equally suitable to young men of their circumstances. It was a cliché of progressive reformers that the most talented young Americans of the nineteenth century eschewed careers in public service for more lucrative work in private business.[4] Men who wanted a diplomatic career had to create one.

Many of the first generation of professionals found in the Foreign Service a way to escape from routine and from cloying family relationships. Diplomacy not only offered a change of scenery, but supplied a possibility for a strong commitment to national service. Some of the most successful diplomats entered the Service not because they had previously desired to become overseas agents, but because it was the most socially respectable way they knew of leading a carefree life. Since such men had to overcome strong parental objections to leaving the web of family relationships, merely leaving home as adventurers or men of the world would have created scandal, but having a diplomatic career was respectable.

In one way or another, the first generation of career American diplomats considered themselves exiles from their homes. Either they had grown up outside the United States, or they felt uncomfortable in their birthplaces. They did not share the fascination with the American West which overcame certain rich Easterners afflicted by wanderlust, nor did they choose to soothe their sense of estrangement by adopting a cynical attitude toward home.[5] Rather, they explored the old nations of Europe and met the statesmen of the Old World on their own grounds and on their own terms.

Henry White was one representative of the young Americans who resolved their ambivalent feelings toward their country by becoming successful diplomats. White later lent great moral support, if not much actual energy, to the cause of Foreign Service reform.[6] Born in 1850, he came from a wealthy Baltimore family and grew up in comfort in the Maryland countryside in the decade before the Civil War. After the death of his father in 1864, his mother married an English doctor, who decided to educate his stepson in Europe. After two years of study in France, White entered Oxford in 1870, but because of illness, he remained there only one year. For the next eight years White lived in "almost complete idleness" as a country gentleman in England.[7] He would rent a shooting box in the English countryside for six months, and for the other six, would go to London or return to Hampton, Newport, or New York for the social season. While engaged in this social whirl, he acquired a set of English friends who included some of the most promising young politicians of the Liberal and Conservative parties. Cecil Spring-Rice, Henry Asquith, George Nathaniel Curzon, and

Edward Grey were those among his intimates who later helped direct British foreign policy. Such well-placed Englishmen later made his way easier in negotiations. They admired White and found him good company, not because of his intellect or wit, which by all accounts were scant, but because of his common sense, his charm, and his "solid dependability, which led people to call him sometimes, even at that early age, 'good old Henry.' "[8]

White's pleasant round of dinners, dances, shooting parties, and travels continued until 1879, when he married Margaret Stuyvesant Rutherford, the daughter of a wealthy New York physician. Since, immediately after the wedding, she complained that it was improper for an intelligent man of twenty-nine to have no vocation, White decided to seek an appointment as a junior secretary in some overseas American mission. There he hoped to find the dignity of a position which would enable him to convert "all his previous training—his travels, his knowledge of different countries, his acquaintances with the English and French character, which otherwise might have been mere luxury—into an admirable preparation for a future career."[9]

His choice of diplomacy as a career might have seemed less bold had he been by nationality the upper-middle-class Englishman he was by inclination. By the late nineteenth century, Great Britain's Foreign Service was already a professional body. It had standard entrance requirements and a recognized procedure for in-service training and promotion. Once appointed, a professional diplomat for Great Britain knew he would be assigned to a mission in which his superiors would teach him the art of negotiations, keep track of his progress, and make annual reports on him to the Foreign Office. Presumably, promotion was based on ability, and tenure in office was secure from changes in political administration.[10]

White's entry into the diplomatic branch of the American Foreign Service was made possible by a political favor. One of the Maryland senators, a friend of his mother, recommended him to Secretary of State William M. Evarts for the job of second secretary at the American legation in London in 1880. White feared that, since he was a Republican, his job would go to a member of the other party as soon as the Democrats gained the presidency. He was also likely to lose his job if another Republican became president, for diplomatic secretaries were expected to submit their resignations upon change in administration. Nevertheless, White went to London, hoping something might turn up to keep him employed.

For most young secretaries the political forces which effectively limited their tenure to slightly more than three years caused no real hardship.[11] Often they did their diplomatic work for no pay, as private secretaries of ministers who recruited them personally. They did not consider diplomacy their lifework; rather, it was a useful means to gain experience as well as friends to assist them later on, when they would engage in politics or private business.[12] White, however, represented a new kind of entering diplomat, since he intended to make a career of the Foreign Service. The training and contacts he hoped to gain during his years in the service he believed would help him in diplomacy, not in his private affairs. He entered determined to learn diplomatic methods from his American superiors, if they had anything to teach him, or from his colleagues in the more professional services of Europe, if they did not.[13]

After a few years in the London legation, White became disturbed at the difference in quality between the American and European diplomats. The Americans seemed timid and insecure, while members of the British and French Foreign Services were efficient and self-confident. He also became alarmed at the possibility of wasting his efforts at turning his gentlemanly accomplishments into a diplomatic advantage. Moreover, White believed he was likely to be dismissed as soon as the Arthur administration was ended. He became convinced that the generally low level of American Foreign Service personnel was due to the impermanence of diplomacy as a career. He therefore resolved, in 1883,

> to become the nucleus, if possible, of a permanent service. Such an idea was considered chimerical by all my friends, but I had a feeling it would be possible for the United States to have, as the other leading powers of the world had then, a non-partisan . . . service, to which appointment should be made on the basis of fitness only.[14]

Luckily for White, his political friends saved him from falling victim to the spoils system when Grover Cleveland took office in 1885. They told the new Secretary of State, Thomas F. Bayard, what a good job White had done in London, appealed to Bayard's desire to bolster the quality of American overseas representatives, and persuaded him to retain White in London.

White's early experience in the Foreign Service set a pattern of uneasiness in his home life, emulation of Europeans, desire for public service, and unhappiness over the poor quality of American overseas staffs which characterized other men who entered the diplomatic branch before World War I. For a few, like White, the low caliber of the American Foreign Service they entered encouraged them to become reformers committed to improving it. Those who followed this path became the leaders of the reform movement. But many more of them "fell into" diplomacy, hoping it might prove to be a rewarding career, and when they encountered boring work and a mediocre service, they abandoned the diplomatic branch.

An example of the type who failed to find the rewarding career he had expected in the diplomatic service was Henry White's half-brother, William H. Buckler.[15] The son of Henry White's mother and her second husband, Buckler was educated by his mother during the family's European travels in the 1870s. Fifteen years younger than White, he entered Trinity College, Cambridge, in 1887, completed a four-year course in history and law, and returned to Baltimore to enter the University of Maryland's law school in 1892. After finishing in 1895, Buckler engaged in private practice for ten years; but since he had no heart for the daily routine of a civil practice, he began studying Roman law and archaeology, and spent the year 1898 writing a book on *The Torts of Lunatics*. However, the Baltimore of the 1890s, which H. L. Mencken considered an exciting place for a boy, proved boring and constraining for a thirty-five-year-old lawyer. More depressing still, Buckler believed he was too well-educated for the work he was doing.[16]

In 1906 he asked his half-brother, who was at that time United States Ambassador to Italy, to find him a diplomatic post. White, who was on good terms with President Theodore Roosevelt, asked him to appoint Buckler secretary to the Special United States Envoy to Spain to attend the marriage of King Alphonso XIII to Princess Ena of Battenberg. This mission, which lasted only a month, got Buckler away from the stodginess of his Baltimore law office and whetted his appetite for more diplomacy. The next year, again through the intercession of White, the State Department offered Buckler the job of secretary to the Minister in Madrid. Although he had longed for a change from Baltimore, he found his new job deadening. The duties of the legation staff consisted mainly in taking the Minister's calling card round to all the other diplomats and acting as guide for an occasional visiting American dignitary. In the three years he worked in Madrid, there was never enough business to occupy the Minister, Buckler, and their staff for more than three hours a day. In 1909, having decided that diplomacy was rotting his mind, and having little desire to reform the Service and make it more professional, he quit in disgust after his last three years of enforced idleness. Buckler had hoped to find excitement, intellectual stimulation, and the chance to be a respected servant of the government; instead, he found himself involved in trivial labor, which went unappreciated in Washington and unnoticed by the public. He therefore left the Spanish mission to pursue

his interest in archaeology, joining the Johns Hopkins faculty as an ar-
chaeologist in 1909, and returning to government service only during the
First World War, when President Wilson sent him on a special mission to
London to report on the wartime attitude of the British Left.[17]

The easy pace of diplomatic life, which had so offended Buckler,
appealed to other wealthy young men who were looking for some type of
public service that demanded neither fierce competition nor great physical or
intellectual stamina. Lloyd Carpenter Griscom, a future United States Ambassador to Japan and Italy, entered the diplomatic branch in order to find
excitement at court, while at the same time conserving his health. Griscom
had deep family roots in the Quaker society of Philadelphia. His great-
grandfather was a Biddle, and his father a Philadelphia steamship magnate
engaged in the China trade, whose closest friends were wealthy Philadelphia
gentlemen.[18] Griscom attended private schools in Philadelphia and Switzerland and entered the University of Pennsylvania in 1887, at the age of
fourteen.[19]

As a young man, Griscom was not only awed by his father's business
acumen, but felt intimidated by the pious deference his father commanded
from employees, servants, and family. As a result, he decided while in
college that a career in the steamship business would condemn him to a meek
existence in his father's shadow.[20] Griscom's future plans were unclear
upon his graduation in 1891 from the Wharton School of Finance and
Commerce at Pennsylvania. During his undergraduate years he had acquired
a taste for political adventure while a guest at the Washington home of
Pennsylvania Senator Donald Cameron. A poor student until his junior year,
he then transferred from the liberal arts program to the Wharton School,
where a part of the curriculum required trips to Washington to observe the
government in operation. While staying at the home of Senator Cameron,
who at that time was pushing for a federal subsidy for the Griscom Steamship Company, Griscom was introduced to Henry Adams, who immediately
adopted him as a "nephew" and often invited him to lunch. At Adams's table
Griscom became friendly with Cecil Spring-Rice, a junior secretary at the
British legation, who painted a glamourous picture of a diplomatic career.[21]

Griscom caught other glimpses of the romance of diplomacy while on a
round-the-world tour after he graduated from college. On his first stop in
London, the American Minister, Robert Todd Lincoln, took him to a
dazzling diplomatic reception. "I went back to the Bath Hotel that night,"
he reminisced, "so wrought up that for hours I could not sleep. No matter
how successful I might be at the law, I was certain I could not find it as
exciting as diplomacy."[22]

Upon returning to Philadelphia in 1892, Griscom entered the Law School of the University of Pennsylvania to study admiralty law. After one year, he contracted typhoid fever at a resort and nearly died. While delirious, he claimed to have had a vivid dream of himself at a London diplomatic reception. When he had somewhat recovered, his doctor advised him that he was too weak to return to law school; he had to conserve his strength for the next year. "I was at loose ends," he wrote, "when Mrs. Cameron came to the rescue. 'Maybe there's something in that dream of Lloyd's,' she said to my mother, 'why don't you get him into the diplomatic service? Thomas Bayard's packing to go to London and I hear he wants a private secretary. There's no salary, but it would be a marvelous opportunity for Lloyd.' "²³

It was in this haphazard manner that Griscom embarked upon a diplomatic career in 1893. Bayard accepted Griscom as his private secretary, but gave him no work. Since the Minister handled his own personal correspondence and appointments, Griscom, left with nothing to do, asked the first secretary if he could be his clerk. The First Secretary was Henry White, who welcomed the opportunity to teach an ignorant but eager newcomer the art of diplomacy. White's training helped mold Griscom's opinion of diplomats and the society in which they operated. There was little formal business for the two men; so after a four-hour session of work and study, White would take Griscom abroad into London society.²⁴

By September 1894, a year after he had arrived at the embassy, Griscom was thoroughly bored with the court life he had at first found so exciting. Having recovered his health, he left diplomacy and returned to New York to read law at the family firm of Biddle and Ward. But he soon discovered the practice of civil law to be as dull as society. Within a year of his return, he was off to Central America seeking adventure with Richard Harding Davis. It was not until his return from this expedition, in 1896, that Griscom decide he had spent enough time searching for romance, concluding that the many advantages enjoyed by European diplomats—travel, intrigue, stimulating colleagues, and the chance to make foreign policy— accrued to them only because they had conscientiously acquired political skills.²⁵ He therefore applied in 1896 for another diplomatic job as a student interpreter in the consular service in China, where he could learn Chinese and get serious political assignments. Working harder than he ever had before, Griscom became even more convinced in Peking that the glamour of diplomacy came only to professionals. Without superior competence in political and economic analysis and international negotiations, a Foreign Service officer was condemned to boredom and disappointment. By 1896, Griscom had learned that the only way to public approval and esteem in a diplomatic career was to be an officer committed to learn the art of diplomacy.[26]

The early experiences of men like Griscom who became professional diplomats in the late nineteenth century profoundly influenced their attitude toward career diplomacy. Their initial frustrations in a somnolent, unbusinesslike bureau caused many of them to follow William Buckler's course and leave the State Department altogether. Those who remained adopted a pioneering and proprietary air toward the work of reorganizing their Service. They searched for allies who might help them improve their career diplomacy, while at the same time they resisted the efforts of outsiders to control the destinies of the Foreign Service. Diplomats hoped for outside supporters who would advance the cause of professional diplomacy without dominating the Service. At the turn of the twentieth century, diplomats thought they had found just such a group of allies in the American universities.

America as a World Power

In the years immediately following the Spanish American War, several American professors examined international relations and concluded, as had the career diplomats, that the United States needed a new foreign policy and a new Foreign Service. They also noticed that, in the past generation, competition among states had become keener, the chances for a clever nation to gain international preeminence by skillful diplomacy had increased, and the dangers awaiting nations that pursued ineffective foreign policies had worsened. The recent activities of the United States in the Caribbean and the Far East had convinced both diplomats and professors interested in international affairs that a serious study of world politics would benefit their country's foreign policy. Before the First World War only a few scholars undertook a systematic study of international relations, but the war and its aftermath persuaded many more American academics that the United States stood to lose its international influence were the study of world politics to be neglected.[27]

The study of international relations grew until, during the 1920s, it became a thriving academic field of specialization. Students of world politics devoted themselves to training specialists in international affairs and filling bookshelves with consciously sophisticated accounts of the theory and practice of international relations.[28] Such professors as Archibald Carey Coolidge, John Bassett Moore, Paul S. Reinsch, and Ellery C. Stowell befriended some of those who made up the first generation of American professional diplomats, and together the scholars and the Foreign Service officers created a specific outlook on world affairs. Indeed, their understanding of international relations provided intellectual justification for the movement, during and after the First World War, for a professional Foreign Service.

American universities formally acknowledged the academic legitimacy of international studies in the twenties, when several institutions set up separate schools of world politics.[29] The theory of international behavior and American foreign policy taught at these schools had been formulated in the fifteen years before the First World War. During that time, several professors with close ties to the Department of State—Coolidge, Moore, Reinsch, and Stowell, as well as some members of that department itself, notably, Lewis Einstein and DeWitt Clinton Poole—detected an increased fierceness in international rivalry. They argued that competition among states anywhere in the world had wide repercussions, and that the interdependence of the world's regions compelled the United States to pursue an active overseas policy. Their main fear was that other Great Powers might shoulder Americans out of overseas markets, and they worried less about threats to the physical security of their own country. The early theorists suggested concrete policies for the American government to pursue in order to exploit fully the opportunities offered by international commercial competition outside Europe. As a result, the advocates of this moderate program of diplomatic reform influenced, personally or intellectually, an entire generation of Foreign Service officers. The academics and the diplomats elaborated a theory of world politics which explained the reasons for international rivalries, the means by which a naturally competitive state system could be made stable, and the role America and America's professional diplomats could play in assuring the peace of the world, while preserving the interests of the United States. Since their suggestions coincided with those of other men and groups in business and politics who took an active interest in foreign affairs, together their recommendations bore fruit in an active American foreign policy and the creation of a staff of career Foreign Service officers to direct those sophisticated overseas operations.

Paul S. Reinsch, a young professor of political science at the University of Wisconsin, was one of the first scholars after the Spanish-American War to prescribe a new American foreign policy. Thirty years old in 1900, Reinsch had had a brilliant undergraduate career at Wisconsin. He received a law degree in 1894, practiced for two years, and returned to the graduate school at Wisconsin in 1896. He then embarked upon an academic career out of dissatisfaction with the routine of legal work, yet he did not want to isolate himself in academia. His desire to pursue a university career was utilitarian in nature: he wanted to train functionaries who could efficiently administer the social affairs of the nation.[30]

At Wisconsin, Reinsch studied and taught with Richard T. Ely, John R. Commons, Frederick Jackson Turner, Charles Haskins, and Charles McCarthy—men who profoundly influenced the development of his progressive thought. They elaborated the "Wisconsin idea" of graduate education, which aimed at training administrators to apply social science to political problems.[31] Reinsch studied Oriental politics in particular and international relations in general. He applied the model of Ely, Commons, and McCarthy to international affairs,[32] and helped provide American diplomats with a faith in the ability of trained overseas administrators.

In 1900 Reinsch published his doctoral dissertation, *World Politics at the End of the Nineteenth Century: As Influenced by the Oriental Situation,* and in the next twenty years wrote several more books on colonialism and diplomacy,[33] seeking to explain the rise of "national imperialism" and the promise and danger this new development held for the United States. When Woodrow Wilson appointed him Minister to China in 1913,[34] his scholarly work provided the bulk of the intellectual baggage he carried with him to Peking. Through the agency of one of the best of his graduate students, Stanley Kuhl Hornbeck, who served almost continuously in the State Department from 1918 to 1945, Reinsch's thought made its way into the Foreign Service. His writings explained how the United States was compelled to enter the European colonial rivalry while at the same time exerting an uplifting force on imperial statecraft. What he hoped was that trained diplomats could resolve the contradictions between American self-ishness and American disinterest.[36]

Reinsch believed that the end of the nineteenth century marked the culmination of the nationalist movements which had been growing in Europe since Napoleonic times. The twentieth century, he predicted, would be a hundred years of "national imperialism,"[37] during which fully developed states, choking on their own surplus of manufactured products, would contend with one another for the markets of the world's poor areas. National imperialism held either a promise or an illusion of world preeminence. The scramble for colonies and spheres of influence outside Europe and America might produce effects directly contrary to the desired goal of expanding the influence of an individual state. In the drive for preeminence, the relative stability of the European system would be upset, and one state or bloc of nations might grow so powerful as to dominate other Western powers, thus rendering their highly valued national independence and sovereignty nugatory.[38] The rush for overseas possessions also endangered the movement for international law and conciliation, since national imperialism gave rise to chauvinistic feelings within states.[39] The state system needed a balancing force. Reinsch hoped that the United States could both enter the race for preeminence and stabilize the international system.[40] To achieve those inconsistent ends, United States policy required the guidance of skilled overseas officers.

Despite the threat national imperialism posed to international equilibrium, Reinsch had no doubts that the United States should enter the race for overseas influence. He saw industrial concentration proceeding as rapidly in the United States as in Europe, and believed that the United States had to sell its unconsumed surplus abroad or face serious economic dislocations at home. Rising protectionist sentiment in Europe eliminated the advanced countries as potential markets, leaving only underdeveloped areas as suitable trading partners.[41] In order to sell goods to China or Latin America, Reinsch insisted that American traders conduct themselves differently than had their predecessors in the days of the Clipper ships. No longer could Western merchants wait in their boats for wide-eyed natives to paddle out to buy trinkets. Selling in underdeveloped areas now required that the merchant *create* the market by investing in the communications network, which could bring his goods to the interior. To realize her dream of securing foreign markets, America would have to send capital and specially trained administrators overseas to protect the interest of the United States.[42]

Since the movement toward overseas influence was inevitable, Reinsch sought ways to eliminate the dangers of militarism and plutocracy implicit in national imperialism. He argued that the United States should undergo some progressive political reforms before she embarked upon an active foreign policy. As a Wisconsin progressive, with abundant faith in the capacity of education to help men in public life, Reinsch called for the improvement of American politics through an improvement in the quality of public men. "Statesmen," with a profound understanding of the national interest and public needs, should replace "politicians," whose primary concern was the advancement of their party. Trained experts, divorced from politics, should administer public affairs and be in charge of regulating business competition to assure balanced output, steady growth, and social stability.[43]

Reinsch's proposals for domestic reform were part of the general progressive creed of efficiency,[44] and he applied the same principles of domestic administration to the direction of United States foreign policy. Trained, expert diplomats should be placed in charge of encouraging United States business abroad in order that they might prevent national passions from upsetting world equilibrium, since they themselves would understand the dangers of untrammelled nationalism. Nonpartisan, impartial with regard to the claims of various American enterprises, learned in diplomatic history and international law, they would be unlikely to follow the narrow and dangerous path of chauvinism pursued by politicians. Professional diplomatic administrators could best apply international law to international disputes, since they would understand that the purpose of international law was to regulate, not eliminate, competition among states for the mutual benefit of all nations. These trained experts were the means by which a volatile international system could be turned into a stable international order.[45]

Reinsch and subsequent professional diplomats applied his views on Oriental questions to the rest of the world. For whereas Far Eastern problems caught the attention of many articulate Americans around 1900, at the time of the Open Door Notes, the increased tempo of diplomatic crises in Europe after 1905 (the date of *Colonial Government*) tended to direct the focus of serious American interest in international affairs back toward Europe. In the seven years before the outbreak of general war in Europe, an historian with close ties to men in the State Department, Archibald Carey Coolidge, and a young diplomatic secretary, Lewis D. Einstein, each wrote a book on American diplomacy,[46] attempting to establish the position that the United States should occupy in world politics. They thus influenced an entire generation of professional diplomats.

Coolidge's early teaching career resembled that of Paul Reinsch. Both men were drawn to the study of remote areas of the world in order to provide their students with the knowledge to solve practical problems. In 1910, when Coolidge published his lectures on the United States as a world power, delivered three years earlier at the Sorbonne, he had been teaching Russian, Turkish, and early modern European history at Harvard for seventeen years. He had entered the teaching profession six years after his graduation from Harvard. In the meantime, he had toured the world, studied for brief periods at the Universities of Paris and Berlin, and tried unsuccessfully to obtain the post of Third Secretary at the American legation in St. Petersburg.[47]

Because his parents were Democrats, the Harrison administration rejected Coolidge when he applied for the job. The reasons the young man gave for wanting it comprised a candid assessment of what he hoped to accomplish by pursuing his interest in international relations. His fascination with the history he had studied in college, he explained, had, during his years of foreign travel and study, become ever more focused on contemporary international politics. A brief stint in the diplomatic service, examining events from the inside, might bring him practical understanding and personal contacts, both of which would inform his judgments when and if he attained his life's ambition of being given a professorship of modern history at Harvard. His letter to his father asking for permission to detour through the Foreign Service before returning to Harvard revealed a spirited young man, painfully aware of his own callowness, and hoping that contact with the dynastic diplomats of Europe could provide him with wisdom in short order. Coolidge's tone of self-conscious timidity in the face of the smoothness of European officials found echoes in the experience of other career diplomats.

> After all, it is a great thing to be a Harvard instructor, but it is not the only thing in the world. I want to be that but I also want to be something more, a man of experience and cultivation in the broadest sense of the term. Don't think I am putting an extraordinary value on the insignificant work of undersecretary at an American legation. I know that it is routine duty about trifles, drawing up papers and presenting the minister's visiting card, but I still think it would give me the kind of opportunity I want to meet people of all kinds . . . the different men, if only the younger ones like myself, in the diplomatic service from all parts of the world. I want to get over my shyness and poor manners, to go out into society, to pick up odd bits of information behind the gov'ts [sic] scenes, to get a look at the true inwardness of things.[48]

Once Coolidge had attained some renown as a professor, his friends recommended to President Theodore Roosevelt that he be offered a position in the legation at Constantinople. Because of politics, that post was denied him, and subsequent attempts by his friends to have Presidents William Howard Taft or Woodrow Wilson appoint Coolidge Secretary of State came to naught.[49] The only government post he did hold was his membership in the Inquiry which Colonel Edward House established in 1917 to help in the planning for the postwar period.[50]

Coolidge's influence upon the practitioners of American diplomacy far exceeded anything he himself achieved in government service. At Harvard he taught William Phillips, Joseph C. Grew, and Robert Woods Bliss, and he followed their subsequent successes in the State Department with close attention. He also cultivated the friendship of diplomatically-minded men like Edwin Morgan, Ellis Dresel, Hiram Bingham, and Julius Klein, exchanging frequent visits with them in Washington or Cambridge, and maintaining an active correspondence with them on world affairs from 1907 until his death.[51]

Coolidge's book on America as a world power presented a view of world politics consistent with his murky personal political philosophy of "liberal conservatism."[52] All of his work combined a fundamental faith in "progress"—in other words, the ultimate resolution of social conflict—with a deep appreciation for what his official biographers called the "realities of human nature." This immutable character of political men consisted in their contentiousness and quest for the satisfaction of self-interests. Although the nature of a man's or a state's self-interest was impossible to define precisely, it could be grasped through patient study. Coolidge prided himself on his sharp intuition with regard to the differing psychologies of nations, and he hoped to teach his students to cultivate that same sure grasp. Such knowledge of men and events was the intellectual tool Coolidge used to break the power of destructive self-interest. Men who understood the idea of self- or national interest were, to him, the ones most capable of regulating the competition that resulted from the pursuit of interest.

The principal theme of *The United States as a World Power* was an explanation of how America became a power "which is interested in all parts of the world and whose voice must be listened to everywhere."[53] Following Reinsch, Coolidge explained how growing political unity in the three decades after the Civil War, economic expansion at home, commercial competition from Europe, and the late nineteenth-century scramble for colonial markets had compelled the United States to take an interest in political events everywhere.[54] Coolidge was aware that some Americans, notably the anti-imperialists, had shunned these new global interests as a threat to the nation's republican traditions, but he cautioned against resisting an "inevitable" development in international relations.[55] His study of history had convinced him that the domination of strong states over weak ones was not only inevitable but beneficial to all parties. The alternative to having more powerful nations "arrange many matters without consulting every wish of their numerous smaller brethren" meant international anarchy, analogous to the national impotence which had characterized the politics of Poland in the eighteenth century.[56]

Once Americans recognized their new interests in terms of being a world power, they would clearly be obliged to revise some old and create new foreign policies. Not only would the Monroe Doctrine have to be amended to remove the restrictions on American activity in Europe, but at the same time, the paramount interests of the United States in the western hemisphere would have to be maintained. The revision of this cherished principle of American foreign policy would have to be handled with cautious diplomatic coordination through the European powers. The United States would have to avoid daily involvement in European affairs to prevent the Europeans from claiming the same right in the New World.[57] What Coolidge proposed, then, in keeping with his conservative view of historical progress, was a better understanding on the part of American diplomats of the complexity and interdependence of the world, rather than a precipitate diplomatic revolution.

In the years after the Spanish-American War, the United States had gradually developed a new foreign policy which Coolidge believed met the test of protecting American global interests, without arousing resentment from the other Great Powers. The new direction was the Open Door policy, which, with the conclusion of the Algeciras conference in 1907, had been extended beyond its original application in China.[58] Moreover, the maintenance of the Open Door demanded that the United States pursue an active foreign policy requiring the daily attention of experts.

"With the expansion of the national trade and the keen commercial rivalry which this brings," foreign affairs became exceedingly delicate matters requiring more competent personnel than those who had previously directed America's foreign interests. A new corps of trained diplomats, who could apply Coolidge's insights to the economic, psychological, and racial characteristics of nations, was needed to supervise the new active foreign policy. Since the United States in the future would insist upon equality of treatment in overseas commercial ventures and the right to be consulted during the disputes of the other world powers, she was destined to become embroiled in international controversies. The directors of her foreign policy would be called upon daily to reduce international discord. "Troubles and responsibilities" were the price America would pay for her prestige, wealth, and "new greatness." Professional diplomats were the men who would shoulder most of those new burdens.[59]

Coolidge was reluctant to state precisely how deeply the country might become embroiled in the rivalries of the great powers. He hinted that the pace of international rivalry was quickening, perhaps to the point of war.[60] He expected the United States to outstrip all other world powers in the race for preeminence,[61] and he hoped the measured use of America's new power could benefit other nations as well as the United States and would harm no one.

Lewis Einstein was one young diplomat who shared Coolidge's progressive conservatism. A member of the first generation of American professional diplomats, he entered the diplomatic branch of the State Department in 1903, five years after graduating from Columbia University with high honors. In the next three decades he served in various posts in Central America, the Balkans, Turkey, and Czechoslovakia. Einstein, more than many other career diplomats, achieved the high degree of culture and breadth of interest which was the professional ideal. He published poetry, aesthetic criticism, and a history of the Tories during the American Revolution, and his literary work brought him the friendship of Joel E. Spingarn, a poet and the first president of the National Association for the Advancement of Colored People. In addition, his close ties to Justice Oliver Wendell Holmes spanned thirty years, during which time the two kept up a voluminous correspondence.[62]

The outlook Einstein shared with Coolidge underlay the political recommendations Einstein made in *American Foreign Policy*. In this work, which he published anonymously in 1909, he proposed changes in America's overseas relations to meet the demands of twentieth-century commercial and political rivalries. Writing in the aftermath of the financial panic of 1907, Einstein described that brief business slump as a disguised blessing which had shaken America's misplaced confidence in her own self-sufficiency. The panic had shown the general public what had been clear to certain statesmen and thinkers in the 1890s, namely, that America's "natural resources are limited, that the end of the nation's possibilities for internal development is almost within sight, and that its capacity of consumption has been unable to keep pace with its production."[63] In the remainder of his work, Einstein argued that while isolation and indifference to European conflicts had been a realistic foreign policy in the nineteenth century, in the twentieth century, aloofness from foreign affairs was a romantic notion that caused business depression and panic.[64]

More than Reinsch or Coolidge, Einstein presented a flexible and subtle policy for America, emphasizing the complexity of international relations. While arguing that commerce underlay diplomacy, he claimed that a diplomat's primary job was political reporting, not trade expansion.[65] And while insisting that the United States faced a threat to her security, he denied that her only possible response was military in nature.[66] In sum, his complicated recommendations ideally justified the creation of a corps of full-time career diplomats.

Einstein distinguished between an end to indifference to European rivalry and an end to diplomatic isolation. Only in the most trivial sense did the replacement of aloofness with concern for the effects rivalries might have on American overseas commerce and possessions imply that the United States was abandoning an isolationist policy. The United States could conceivably take an active part in world affairs while remaining alone, concluding no understanding with other nations and relying upon naval power to protect her foreign trade, her prerogatives in Latin America, and her recently acquired dependencies in the Pacific.[67] On the surface, this traditional policy of independence had an appeal to the nation's "manliness," and struck a responsive chord in the minds of those who recalled President Monroe's statement that the republican United States was uninterested in the problems of dynastic, militaristic Europe. But the traditional policy of independence was to have the ironic effect of undermining republican institutions in the United States. "A triumph of militarism would be the only effective means by which we could assure the safeguarding of our pretensions and over-sea possessions . . . A traditional policy inevitably means for us a military policy."[68]

Even if the United States embraced militarism to achieve security, it might well have found itself dangerously exposed. As Einstein reminded proponents of an independent strategy: "Our strength, however great, is only relative—proportionate neither to the magnitude of our ambitions nor to the defenselessness of our foreign policy."[69] The alternative Einstein proposed to an exclusive reliance upon naval power was the development of political alliances. American foreign policy in the twentieth century, he believed, ought to consist of an intelligent diplomacy which sought to make arrangements with one or more European powers for the mutual protection of interests in Latin America and the Orient. He would have had any European-American agreement patterned upon the series of ententes and insurance treaties that the powers in Europe had been concluding among themselves since 1890. To those Americans who complained that the diplomatic arrangements he proposed resembled the offensive alliances which made eighteenth-century diplomacy so unstable, Einstein responded by pointing to the pacific and static character of an entente "which aims within certain determined regions to preserve actual conditions and to eliminate possible causes of conflict, chiefly in colonial spheres by taking cognizance of the special or mutual interests of the powers concerned and lending to the preservation of such agreements the force that is derived by cooperation of effort."[70]

Einstein warned American policy-makers to reject the premise that since some sort of entente with a European power was necessary, any willing world power would make a suitable partner. Americans, he implied, might eagerly embrace ruthless Machiavellianism once they decided that indifference to world affairs had proved ineffectual. It would be not realism but diplomatic naïveté, however, for the United States to neglect to determine which power's political institutions and overseas interest had the most in common with this country's when deciding upon an ally.[71] By making these balanced judgments of a potential ally, Americans could place their forward foreign policy upon a firmer moral footing than pure selfishness.

Einstein proposed Great Britain as the best candidate for a diplomatic partnership, since bonds of blood and juridical institutions united the two countries. In the two unstable areas of the world in which the United States had commercial interests, the Orient and Latin America, there was no conflict between American and British aims. The two powers would therefore find it easy to reach an understanding that would restrict United States military liability to the North American continent and the Pacific islands in return for a mutual guarantee of the political status quo in Latin America, the Philippines, and the British possessions in the Far East.[72] European affairs would not be included in the understanding; so in the event of armed confrontation in Europe, the American continent and the Pacific islands would be removed from hostilities. Nothing in the agreement would imply United States involvement in strictly European questions, but an entente with Great Britain would assure America that the European powers could not all combine to prevent her from attaining her legitimate demand for commercial equality throughout the world.

Einstein greatly admired Theodore Roosevelt and shared the President's regard for the naval theories of Alfred Thayer Mahan.[73] Mahan had argued since 1890 for an enlarged American Navy and an active foreign policy.[74] Although an aggressive navalist, he wanted not only that the United States pursue an active diplomatic as well as naval policy, but that she reach an understanding with Great Britain.[75] Einstein's thought also resembled the prescriptions of Henry Adams and Brooks Adams, two brothers who had observed that international politics forced the United States to follow a forward overseas course. They, too, hoped America would align itself with Britain.[76]

Einstein expanded the arguments of Mahan's circle by suggesting that an active overseas policy required the guidance of a prestigious corps of career diplomats as much as it needed a strong navy, and proposed improvements in the diplomatic machinery of the United States necessary for carrying out a sophisticated policy of overseas alignments. Since the war of

1898 at least, the nation had recognized the need for a modern navy; but, as of 1908, it had done little to provide itself with a trained, efficient corps of experts to direct its new foreign policy.[77] His analysis of the reasons for the inadequacies of current diplomatic staffs followed the pattern of arguments advanced by civil service reformers.[78] Einstein noted that the prestige attached by Europeans to government work and the sordidness they associated with a business career were quite the contrary of the attitudes of educated Americans in the nineteenth century.[79]

Now, in the beginning of the twentieth century, it was essential that the talented men who had been responsible for the economic growth of the country devote some of their energies to foreign policy, in the interest of continuing that economic expansion. An active policy demanded that the political appointees in the higher ranks supervise a corps of lieutenants, well-trained in international history, economics, and politics, who could provide the practical knowledge of foreign countries and diplomatic procedure essential in important negotiations.[80]

Career diplomats would have to present their chiefs with the information upon which sound policy could be built. The experts would have to gather information on foreign countries from sources unavailable to the daily press, and, using the wisdom they had gained through the study of international relations, write coherent reports to guide policy-makers. In addition the professionals would have to free politicians from the task of settling minor difficulties between the United States and foreign countries. Trained specialists did such work routinely, but it involved hidden snares for the unwary amateur. If the professionals could eliminate minor irritations in relationships, they would provide the men who made policies with the climate necessary for concluding general agreements with other states. When the American policy-makers realized that diplomacy required daily attention rather than intermittent bursts of energy, they would understand that they needed a specialized foreign affairs bureaucracy "to obtain a certain standard of action, a certain norm of method and coordination of policies, which in the conduct of affairs of state takes the place of genius."[81]

A permanent State Department bureaucracy would not only make any new initiatives in foreign policy more coherent; it would also remove international affairs from the sphere of domestic politics. A nonpartisan, career Foreign Service offered an extension of the efficient use of executive power overseas, without providing the President with increased political influence to upset party harmony at home.

Einstein completed his account of American foreign policy with a "utopian" vision of the future. Although his book was filled with scorn for those who believed that the United States could escape international turmoil and domestic depression through isolation, Einstein, in his conclusions, sought international harmony by way of a different route. In his scheme, professional diplomats, pursuing the national aspirations of the United States, and always aware of the interests of other Great Powers, could arrange a world order which balanced the aspirations of all states.

Einstein made predictions about the prospect for peace in Europe and the chances of American involvement if war broke out. In his *American Diplomacy,* in 1909, he stated his belief that the European alliance system was stable. Since the agreements seemed purely defensive, he doubted they would lead to war.[82] In 1913 he observed the military buildup of the powers over the past four years, and concluded that the Europeans were likely soon to come to blows.[83] Once war did break out, Einstein quickly noted that America had a stake in its outcome. The United States, he said, had to preserve a power balance in Europe. Einstein wanted her to support the Triple Entente, predicting that a German victory would unify Europe under the aegis of the nation that had hitherto shown the least respect for American demands for equal treatment.[84]

During the two and a half years of American neutrality, Einstein aligned himself with Theodore Roosevelt and some nominally Republican professional diplomats, like Joseph C. Grew and William Phillips. These men found that President Wilson's original injunction for Americans to be strictly neutral in thought as well as in deed overlooked the legitimate interests which America had in the outcome of European conflicts. They condemned the President's belated support for military training and pre-paredness as hesitant and cowardly, and found his final decision to enter the war insufficiently grounded in an appreciation of the identity of interest between the United States and Great Britain.[85] Einstein and the diplomats who shared his point of view were most annoyed not at Wilson's "idealism," since they themselves had abiding faith in the ideal of a Concert of Europe. What bothered them was the President's sedulous refusal to announce that the United States was fighting to restore a power balance in Europe, and in their eyes, he had erred in not recognizing the legitimate self-interest of the United States.

By the time the United States entered the war, the three writers—Reinsch, Coolidge, and Einstein—had outlined the basic principles of the professional diplomat's theory of international relations. They held that economic and political pressures were forcing the United States to follow an active, global foreign policy. In order to play a worldwide role, this country had to create a corps of expert diplomats who understood the complexity of international relations. Their own attitude toward the state system was curiously ambiguous. They saw the world as a harsh, contentious place in which the United States, as a world power, pursued its own self-interest. Yet American self-interest was simultaneously the interest of every state: the United States was not a "selfish" power, but acted as a balance wheel for the whole state system.

By thus denying a contradiction between "ideals" and "self-interest," the theorists maintained an optimistic outlook in keeping with that of progressive thinkers. Their description of the states system and their recommendation for a forward policy resembled Herbert Croly's analysis of a new American nationalism presented in *The Promise of American Life*.[86] And that similarity was not accidental. Journalists, academics, and professional diplomats shared the progressive faith in the meliorative impact of acquired knowledge, or "expertise," applied to social problems at home or abroad.

Disillusion, Utopia, and the Career Diplomats

The war and its aftermath made the diplomats and those academics close to them reiterate their theories of world politics, for they faced challenges from both disillusioned liberals and idealistic Wilsonians. Such discouraged liberals as Harold Stearns, Harry Elmer Barnes, and the editors of the *New Republic* charged professional diplomats with a major responsibility for the war.[87] They said the European alliance system had led to world war, which had ripped the fabric of international law, and that American participation in the Versailles settlement had made a mockery of President Wilson's proclamation of national self-determination. Such Wilsonians as James T. Shotwell, William E. Dodd, James W. Garner, and Charles W. Seymour also criticized the evil machinations of the "Old Diplomacy." They suggested that the United States seek world order by participating in multilateral conferences, expert commissions, the World Court, and the League of Nations, placing more faith in collective bodies than in the wisdom of any single country. Across the Atlantic, English liberals echoed the American disillusionment with the manueverings of prewar diplomats.[88] One discouraged veteran of the trenches, Siegfried Sassoon, expressed a popular scorn for the Old Diplomacy in his poem "On Reading the War Diary of a Defunct Ambassador":

But I, for one, am grateful, overjoyed,
And unindignant that your punctual pen
Should have been so constructively employed
In manifesting to unprivileged men
The visionless officialized fatuity
That once made Europe safe for Perpetuity.[89]

The diplomatic theorists rebutted these attacks on the Old Diplomacy by occupying a position midway between the former liberals and the Wilsonians. They criticized the disillusioned writers for their cynical despair and the Wilsonians for their naïve optimism. To them the war had proved the need for more, not fewer, career diplomats. Had there been more overseas experts, they said, the outbreak of the war might have been predicted.[90] Had the American people paid more attention to their advice, they suggested, there would have been less popular surprise at the events in Europe, and less disillusionment at the war's outcome.[91] They responded to the Wilsonians by saying that the idealists confused the European diplomats' means with their ends, and claimed that American diplomats should emulate the methods of the European professionals. However, the goals of American foreign policy, they felt, ought to be more democratic and commercial than those of the Europeans.[92] The theorists placed more emphasis on the skill of individual diplomats than did the Wilsonians, for the diplomat's theory held that the postwar world was continuing to be competitive.

In order to place their model upon as firm a legal foundation as that of their critics, the diplomats and academics had to define international law in a manner which recognized the inevitability of international conflict. They rebutted the disillusioned liberals who said the war had killed international law. They also disputed such Wilsonians as Shotwell, Garner, and Hudson, who considered international law a remote and immutable set of principles which statesmen were ethically bound to follow.

John Bassett Moore was one professor of international law with close ties to the Department of State who explained how the recent war had neither irrevocably destroyed international law nor rendered obsolete the old style of diplomacy. In 1923 Moore examined "some of the currect illusions" about international law, namely, the arguments of disillusioned liberals who held that the war, with its brutality and violations of human rights, had destroyed the body of international usage which had been codified into international law.[93] Not so, said Moore. Even during the height of the conflict, all belligerents had respected the parts of international law which afforded protection to prisoners of war and civilian noncombatants.[94]

Some Americans had become that disillusioned with the power of international law to reduce international strife because, as idealists, they expected the law to do something it was not designed to do. International law, said Moore, had been conceived by statesmen to regulate competition, not to abolish it. Like most of the diplomats, Moore believed in an immutable human nature which made conflict between states inevitable. According to him, the rules of war and international intercourse which diplomats had evolved over the previous two centuries could and did provide the setting within which the disputes could be resolved.[95] For Moore there would be far more strife among nations were it not for the desire on the part of professional diplomats and international lawyers to uphold the principles of international law.

Another academic who tried to define international law in a postwar context was Ellery Stowell, who taught international relations and law from 1910 to 1923 at Columbia University. He left Columbia in 1923 after an intellectual disagreement with the "utopianism" of James T. Shotwell,[96] and went to the American University in Washington. There, he constantly visited the State Department, lecturing at the Foreign Service School in 1925 and 1926. Moreover, he had a long and intimate association with the movement for Foreign Service reform. From 1919 to 1924 he was chairman of the National Civil Service Reform League's Committee on Foreign Service. From 1926 to 1937 he acted as something of an unofficial press agent for the new Foreign Service in the pages of the *American Journal of International Law*.[97]

In 1931 Stowell published an 829-page book which represented the culmination of his thinking on international law since the outbreak of the war. The title of his work, *International Law: A Restatement of Principles in Conformity with Actual Practice,* revealed his view that international law was the only way that states could regulate their relations with one another, not "a set of platonic principles to which nations [could] only aspire."[98] For Stowell the law of nations consisted in methods of fostering international peace and commerce which a majority of states agreed they would enforce upon dissident nations.[99]

As Moore had contended, international law did not eliminate the cause of war; it provided the basis for just wars. The aim of statesmen who believed in the principles of international law, said Stowell, was the creation of what Theodore Roosevelt had called a "righteous peace." This happy state of affairs could be achieved by responsible statesmen in morally superior lands which relied upon skillful diplomacy and vigilant preparation for war to persuade recalcitrant states to accept the principles of international equity. To his mind, international law required a firm will on the part of the foremost states in the world to enforce it, for

> Notwithstanding all these achievements [of the League of Nations] and the efforts to preserve a just peace, war remains the penalty for ignorance and crass selfishness. Perhaps it is our duty to consider whether preparation for war is not possibly destined to play an important part in selecting those who are fit. Because of its onerous burdens, may it not help to eliminate from the direction of world affairs those states which are unable to hold their own in the race?[100]

Stowell's vision of international relations, which he hoped to inculcate into his university and Foreign Service students, was at once fiercely competitive, evolutionary, and progressive. States could be classified as responsible or selfish depending upon whether or not they sought to apply the principles of international law to the resolution of disputes among nations. The outcome of the inevitable clashes between law-abiding and irresponsible states would eventually provide a general climate of international tranquillity, for

> gradually nation states begin to appear more and more in their true aspect as agencies to police mankind and preserve a righteous peace; until at last man emerges as the subject of the laws of humanity, and nations are understood to be instruments for the orderly control of the geographical divisions into which the human race has been for a certain period of its development necessarily divided.[101]

Throughout the first three decades of the twentieth century, serious American observers of international affairs tried to reconcile the clashes they saw between a nation's self-interest and the common interest of all states. To theorists of international law like Moore and Stowell, to a foreign policy analyst like Coolidge, or to a diplomat like Einstein, the threat of physical force was, in the last instance, the means by which recalcitrant states were brought to realize that their self-interest coincided with the common aims of nations. These men upheld a view of international relations that was dynamic and progressive, and they believed that the use of force could gradually be diminished in world affairs. The threat of armed intervention was to be replaced with advocacy by professional diplomats, whose job would consist in persuading morally backward states that their self-interest consisted in accepting the precepts of a majority of the Great Powers.

This meliorist view of the progressive nature of world politics was held by many American professional diplomats,[102] and nowhere was it more fully stated than during the round table discussion that DeWitt Clinton Poole, Chief of the State Department's Division of Russian Affairs, conducted at the Williamstown Institute of World Politics in the summer of 1923.[103] In the book Poole compiled from his lectures, he tried to explain how modern conditions—namely, the war, liberal democracy, and the revolutions in Russian and Germany—affected the conduct of diplomacy. All these changes in the political climate of Europe and America had altered the framework in which diplomacy was carried out, but they had not destroyed the need for diplomats. Force was still the ultimate foundation upon which to construct successful negotiations,

> and the threat of its use in one way or another the most direct and cogent appeal to self-interest. A widening intelligence, more intimate international relationships, and the vastly increased cost of force, more and more, however, dispose governments to purely pacific methods. With each generation the community of interests among states is more keenly felt.[104]

The agents who would make a higher form of international conciliation increasingly likely were sophisicated professional diplomats. To succeed in their task of reducing tension, they would have to be taught that the national psychologies of various states were immutable. They would have to learn, for example, that the revolutions in Germany and Russian had not changed the outlook of the statesmen in charge of those two countries, nor had they caused a reversal in any of the fundamental goals of either of the states. Diplomats had to be trained to recognize the differences among states caused by race and language, and to appreciate an individual nation's "own modes of thought and feeling, its conceptions of what is right and decent, its conceptions of what constitutes liberty and what constitutes right between man and man."[105] Only professionals, possessing this subtle grasp of the psychologies of various nations, would have the means to convince foreign states "to sacrifice expediency to principle on the ground of ultimate advantage."[106]

For Poole and other members of the diplomatic corps who shared his outlook, international relations were gradually improving. Neither panaceas, in the form of international bodies, nor a Fortress America, indifferent to the world around it, would assure physical security and a climate favorable to international peace and commerce. Instead, an elite corps of diplomats, selected for their abilities and trained as experts in world politics, would fulfill these thinkers' dream of a slow evolution toward a stable international order.

II

Training for Foreign Service, 1906-1924

THE intellectual argument for a new Foreign Service changed into a political movement for diplomatic reform during the administration of Theodore Roosevelt, culminating in 1924 with the passage of the Rogers Act. This political agitation had wide repercussions outside the Department of State, since it created a national system of Foreign Service training in American universities. Diplomats, academics, and businessmen, each with his own needs and interests, formed an uneasy alliance to promote Foreign Service training, and the system they created emerged as an intellectually confused and unsatisfactory compromise of the competing aims of all three groups.

Diplomats and consuls initiated the movement for Foreign Service training while they were searching for a means to stock a pool of talented recruits for a new Service. They wanted universities to teach young men fundamental skills that would be useful for diplomatic work, but refused to permit outsiders to assume complete responsibility for the training of Foreign Service officers. Foreign Service men jealously guarded their prerogative to inculcate their own outlook on world affairs into new recruits. They believed that intellectual training was necessary but hardly sufficient to create a professional diplomat. More important was a sense of belonging to a professional corps, and building morale was the job of the diplomats themselves.

Professional educators differed with diplomats over who should take responsibility for training Foreign Service recruits, since the educators wanted equality in their partnership with the government. In the case of both groups, their aims were the advancement of their own institutions. The diplomats wanted to enhance the prestige of the service by recruiting officers with college educations, while the academic entrepreneurs looked to an official connection with the State Department as a means of promoting the public esteem of their universities.

The educators encountered resistance to their attempts to associate with the State Department on educational and governmental fronts. Some university authorities feared that too close a relationship between their schools and the State Department would threaten academic freedom, and, if official programs did not reduce the participating colleges to parasitism, there was some danger that the connection between the government and a few colleges would arouse the jealousy of nonparticipating schools. Therefore government officials flirted with the universities, but shied away from permanent union. In the early years of the reform movement, State Department officials had enticed educators into training men for the Foreign Service. But as the programs began to expand under the stimulus of the First World War, they grew leery of an intimate association in which they feared that they, not the academics, would be the junior partners.

Businessmen, the third distinct interest group, wanted universities to provide a corps of commercial experts who could handle the increased volume of American foreign trade. The curriculum they favored, which emphasized commercial subjects nearly to the exclusion of political education, was supported by the State Department for a bureaucratic, not an intellectual, reason—namely, that any man who pursued that course of study would not be fully trained either for a business or for a government career abroad, although he would have had a college education.

The diplomats' tortured, contradictory understanding of world affairs had it roots in the wrangling over who should decide what was taught to aspiring Foreign Service officers. The first attempt to teach men to do international work served as a model for the subsequent professional instruction in Foreign Service techniques, which was determined by the internal needs of various organizations. In the end, diplomats, academics, and businessmen decided it was more important that Foreign Service officers go to school than that they learn anything while there.

Infancy of Foreign Service Training

Immediately after the war with Spain, businessmen interested in overseas trade began agitating for a professional consular service, with admission based on merit.[1] They attempted to have legislation passed for this purpose, but the Congress balked at stripping the president of patronage powers in the appointment of consuls.[2] After considerable business pressure, President

Theodore Roosevelt signed away his patronage rights by issuing an Executive Order placing admission to the consular service on a merit basis.[3] Six months later, the Congress passed a weak reorganization bill for the consular service,[4] which said nothing regarding appointment by merit, but did provide for the regular inspection of the efficiency of overseas consulates. Roosevelt supplemented this law with another executive order establishing an Examination Board for the Consular Service.[5] The order was merely the first victory for the professionalization movement, for it bound only one administration, and T. R. could rescind it at will. Nor was the new policy democratic in nature: only candidates from an approved list were eligible to take the new examinations. Despite its inefficiencies, Roosevelt's decision to set up an Examination Board partially satisfied the consuls, diplomats, and businessmen who wanted reform, and who turned their attention next to recruiting good candidates. Once the testing machinery was established, the Department needed the cooperation of both businessmen and educators to train men to meet whatever standards might be set.

The results of the first consular examination given in 1907 disappointed the reformers. The examination papers seemed to prove that American universities were not turning out men especially qualified for foreign service and that some special training was necessary. John Ball Osborne, Chief of the State Department's Bureau of Trade Relations, contrasted the fine showing of graduates who took the French consular examination at the Paris Ecole des Sciences Politiques with the dismal record of those American university graduates who took the first consular tests in Washington: in France over half the men who were certified had passed, whereas in the United States half the candidates failed the first test, and two-thirds, each of the next two.[6]

In 1906 the National Business League of America, a Chicago-based trade expansion organization formed in 1897, took the first step toward coordinating the various proposals for improving consular training.[7] In January of that year the League's secretary, Austen Burnham, polled the presidents of eighteen American universities for the "purpose of ascertaining the facilities for fitting young men for the American Consular Service."[8] The results clearly indicated that international subjects had been neglected at American universities: no university offered a special course in international relations, nor did any institution have a separate school to study the subject. Moreover, little attention was given to the study of history, politics, or economics of countries outside Europe.

Three years later, the League conducted a new poll at the same eighteen universities with more encouraging results. The university heads all replied that their institutions had begun to recognize Foreign Service subjects as legitimate academic specialties. Each school concentrated on language instruction, and some offered a broad range of courses in commercial and political geography, commercial law, international law, colonial government and administration, and consular organization and procedure.[9]

Educators polled by the Business League differed over the desirable extent of government supervision of Foreign Service training programs. They all opposed a bill for a national consular school similar to the military academies,[10] for not only the educators, but the businessmen[11] and the State Department,[12] agreed that a formal consular school would either become a refuge for spoilsmen or would discriminate against graduates of business schools. Some educators, however, wanted a close, informal relationship with the State Department. They acknowledged that there was insufficient demand for a separate Foreign Service institute, but they wanted the State Department to designate certain universities as official training centers for consular personnel. Other college presidents, jealous of their institutions' independence and believing that business, not government, was more concerned with the education of overseas officials, wanted each school to set its own standards for professional training in Foreign Service subjects.

Richard D. Harlan, the first Dean of the College of Political Science at George Washington University, was one of the proponents of the idea that the Department establish a single center for the training of prospective diplomats. Harlan surveyed the work in international commerce offered in the United States and concluded that it was sufficient to fit a young man for "effective work in his own country (in case he should fail of a consular appointment, or afterwards decide not to seek one)."[13] He found, however, that not only were the courses too general and failed to give special training in consular procedure, but that instructors were too unfamiliar with the daily routine of the Department of State to be of much assistance in introducing a young man to the type of work he would do in the consular service.

For special training, Harlan suggested that the government endow a Consular Training School to supplement the work of the universities.[14] The small number of consuls needed each year would prevent such a school from ever becoming an independent venture like the military academies, and Harlan did not believe that a service academy-like school was a very good idea. Even if enough students could be found to enter such an academy, he foresaw dangers to academic freedom in a school of international affairs operated by the government. What he recommended was that a happy balance be struck between the demand for special consular instruction and the need for academic independence by having the Department of State recommend to candidates for the Foreign Service that they attend a designated university in Washington.[15]

The institution Harlan had in mind for a training center was naturally his own College of Political Science,[16] the establishment of which in 1907, he claimed, realized the vision of the Founding Fathers of a national institution to educate young Americans in the science of government.[17] Harlan hoped that the State Department would want to support the school by encouraging high officials to lecture there and to open their offices to any visiting students who wanted an introduction to diplomatic work. He foresaw the possibility of his school becoming a national postgraduate center for Foreign Service instruction, where young men anticipating a consular career would spend a year or two before presenting themselves for the exam.[18]

The idea of an informal arrangement between the government and George Washington University was a convenient device for increasing the prestige of the new college. Unfortunately, Harlan's plan barely took into account the increased work load of the Department of State. New, complex relations with the rest of the world were the reason for a specially trained consular corps. Since high State Department officials wanted trained junior officers to reduce the tedium of routine work, they shrank from the prospect of adding to their own burdens by acting as unpaid consultants at the College of Political Science.[19]

Other college presidents naturally had grave reservations about entrusting all consular training to an institution in Washington. Given the fact that the Universities of California, Chicago, Illinois, Iowa, Kentucky, Pennsylvania, Wisconsin, and Columbia, as well as Harvard and Yale, had had some type of program for Foreign Service training since 1907, the heads of those programs thought it would be manifestly unfair to their students for the government to establish a special relationship with a single school.[20] One professor at Chicago recommended that the State Department treat all graduates equally and provide its own special short course in its headquarters before sending new recruits to the first overseas posts.[21]

Although the leaders of the State Department ultimately concluded that the informal arrangement between the Foreign Service and a Washington university was unworkable, they took a keen interest in the founding of the

College of Political Science at George Washington. When the College opened, Secretary of State Elihu Root congratulated Dean Harlan for starting the school, and told him that the government was now beginning to "limit appointments in the diplomatic and consular service to men of special fitness." He added, however, that in order to maintain the high standards of the men admitted under merit provisions, many talented candidates had to be trained, and he hoped that Harlan's college would help stock the pool of recruits.[22]

Part of the initial enthusiasm for the new college arose because the founders of the school tried to pattern it after European institutes of government service. Harlan explained that the college was "modelled after the famed *Ecole des Sciences Politiques* in Paris and the London School of Economics and Political Science."[23] Root told Harlan that the European experience proved that a professional Foreign Service could not rely upon classical education alone to provide suitable candidates:[24] Europeans had learned the value of special technical instruction.

When the businessmen and consuls agitated for a special training school, they implicitly condemned the classical liberal arts curriculum in American colleges and universities, in the belief that practical knowledge was more important than broad cultural attainments for success in both consular and business careers. The State Department's John Ball Osborne described the new university courses in Foreign Service subjects as the vanguard of the movement for a utilitarian form of higher education. He found the new courses particularly attractive, since they satisfied young men impatient with the "idea of pursuing a college course for four years that offers little more than fundamental cultural courses." These "hustling sons of America's businessmen" sought preparation for a lifetime career, and demanded a curriculum that combined "technical and informational studies with those that are intended for general mental discipline."[25]

The practical nature of consular training suggested two political weaknesses of the consular service. In the first place, training for a consular career was considered indistinguishable from that required for a career in international trade. Reformers realized that the State Department would never need enough personnel to warrant a national educational system devoted to producing recruits. The consular service could flourish only by allying commercial interests with political influence. Secondly, the emphasis upon technical education revealed the tension in the reformer's minds between the need for special knowledge and general competence.[26]

Throughout the reform period, consuls wanted to supplement their commercial skills with the genteel grace of the members of the socially superior diplomatic branch.[27] Diplomats, on the other hand, wanted commercial knowledge in order to gain the respect of businessmen. Both consuls and diplomats needed the approval of two separate groups—the international guild of professional diplomats, and American businessmen interested in foreign affairs. To satisfy those two constituencies, the consuls and diplomats sought a training system that provided specialized knowledge for generalists.

International Studies Come of Age

Proposals for Foreign Service training followed the pattern of the development of theories of international relations. Before the outbreak of the European war, the interest in training for the Foreign Service, although considerable, was diffuse, unorganized, and local. Moreover, the results of the prewar activity in that realm were disappointing to reformers. The United States Commissioner of Education, Philander C. Claxton, complained at the end of 1915 that the interest in Foreign Service training had been "largely local and detached. It has shown itself only in the introduction of some new course of study or in a modification in the presentation of an older one, often out of relation to the end to be accomplished and failing, therefore, in its purpose."[28] Besides, the Business League's poll of universities had been too general to be a guide to future action. While the State Department had privately commended the universities for setting up courses dealing with Foreign Service, and had publicly appealed to more institutions to do the same, no official or informal group had created a policy regarding the aims and character of Foreign Service training.

The increased American concern with foreign affairs caused by the war impelled government officials to set an educational policy for diplomatic and consular work. In the spring of 1915 Claxton, with the cooperation of the Director of Consular Service, Wilbur J. Carr, invited representatives of twenty-five universities to attend a national conference on Foreign Service training.[29] When the meeting convened in December 1915 as part of the second Pan-American Scientific Conference, it began organizing a national curriculum of subjects dealing with foreign service.

The opening business of the conference was the appointment of a Steering Committee consisting of David Kinley, Dean of the University of Illinois' School of Commerce, and two historians, Professors Ephraim D. Adams of Stanford and G. W. Hoke of the University of Miami. These three men were to continue the work of the conference after its one-day meeting adjourned,[30] acting as a clearing house for information with regard to university courses on foreign affairs. The members of the conference also appointed a Committee of Fifteen on Educational Preparation for Foreign Service to suggest courses that colleges might offer to those who wished to prepare for a consular or international business career.[31]

The remainder of the conference was devoted to speeches from State Department officials, university representatives, and exporters. Each man indicated what his particular organization hoped to accomplish through training programs, and what each institution ought to expect of the others, thus giving a clear indication of the relative strength of each group. Every one of the organizations was trying to mold the training program to its own ends, but no single group had the resources to provide training on its own. Each of them wanted to use the prestige of the others to gain advantage for itself. In other words, the partnerships formed at the conference were for political convenience, not intellectual coherence. The subsequent internal conflicts in the training given Foreign Service officers originated in the tension between proposals for political and commercial education. The conference of 1915 did not originate those tensions; it exposed them.

The first expert to testify was Wilbur J. Carr. A small neat man with the colorless, moon-shaped face of a copy clerk, who had served twenty-two years in the Department of State, Carr was already considered the Department's foremost expert on consular legislation and appropriations.[32] He, more than any other man, was responsible for the drafting of the Rogers Act of 1924.[33] He also played a major role in the development of a professional Foreign-Service outlook, representing the interests of the consular service he had headed throughout the period of professionalization. Carr's greatest hope was to see a unified, professional Foreign Service which would serve the needs of his consular corps. When this hope soured after 1924, he aged quickly and became embittered. During his most effective years, from 1914 to 1924, Carr's talent consisted in representing his service to businessmen and to those Congressmen who shared a business outlook. He was fiercely devoted to the welfare of American consuls, but lacked all the humor and smooth charm of the professional diplomats. Carr paid dearly for his awkwardness when the interests of the consular and diplomatic branches clashed.[34] He understood businessmen better and respected them more than he did diplomats; for he appreciated the businessmen's economic and political influence and wanted to use their power for the good of his Service.[35]

Carr explained at the conference that the quality of the men applying for consulships was low. They had not received sufficient specialized training to make them equal to their European counterparts. While educators had to raise the standards of consular candidates, they also had to be aware that the need for consuls in any year would be slight. A mere hundred applicants a year would provide the Department with a large enough pool to find the thirty consuls it required. The problem facing the Department and the educators, then, was how to create an educational system to provide the consular corps with superior recruits, without at the same time wasting the resources of universities or shattering the hopes of those students who would necessarily be turned away by the consular service.[36]

Carr hoped to solve the problem by suggesting that consuls be recruited from institutions designed to train commercial agents, having observed that new American interests overseas had increased the demand for international businessmen faster than it had created the need for more consuls. His idea, therefore was that universities devise programs to prepare men for both careers. Thus if a candidate failed to gain a consulship, he could find another job.[37]

Carr's reason for combining consular and commercial education was economic in nature, not pedagogical, but he did not foresee the possibility of the consular corps suffering from any marriage of convenience. He based his optimism on the added prestige that a college education—any college education—would give American consuls in the eyes of foreigners. Moreover, his atitude toward specialized training was curiously ambivalent. While he wanted consuls to learn as much as businessmen, and to supplement their commercial studies with work in international law and diplomatic procedure, he was less interested in the content of courses than in the attitude acquired in college. He told the educators and businessmen, "If I could apportion the weight of education to that of personality I should almost be inclined to say that the proportion should be about two-thirds personality and one-third education."[38]

For the consular branch, college education provided prestige as well as technical knowledge.[39] Carr hoped that consuls could become the educational equals of diplomats, nearly all of whom had degrees from elite Eastern private colleges.[40] The educators present at the conference missed this important conflict between the two branches of the Service, and the university officials felt cheated by the State Department, which had encouraged them to train men for consular work and then provided insufficient space for their graduates.[41] The educators asked for more guidance from Carr's office in the development of a Foreign Service curriculum.[42] Professor Ephraim D. Adams, in particular, charged that the State Department was so cowed by complaints of interference with academic freedom that it refused to give direction to consular training, which led to anarchy, with universities expressing "fads and fancies" when they made up their courses.[43] Actually, wariness about interference with academic freedom had little to do with Carr's reluctance to draft university curricula. He had neither the time nor the inclination to write course syllabi.[44] He responded to Adams's plea for guidance with a bit of enthusiastic buck-passing, given his suggestion that the Commissioner of Education was the man to tell the universities what to teach.[45]

Carr's address to the conference was far more reserved than the earlier ringing endorsement Secretary of State Root had prepared for George Washington's College of Political Science. By 1915 Carr saw reason to hope that the colleges could train the men needed by the Department without the incentive of official government approval, which he was reluctant to grant to programs he could not control. The conference of 1915 indicated the type of cooperation the State Department wanted from private schools and business. Carr needed help, but he did not wish to be controlled. The day ended with the Commissioner of Education asking the Committee of Fifteen businessmen and educators to end the deadlock caused by a very large need for very few consuls.[46] As a result, the Committee, not the Department, was responsible for drafting a sample curriculum.

In the years following the 1915 conference, much progress was made in increasing the number of students enrolled in courses on foreign affairs, but that progress was due to the war rather than to any of the work done by the Committee of Fifteen. From 1915 to 1921 the Bureau of Education noticed a tremendous increase in the number of universities offering instruction in international relations: from under thirty schools offering courses in 1916, the number grew to seventy by 1921. The ten universities that showed the largest increase had over a hundred students enrolled in courses dealing with overseas trade and consular procedure. The total enrollment in such courses at the ten schools was 2,225.[47]

Carr successfully discouraged universities from establishing separate institutions to train men for government work abroad. Only one university, Georgetown, set up a separate School of Foreign Service, and even the Georgetown School tried to prepare men for both commercial and government work.[48] In 1916 Yale and Columbia abandoned their joint program to train consuls,[49] while the other universities offering courses in international studies geared them to preparing students for careers in international commerce or consular work.[50]

After the war the State Department sought to help educators draft a curriculum in practical subjects. In December 1922 the Director of the Consular Bureau and the Commissioner of Education conducted a round-table discussion with a dozen college instructors of international studies at a Chicago hotel. A year later, the government agencies convened a larger conference in Washington, composed of teachers from eighteen states. At both meetings there were discussions about the progress made since 1915 by the Committee of Fifteen in drafting a curriculum.[51] The Committee reported that it had devised two courses of study, applicable either to commercial or government service abroad. The first year of each was identical, consisting of basic studies in English, a foreign language, mathematics, and science, with a special course in economic history. During the next three years the business curriculum consisted entirely of specialized courses in business and economics, while the Foreign Service curriculum was divided equally between general economic training and the study of languages, history, and international law.[52]

When Carr addressed the 1923 meeting, he spoke more optimistically about the prospects for Foreign Service reform, since the war had persuaded the public of the need for a trained and professional Foreign Service. Carr predicted that the movement for reform would obtain new legislation short-ly.[53] One of the tasks of the professional Foreign Service would be to stem the rising tide of economic nationalism, which interfered with the "freedom of commercial intercourse between the people of our country and the people of certain regions of the world."[54] No longer, therefore, did Carr justify the combining of training for the Foreign Service and for foreign commerce strictly on the grounds of educational economy. Instead, he now pointed to the additional importance commerce had assumed in world politics since the Great War. Presently, he said, commerce and politics were so intimately connected that "it is not possible in a majority of cases to draw a line between activities which are purely political and those which ultimately affect our commercial affairs." In those days the "principal activity" of the Foreign Service had been that of "creating and maintaining a condition in which trade could be freely carried on by those seeking to engage in it."[55] To create such an open trade system, a diplomat or consul had not only to have a firm grounding in commercial subjects, but had to understand businessmen and know how to convey their desires to foreign governments.

At this time, Carr actively opposed any new programs for Foreign Service training. Inside the Department, he successfully resisted the efforts to include a provision in the Rogers Bill requiring the Department to grant scholarships to students enrolled in special Foreign Service courses at selected universities. He believed that the Service could get very good men from a variety of universities, and that designating certain schools would tend to narrow the range of institutions from which Foreign Service personnel were drawn.[56] He also believed that the universities had established a workable curriculum for Foreign Service training. Now their task was to make sure that dull or mediocre students did not seek out a diplomatic career. As he had indicated in 1915, what a student studied was not nearly so important for his success as a Foreign Service officer as his personal qualities. Carr wanted the universities to produce men who were "hearty, personable, manly, shrewd, business-like, observant, and well-informed, with a good knowledge of human nature," as well as "the instincts of a gentleman in the finer sense."[57] If the colleges would supply such men as raw material, the State Department would turn them into diplomats.

In contrast to Carr and the Department, professional educators wished to prove that they could turn out Foreign Service officers technically prepared to take over their duties as soon as they entered the Department—[58]a commitment to rational training which frightened the Department of State. Carr realized that if he accepted their argument, his Department would be forced to relinquish some of the responsibility for training new men.[59] And the result of such divided authority would have been unpredictable. Carr feared that neophytes trained in outside academies would feel obliged to two organizations—their schools and the Foreign Service. He did not want the *esprit de corps* within the Service to be diluted by any sympathy with other institutions.[60]

In sum, the Department's alliance with the educators and businessmen was based on convenience, not on common aims and opinions. The Department, of course, knew that those two outside groups were a source of political power and recruits. Yet while it sought out individual scholars for advice, any association between scholars and diplomats was intended to be on an informal, ad hoc basis. And the Foreign Service was of the same mind regarding its relations with such scholars as Archibald Carey Coolidge, Ellery C. Stowell, or Bernadotte E. Schmitt.[61] Since the men who administered the Foreign Service wanted to create their own policy on world affairs, in the 1920s they formed an intellectual defense of their careers that prevented other organizations, whether governmental or private, from interfering with the training of Foreign Service officers.

III

The Movement for Foreign Service
Reform, 1914-1924

The Prewar Recruits

IN the first fifteen years of the twentieth century, the diplomatic and consular branches of the Foreign Service recruited a group of junior officers who displayed a deeper commitment to public service than any previous recruits. These new men became the nucleus of the reorganized Foreign Service, stamping it with their values and experience. Those who entered the diplomatic branch—such men as Lewis Einstein, Henry P. Fletcher, Hugh Gibson, Leland Harrison, Jr., Franklin Mott Gunther, Peter Augustus Jay, Basil Miles, William Phillips, Hugh Wilson, and John Campbell White—had social backgrounds, wealth, and family connections remarkably similar to those of their predecessors Henry White, William Buckler, or Lloyd Carpenter Griscom. Most of the twentieth-century recruits had fine educations and had traveled widely before becoming diplomatic secretaries.[1] The men who entered the consular branch of the Department and went on to help amalgamate both branches came from more modest backgrounds. The most successful of the consuls—Wilbur J. Carr, Joseph Ballantine, Nelson T. Johnson, Tracy H. Lay, George Messersmith, and DeWitt Clinton Poole—were more interested in self-improvement and public service than in liberating themselves from cloying family connections.[2] Whatever their initial reasons for entering the Service, those who remained and became the most successful soon changed their outlook. They responded favorably to the progressive call for talented men to enter the service of their country, and believed that professional diplomats should order foreign affairs in the same way as progressives were trying to reform domestic politics.[3]

Their common social backgrounds and the early career experiences shared by those diplomats profoundly affected the style they adopted in agitating for the reform of the Service. Their wealth and education made them congenial to the progressive advocacy of the benefits of expertise. Only knowledgeable experts, committed to doing their job well rather than promoting their own fortunes, were capable of directing public affairs in a complex commercial society. Their wealth and education had instilled in them habits of command, while their unhappiness in family businesses encouraged them to seek outlets for their urge to make do away from home. In their pioneering work to establish a new Foreign Service, they displayed the dominance and zeal Max Weber described as characteristic of public officials who lived for, rather than from, public life.[4] If the first generation's wealth and education gave them the desire to excel at their chosen calling, their common backgrounds also made them resent the ambitions of outsiders who might try to dominate the practice of diplomacy. The lessons the first generation learned in their initial years of diplomatic apprenticeship became the intellectual and emotional foundation on which Foreign Service officers built a legally recognized career.

Several of the wealthy young men who entered diplomacy with a serious commitment to public service did so directly, in response to Theodore Roosevelt's appeal for talented government officials.[5] Henry P. Fletcher, who later became Undersecretary of State in the Harding Administration, differed from many other diplomats in never having attended college. Rather, his formative youthful experience came from his adventures as a Rough Rider during the Spanish-American War. The thrill of military camaraderie, the sense of contributing to a patriotic cause, and the exhilaration of being exhorted by Theodore Roosevelt never left him.[6]

Fletcher was the son of a wealthy Pennsylvania merchant. He read law privately and practiced it for four years before joining Colonel Roosevelt. At the end of the war with Spain, he resisted the idea of turning to a routine law practice in Greencastle, Pennsylvania, remaining instead in the Army and going to the Philippines to help suppress the insurrection. In 1901 Fletcher returned to Greencastle, but he wanted to retain some of the military *esprit de corps* he had known for the previous three years. In January 1902 he wrote his old commander, T. R., then Commander-in-Chief, asking him for help in gaining a diplomatic post.[7] The President put him in touch with Herbert Squiers, who was leaving for Havana as Minister to Cuba and who promptly launched Fletcher's diplomatic career by accepting him as the

Second Secretary.[8] A year later, Fletcher went to Peking as Second Secretary, and remained in China for three eventful years, until 1906, doing important political work.[9]

Two other future Undersecretaries of State, William Phillips and Joseph Grew, also fell under the spell of Roosevelt's call to national service. They encountered Roosevelt not on the battlefield but at Harvard University, where both were undergraduates early in the twentieth century. Moreover, both had grown up in Boston, where their families were pillars of society, and although both were expected to remain in Boston, as they admitted later on, they nevertheless decided to escape to public careers abroad.[10]

Phillips, who was a member of a Brahmin family and a great-nephew of Wendell Phillips, worried about his future in 1900, during his senior year at Harvard. Not only was his scholastic record desultory, but he felt uneasy about a business career.[11] Later he wrote:

> Something warned me that it would be better to get away from the familiar school environment, away from a life of too much ease, away from friends and family who were urging upon me the pallid career of family trustee. I wanted a freer outlook, and I felt the influence of Theodore Roosevelt, who in 1900, was preaching the gospel of the "strenuous life."[12]

Most of Phillips's college courses had taught him very little, but one professor in particular, Archibald Carey Coolidge, had awakened his interest in world affairs. Fortunately, his financial independence made it possible for him to find out if he were "adapted to a more adventurous life than Boston afforded." Like Henry White before him, however, he realized that wealth held "certain temptations to waste one's life in empty explorations." Upon his graduation, therefore, he sought Coolidge's help in securing a diplomatic post.[13] Coolidge wrote Secretary of State John Hay about Phillips, but when the young man arrived in Washington, the Secretary discouraged him, suggesting that he get a law degree before trying for a foreign assignment, and warning him of the scarcity of positions in the Department and of the political considerations which limited appointments to one presidential term, at most. Since there was no way to train for a career in diplomacy, law school would at least train his mind for international negotiation and provide him with a profession to fall back upon when the presidency changed hands.[14]

Phillips accepted Hay's counsel and reluctantly enrolled in the Harvard Law School in September 1900. Uninterested in the work, he did poorly for two and a half years. At the end of his second year he met Joseph Choate at a house party on the Vanderbilt estate in North Carolina. Phillips told Choate of his interest in a diplomatic career, and impressed the older man with his charm and seriousness. When, in February 1903, President Roosevelt appointed Choate Ambassador to Great Britain, Choate asked Phillips to accompany him as his unpaid private secretary. Disgusted with the law, and finding the ambassador's offer the most promising way at hand to enter diplomacy, Phillips accepted and sailed for London in April 1903.[15]

During the next few years Phillips tried to teach himself diplomatic procedure. He measured himself against his superiors and colleagues in the services of European nations, and tried to find ways to improve his knowledge. Gradually, he developed his own conception of professional diplomacy and how it could be strengthened in the United States. His enlightenment was typical of the one experienced by other members of the first professional generation.

Phillips's experience as Choate's private secretary was both educational and frustrating. To begin with, he had no responsibility for preparing or for gathering information. His major job was that of organizing the ambassador's social schedule, but he was also required to copy all of Choate's dispatches sent to Washington, thus receiving a daily second-hand lesson in the "lawyerlike qualities" of his chief.[16] Within two years Phillips was overcome with boredom in a politically unimportant job, and depressed by the neglect shown him by Washington. Since he was only a private secretary, and the State Department had no interest in his acquiring diplomatic skills, he discovered that if he wanted diplomatic training, he would have to acquire it through his own efforts.[17]

During the next fifteen years of Phillips's career, he aggressively sought positions that would teach him diplomacy, involve him important work, and enable him to catch the eye of his superiors. In 1905, while still in London, he befriended William W. Rockhill, the United States Ambassador to China.[18] Rockhill brought him to Peking in 1905 to replace Henry Fletcher, who was going to Portugal as Secretary of the Legation.[19] Phillips, who remained in China for two years as Second Secretary, enjoyed the political work, but decided in 1907 that his diplomatic education would be incomplete without service inside the State Department. The Department therefore gave him permission to return to Washington, but did not promise him a job.[20]

It did, however, find this Boston Brahmin and great-nephew of the abolitionist a sinecure in the "colored messenger service."[21] From that vantage point, Phillips was able to observe the primitive business methods employed by the Department. Since he had returned from China just at a time when the volume of diplomatic correspondence with the Far East was expanding, he asked Secretary of State Elihu Root for permission to establish a special office to handle dispatches arriving from the Orient. Root agreed to let Phillips head the Department's first specialized office, the Division of Far Eastern Affairs. There, incoming dispatches came directly to Phillips, who then made political recommendations directly to the Counsellor of the Department of State.[22]

Phillips's aggressiveness in procuring himself a Washington job singled him out from the usual junior diplomatic secretary, and he soon caught the attention of the President. Theodore Roosevelt, who had inspired him early on, ordinarily had little patience for indolent diplomatic secretaries who served in overseas missions for only a few years, squandering their talent and wealth.[23] But he was attracted by Phillips's family background, his education, his youth, his serious commitment to public service, and his desire to emulate Roosevelt himself. A few months after Phillips had returned home to the Far Eastern Division in 1907, he was invited to the White House for dinner. Since the President discovered in him the type of wealthy and gifted young man he thought should be encouraged to abandon private gain for public stewardship, he began inviting Phillips to join the French Ambassador, Jules Jusserand, and Archie Butt and himself in rock-climbing, riding, and tennis, thus including Phillips as a steady member of the so-called tennis cabinet.[24]

The meetings of the tennis cabinet launched Phillips in Washington society. His freshness, intelligence, and eagerness to understand national politics next attracted the attention of Henry Adams, who maintained his station in Washington society by inviting to his luncheons the brightest figures in politics and government. When Phillips was introduced to Adams by Elihu Root, the older man was so taken with him that he presented him with a standing invitation to join his table. In that way Phillips met most of the socially respectable political leaders of the day.[25]

Particularly important for the development of Phillips's diplomatic outlook were his meetings with Jusserand, a constant guest at Adams's house. Jusserand explained to him the French and British systems for recruiting and promoting diplomats on the basis of their education and competence, and painted a glorious picture of diplomatic services, all of whose members came from the upper-middle class and the finest universities, from which political favoritism had been eliminated, and where the diplomatic secretaries had some influence in formulating policy. Phillips was also impressed by the social outlook of Jusserand, who held the meliorist view of international relations which Phillips's teacher Archibald Carey Coolidge had outlined in his Harvard lectures. Jusserand told Phillips that he could see him in the role of a professional diplomat, gradually improving relations among nations, insisting that amateurs could ruin good relations, and that experts could improve them with diligent effort. In his view, the international system was competitive, and the guiding principle of all states was self-interest. One of a diplomat's jobs was to teach his nation's politicians the difference between true self-interest and belligerent selfishness. For professional diplomats had a unique perspective on international competition, trained as they were to understand the reasons for competing claims of different states. The perspective allowed them to resolve conflicts by explaining to their governments the causes of other nations' differing views on international questions.[26]

By the end of the Roosevelt administration, Phillips had, through his own efforts, acquired a firm knowledge of diplomatic practice. He had compared his Service and his position in it to that of the Europeans, and found American diplomacy sorely lacking in legal protection for its practitioners. His desire to make a career for himself in the Foreign Service where none really existed had forced him to learn how to deal diplomatically with his superiors and colleagues. His goal was to acquire security and prestige for himself and other aspiring professionals without arousing the hostility of the political appointees and time-servers in the Department of State, and to convince such men that the professionalization of the diplomatic service was actually in their own interests.[27]

From the beginning of the Taft Administration until the outbreak of the First World War, Phillips's career took an erratic course over which he had little control. He found himself at the mercy of the spoils system and his professional talent often overlooked. When William Howard Taft became President in March 1909, political favors were the cause of Philander C. Knox, the new Secretary of State, removing Phillips from the post of Third Assistant Secretary of State, which he had occupied for the last year.[28] As a consolation, Knox offered Phillips the job of Counsellor of Embassy (second in command) in London under the new Ambassador Whitelaw Reid.[29] When Phillips's first child arrived in 1912, he requested a year's leave without pay in order to return to the States and introduce his wife to his New England family and to society, basing his petition upon the practice, common in Britain and France, of granting a year of *disponsibilité* to diplomats. The Department granted the leave, but without guaranteeing Phillips a place in the Service should he wish to return.[30]

When the Democrats won the election in November 1912, Phillips, in the belief that Woodrow Wilson would not offer him a diplomatic post, had an elegant house built near Boston and settled into the position of Secretary to the Harvard Corporation.[31] He remained in that sinecure until January 1914, when the President, at the request of his advisor Colonel Edward M. House, asked Phillips to become the confidential Presidential negotiator with the Mexican representatives seeking *de jure* recognition for the regime of Venustiano Carranza.[32] Having completed his mission in two months, Phillips was astonished when the President asked him to resume his old duties as Third Assistant Secretary of State. Secretary of State William Jennings Bryan, supposedly the arch-spoilsman, had appreciated Phillips's work in the Mexican negotiations, and endorsed the nomination. But opposition came from an unexpected source, Phillips's own Republican Senator, Henry Cabot Lodge, who had a reputation as a solid advocate of the career principle for the Foreign Service. After an argument with Mrs. Lodge, the Senator, who finally agreed that Phillips's career was more important than his nominal Republicanism, relented.[33]

For the first time, Phillips had a position in a Democratic administration, and believed it to be a permanent job that was *de facto* under the civil service principle. For he had created a job where none had existed before. Eleven years after entering the Service, promotion was still not based upon rational bureaucratic criteria. Phillips and the group of men who had entered at roughly the same time and risen by dint of their own energies vowed to create a bureaucratic system for the benefit of the young men who were to follow them, so that the next generation of diplomats could enter the service with a clearer idea of the responsibilities and benefits of professional diplomacy. They would not face the same uncertainties about the security and prestige of their work.

Several other men who entered the Service in the first decade of the twentieth century—Lewis Einstein, Joseph C. Grew, Leland Harrison, Hugh Wilson, and Hugh Gibson—shared Phillips's background and initial diplomatic experiences. All had attended excellent universities, but none except Einstein had distinguished himself as a student. All came from families with deep roots in a specific area. All were encouraged by their relatives to reside near home, and all had decided that to remain in a familiar environment was to be stultified. They chose a Foreign Service career as a respectable means of satisfying their wanderlust, studying mankind, and performing a public service. They all came armed with personal recommendations to politicians. All of them found a nineteenth-century bureau, bogged down in routine and conducting little important political business.

And all of them rose in the Service through their own efforts, making personal studies of the professional Foreign Services of Europe, and trying to convince their political superiors that American diplomacy needed the skills of trained men.[34] After gaining a foothold during the tumultous war years, they sought in the twenties to mold the Service to their liking, to recruit the type of men they thought most capable, and to inculcate in them a realistic outlook in international relations and professional diplomacy.

The Shock of War

Between 1914 and 1924, the Foreign Service of the United States underwent a dramatic transformation, growing in size and political importance, and gaining unqualified Congressional support for the career principle. It was not so much the arguments of the Department of State officials, academics, and businessmen, but the First World War and its aftermath, which persuaded the Congress to reform the Foreign Service. When reorganization came, it took the form it did as a result of the conflicts and accommodations among the groups and personalities involved in professional diplomacy. No single group among the diplomats, consuls, academics, and businessmen possessed sufficient power to make its reorganization scheme prevail, so that the reformers compromised with a bill introduced by Representative John Jacob Rogers of Massachusetts. The way in which this bill became law in 1924 revealed the intentions of the supporters of reform. For example, diplomats and consuls used each other's rhetoric for their own distinct ends. The consuls, who had relative job security but little social prestige by the end of the war, demanded a fused Foreign Service to make them the social equals of the diplomats. The diplomats, on the other hand, considered themselves a social elite and wanted their salaries and job tenure to be commensurate with their high status. They also wanted not to be considered snobs by the politicians and businessmen, but rather to gain approval for their superior grasp of foreign affairs. They did, moreover, accept the consuls' demand for a fused Foreign Service, but merely in order to gain higher salaries for themselves. While agitating for the new bill, the diplomats adopted a pose for the benefit of Congress, portraying their branch as a group of sophisticated commercial agents breaking down barriers to American trade in the hope that commercially-minded Congressmen would defer to their judgment in political affairs.

The period of the Wilson administration was a tumultous time for career diplomats. At the beginning, Secretary of State William Jennings Bryan jolted morale by reinstituting the spoils system for the appointment of ministers. In several countries professionals were replaced as chiefs of mission by politicians with no experience at all in foreign affairs.[35] In the more important overseas posts, where professionals would not be sent in any event, Bryan employed idiosyncratic standards for selecting heads of mission.[36] Membership in the Democratic Party, for example, and fervor for international arbitration were among the necessary qualifications for a position on the Secretary's Washington staff. Five months after Bryan took office, Archibald Carey Coolidge described the organization of the Department as "incredible, and would be anywhere but in the United States." For Coolidge, Bryan was a Secretary whose "good intentions are equaled only by his ignorance." The Counsellor of the Department, John Bassett Moore, who seemed to Coolidge to be the only competent member of the upper echelon,[37] resigned in disgust after eleven months.[38]

No member of the State Department felt more isolated and more betrayed by Bryan's leadership than Wilbur J. Carr, who believed that Bryan disregarded efficiency as a qualification for consular appointments and had no "real regard for the public service."[39] After a year of Bryan's leadership, Carr felt that his chief was consciously trying to humiliate and ignore him, for Bryan saw Carr rarely, was inattentive when he could spare the time, and denied Carr's urgent pleas to make appointments on the basis of merit. Bryan displayed interest in an appointment only when he was personally involved. He once left Carr sputtering by affably stating that the man Carr had chosen for a clerkship in Paris could have the job but not the salary, since he had private means, and requested that Carr keep the clerkship for "someone who wanted to take a trip over there."[40] In November 1914 Assistant Secretary of State William Phillips, a member of the diplomatic branch, took over the presenting of consular appointments for Bryan's approval. Phillips, who was more adept at small talk than Carr and seemed to Bryan less of a civil service fanatic, succeeded where Carr had failed.[41] Indeed, his easy handling of Bryan was tinged with an irony that recurred in the subsequent movement to professionalize the Foreign Service. Although the consular branch, under Carr, carried the burden of the agitation for reform, the diplomatic branch had more influence with politicians.

The outbreak of war in Europe provided an immediate but temporary fillip for Department morale. The protection of American citizens in belligerent countries kept European missions busier than they had ever been in the Wilson administration.[42] Consuls and diplomats abandoned their usual four-hour work day and remained in their offices long into the night to assist stranded Americans. [43] In Washington, at the end of the first week of war, Carr was more cheerful than he had been at any time in the preceding fifteen months. "One feels alive once more," he wrote. [44]

However, the professionals' initial excitement soon gave way to pessimism, since they disapproved of Bryan's insistence upon strict American neutrality. Their commitment to an active American policy, their respect for Theodore Roosevelt, and their closeness to the diplomats of the Entente disposed them to favor the claims of Britain and France. [45] They also believed that Bryan was mismanaging the Department's affairs by ignoring the advice of his professional staff. When he resigned in June 1915, Carr, Phillips, and Assistant Secretary Harrison expected to be consulted more often, especially since Robert E. Lansing, an orderly administrator, was directing the Department. [46]

Lansing did, in fact, pay more attention to professional counsel than Bryan, and he shared his staff's attitude regarding the war. As relations between the United States and Germany deteriorated, Lansing confided to Phillips his belief in the necessity for American intervention. [47] The Secretary of State was powerless, however, to maintain the bureaucratic influence of the Foreign Service and the State Department during the American war effort or the peacemaking. Representatives of the War and Treasury Departments, such special wartime agencies as the War Trade Board, the War Industries Board, and the Shipping Board, and extraordinary presidential envoys handled the bulk of inter-allied negotiations during 1917 and 1918. [48] Naturally, professionals in the Department of State grumbled bitterly over being reduced to playing a subsidiary role in routine consular work, while outsiders conducted important political and military discussions. [49] During July and August 1918 Carr, Phillips, and Department Counsellor Leonard Woolsey tried unsuccessfully to bring the postwar planning work of the "Inquiry"—Edward M. House's special research organization—under the control of the State Department. [50] Indeed, professional diplomats continued to occupy a subsidiary, administrative position even at the Paris Peace Conference. Joseph C. Grew, the Secretary of the American Commission, had difficulty adjusting the competing claims of the Inquiry experts, the Army, and the nine technical advisory staffs of the Commission. [51] But the President and the Commissioners did not appreciate Grew's work, [52] and Colonel House complained about Leland Harrison's supercilious manner. [53] Grew, for his part, disliked doing the organizational, nonpolitical work. [54] At the end of the Paris conference, career diplomats vowed they would bolster their political authority in peacetime[55] in hopes that the Congress and the State Department would follow their prewar advice and reorganize the Foreign Service into a professional body, capable of guiding foreign policy.

The burden of work growing out of the war's dislocations nearly overwhelmed the American diplomatic personnel. When redrawing the map of Europe, the negotiators in Paris had created three new sovereign states in Eastern Europe—Poland, Hungary, and Czechoslovakia. The shattering of the Russian Empire had similarly created four independent states in the Baltic—Finland, Latvia, Lithuania, and Estonia. To all these newly independent nations the United States sent diplomatic representatives who were soon confronted with political problems that taxed their staffs.

In Poland difficulties began while the Peace Conference was still in session. News of an anti-Jewish pogrom sent an American investigating committee headed by Henry Morgenthau scurrying from Paris to Warsaw in August 1919 to report on the condition of the Jews. Morgenthau's account to Herbert Hoover was grim: widespread violence against Jews had taken place; there had been a general breakdown of civil authority; the Poles themselves were without food, fuel, trained government officials, and, in fact, all that was needed by a sovereign state. These problems lay at the roots of the pogroms, and for assistance, as Morgenthau wrote, "Poland must rely on the United States."[56]

Most of the help that was forthcoming was to be dispersed through the new American Minister to Poland, Hugh Gibson. A career diplomat since 1908, Gibson was later, in 1924, called upon to present to the House Committee on Foreign Affairs the career officers' arguments for a new professional Foreign Service. And what inspired the eloquence and intensity of his plea were the dreadful working conditions of the first three years of his Warsaw ministry.

In the aftermath of the pogroms, thousands of Polish Jews flocked to the American Embassy for visas to emigrate to the United States. Gibson's staff of three clerks, one of whom was a young lady with a "very slight idea of the English language gained in Russia," was under strain owing to the burden of processing so many visas.[57] But handling the needs of Polish citizens was not the only drain on the staff. Poland was the most important state bordering on revolutionary Russia, and the State Department wanted perceptive reports drawn up from the mass of information about conditions in Russia that was available to Gibson.[58] Throughout the spring and summer of 1919 Gibson petitioned Assistant Secretary Phillips for more clerical help, but the State Department was slow to respond.[59] At the end of July he complained to his First Secretary, Arthur Bliss Lane, that he was spending more time writing pleading letters to Washington than attending to Polish-American relations. "We are all about to break down," he said, and unless the State Department quickly made an emergency appropriation to pay for more clerks, he would either have to close the Chancery or send all his staff to the hospital to recover from overwork.[60] Even after the 1919 political crisis in Poland had subsided, the Warsaw mission continued to be deluged with requests for immigrant visas, and immediately before immigration quotas were imposed in 1922, the Warsaw consular office was receiving seven to eight hundred applications for visas daily.[61]

The stress on American diplomats and consuls in postwar Europe was perhaps at its greatest during the summer of 1919 in Poland, but nowhere did the workload diminish to the level of prewar days, when a consul could complete his daily tasks by working from ten o'clock to noon and from two to four in the afternoon. In other eastern European countries the new task of processing the visas of so many prospective immigrants rudely shocked complacent consular officers. In Hungary, for example, the American Vice-Consul in charge of visas was one Richard Cameron Beer, a young career consul who had spent the war years in the Bahamas and Cuba.[63] Since Budapest in the winter of 1922-23 was not all that idyllic, Beer complained to his family that the Hungarians, Gypsies, and Jews whose visas he had to approve were all barbarians who gave his office a smell "no zoo in the world can equal." Immigration work, he claimed, was the most wretched in the Service, and was at its worst in Poland and Hungary. Beer longed for a transfer to a less hectic spot, preferably near a golf course.[64]

As exhausting as immigration work may have been for American consuls, it had its political purposes. Carr explained in 1922 how a system of visa control had been established during the war for Americans traveling in belligerent areas. The system had proved so useful that "when the armistice was signed it was decided to retain . . . the system as a protection against world revolutionaries and fanatics who were attempting to spread their propaganda to create unrest and inaugurate movements subversive of the best interests of the country."[65] Thus, when the postwar wave of immigration began, it became the consuls' duty to sift out from among the millions of prospective immigrants the Bolsheviks and the anarchists.[66]

Given the fact that the New Diplomacy which followed the war was conducted openly, often in multilateral conferences or by way of international organizations, American diplomats soon saw it as increasing rather than diminishing their burdens. Six months after the Peace Treaty was signed, Secretary of State Lansing wrote the Chairman of the House Foreign Affairs Committee, Representative Stephen G. Porter, a hearty endorsement of the idea of a complete reform of the Foreign Service. In 1914, he said, lack of information and a tendency to conjecture had blinded some American diplomats to the instability of the European system. The "present perplexities of world politics" and America's new role in it did not allow "any degree of conjecture" in judging the intentions of other nations. American diplomats had to have the highest skills in the future in order to avoid such misjudgments as that of 1914—mistakes which could have been disastrous for the United States.[67] For his part, Lansing's Republican successor, Charles Evans Hughes, did not believe that international conferences or organizations or the speedier communications in the age of the wireless would render diplomats superfluous.[68] Since the war, claimed Hughes in 1922, the State Department had had more than twice as much business to conduct as before 1917, and the new work was politically more important.[69]

International commerce also underwent a great transformation in the years following World War I. Carr noted in 1921 not only how the economy of the world had been upset, but that the United States found itself economically dominant, possessed of a large merchant marine, with a huge debt owed her.[70] The fact that it was the collapse of the European economy more than a phenomenal boom at home which had catapulted the United States to the economic summit was hazardous to American diplomacy. Secretary of State Lansing wrote at the beginning of 1920 that "the greater portion of the world now finds its financial structure seriously weakened, its stocks exhausted, its productive forces impaired," and that the resulting feeling of political insecurity had made many nations artificially divert their economic interests in a direction that served the ends of national ambition and greed.[71] Since the war, Lansing claimed,

> [European] statecraft is being directed by those who are dealing with fresh and unfamiliar factors in the shaping of novel and untried policies. There has been devastation of territory, displacement of frontiers, disruption of institutions and disintegration of empires. The commercial treaty structure has been laid waste, trade agreements abrogated, tariff policies altered or become obsolete, lines of communication suspended, and routes of trade transformed.[72]

If the closest attention were not paid daily to cultivating friendly relations with new and intensely nationalistic regimes, America's fortunate economic position could be damaged by discriminatory tariff and investment policies imposed by the new nations.

Outside Agitators

The war and its aftermath awakened a vast public interest in the workings of the State Department, which Carr felt certain would result in some reform of the American Foreign Service.[73] He foresaw a danger, however, were outside groups to control the reorganization of the Foreign Service. Since he wanted reform to protect the needs of the Service, especially those of the consular branch, he carefully orchestrated the outside campaign of support to serve consular interests.[74] No doubt the interest of the outsiders was quite genuine, but the channels through which they expressed their opinions were controlled by the State Department. Carr therefore worked closely with civil service reformers and businessmen in deciding exactly how those groups should phrase their recommendations. He and his staff decided who testified in favor of the Rogers Act. In sum, he refused to permit outsiders to preside at the birth of a new career service based on the principle that inside experts best understood their bureaucracy and the practice of diplomacy.

The most vocal nongovernmental organizations advocating the restructuring of the State Department and the consular and diplomatic services were the National Civil Service Reform League, and various business, trade, and labor groups. In 1919 the League published a 322-page *Report on the Foreign Service,* drafted by a committee of five, headed by Professor Ellery C. Stowell.[75] The *Report* was a culmination of a long effort, dating back to the 1890s, on the part of the League to assure that all civil service positions, including those in the diplomatic and consular services, were placed under a provision of appointment and promotion by merit alone. At the end of the war, only the Foreign Service, of all government agencies, did not have the merit provision firmly established, and the League was determined to rectify the situation in order to complete its original task.[76]

The *Report,* which indicated current Foreign Service practice and offered several reform recommendations, many of which were later made into law by the Rogers Act, had Carr's full support, and its arguments often appeared in the voluminous literature dealing with diplomats and consuls published in the five years after the Peace Treaty was signed.[77] According to the *Report,* the major failing of the Foreign Service lay in its repudiation of the career principle, since the top diplomatic positions were barred to career men, and career diplomacy itself was barred to all but the very rich. In theory, the *Report* allowed, the Service's idea of going outside the ranks of professional diplomats to appoint the nation's leading citizens to ambassadorial and ministerial posts was sound, but in practice, what the Service did was to measure a man's stature by the amount he had contributed to the campaign fund of the winning party.[78] Seldom were political appointees qualified to serve the United States in important posts overseas. And in the rare cases where they were competent, their tenure of office was so brief as to make their services inefficient.[79]

In its appendices the *Report* gave several examples of the retreat to the spoils system which had occurred during William Jennings Bryan's tenure in the State Department. The League was particularly enraged by the "unjust" replacement of W. W. Rockhill as Minister to Turkey by Henry Morgenthau, a man described as "undistinguished in politics, letters, or diplomacy," and whose only claim to renown was being the largest contributor to the 1912 Democratic fund drive.[80] Most of Woodrow Wilson's other diplomatic appointees were judged and found wanting as mediocre Democratic hacks. At least one of them E. J. Hale of North Carolina, was charged with downright dishonesty for continuing to draw his pay as Minister to Costa Rica for two years after returning home from his post.[81]

The League recommended that a statute to the effect that only career diplomats be advanced to ministerial positions be enacted. It also recommended that the assistant secretary of state in charge of personnel be a career, rather than a political, appointee.[82] As for the State Department, it welcomed the League's plan for a legal limitation of ministerial posts to career men. In the winter of 1919-20, Secretary Lansing and Undersecretary Polk had discovered how difficult it was to reward excellent career men so long as politicians considered any vacant diplomatic assignment a proper spot for constituents with a yen to serve their country abroad. In December 1919 Lansing and Polk decided to suggest that the President appoint a career diplomat, Assistant Secretary of State William Phillips, as Minister to the Netherlands. Throughout January 1920 both Lansing and Polk received letters from a Baltimore businessman, Francis King Carey, who insisted that Senator John W. Smith of Maryland had been promised by Lansing that Carey would be appointed to the job at the Hague.[83] After he had heard that a career diplomat was scheduled to get the post, Carey said he was pleased that a professional diplomat had been deemed qualified to serve as Minister, but insisted that his own business experience in the Netherlands made him especially fit for the job. He asked Lansing if it would not be possible to send the career man somewhere else—perhaps as Minister to China.[84] Shortly after this harrowing attempt to reward a diligent diplomat, Polk confided to Wilbur J. Carr his belief that the merit system ought be established in the State Department,[85] for promoting career diplomats to ministerial posts through merit was a means of instilling *esprit de corps* in diplomatic officers.

Another task the Civil Service Reform League set out to perform was to find ways of improving the quality of the men who entered the diplomatic corps, and one way was to pay them adequate wages. In its indictment the *Report* pointed to how low the salaries in fact were. The highest-paid Secretaries received $4000 a year, with no allowance for entertaining foreign government officials or for especially costly posts.[86] In the lower grades of the Service the salaries were so low—$1500 a year for fourth secretaries—that, according to the *Report,* a man simply could not live on his earnings.[87] It compared American diplomats' salaries to those paid by Great Britain and found that the Americans' lagged far behind.[88] It also compiled charts showing how the real wages of American professional diplomats had declined from 1908 to 1919, when they had fallen to the low level of 1875.[89]

Low salaries, of course, had direct consequences on the quality of the Foreign Service. For example, a career diplomat was in a difficult position if he wished to marry. According to the *Report,* he could either wed an heiress and remain a diplomat, marry a woman of moderate means and resign from the Service, or remain a bachelor.[90] The salary scale had the further effect of making diplomatic careers the exclusive preserve of the rich, since men without private means were cautioned by the State Department against applying for a secretaryship in a foreign mission.[91] The League hoped to democratize recruitment and increase professional diplomacy's appeal for the men already in the Service by increasing salaries to a level which would support a man with a family, granting post allowances for use in expensive capitals, and establishing a pension system to offer old-age security.[92]

On the need for reform in the consular branch, the *Report* was largely silent, but the business organizations interested in foreign trade were all very strong friends of the consular service. The plans for reform they drew up involved some sort of amalgamation of the two branches of the Foreign Service, so that a close connection could be maintained between foreign commercial and political policy. The business groups wanted a Foreign Service that would consist of men who had experience in both consular and diplomatic posts, and whose political and economic work would be carefully coordinated by the State Department. Such an amalgamation followed from the belief that in the postwar world, international politics rested on a foundation of international trade.[94] As Carr and Hughes explained several times to business audiences, no diplomat would have the knowledge to successfully defend America's interests, which were largely economic, unless he had a firm grounding in the business side of diplomacy. A diplomat could best receive this training if he spent the first years of his career in the consular service. Likewise, consuls could not do their job properly so long as they remained isolated from political diplomacy. The consul's mission was to gather information about economic conditions abroad and to try to expand opportunities for American trade and investment, but so long as they received little official news about what American foreign policy was, their effectiveness remained severely limited.[95]

The response of many business groups to those arguments was favorable. All the Chambers of Commerce at home and overseas had been sent copies of the Civil Service Reform League's *Report* in 1919.[96] In the fall of 1920 the State Department began receiving word that the American Chamber of Commerce in London endorsed the principles of professional diplomacy and the amalgamation of the diplomatic and consular services embodied in the reorganization bill introduced by Representative Rogers.[97] Soon afterward, American Chambers of Commerce in Mexico and Turkey were endorsing the bill.[98] More important, in late 1922 the Executive Committee of the United States Chamber of Commerce voted its full approval of the Rogers Bill and urged its immediate passage.[99] Where business went, labor was not far behind, and in the spring of 1923 Tracy H. Lay of the Consular Bureau convinced Samuel Gompers's legislative assistant to have the American Federation of Labor lobby for the bill.[100]

Diplomacy Within the State Department

Despite all the agitation for reform among organizations outside the government, the major impetus for change came from the State Department itself. When Carr outlined for the Secretary of State in December 1919 the "Reasons Why the State Department Should Be Reorganized," he explained how no agency other than the State Department could command as much information regarding the needs and aspirations of the Foreign Service.[101] Although the bill, which became law in 1924, earned for its sponsor, John Jacob Rogers, the title of "Father of the Foreign Service,"[102] most of the drafting and lobbying were done by State Department officials. When outsiders such as the Chairman of the United States Chamber of Commerce testified for the Rogers Act, they appeared at the request of Carr of his staff.[103]

These departmental officials came from diplomatic and consular branches of the Service and consequently disagreed over the purpose of reorganization. Both diplomats and consuls wanted a new law which would end the endemic competition between them. The question was, on whose terms was the squabbling to be stopped. The National Civil Service Reform League's recommendations for amalgamation were vital for the consuls, who could be advanced to do the political work of diplomatic officers if the branches were merged. Diplomats, on the other hand, saw fusion as a threat. What they considered as their aims were increased salaries, a pension plan, and a strengthening of the merit promotion system, and at the same time, a neutralization of any encroachment on the part of consuls through amalgamation. The maneuvers of both sides to have their views expressed in the Rogers bill resembled the subtle negotiations of great power diplomacy, and accounted for some of the inherent contradictions, as well as the strengths, of the new Foreign Service.

Such diplomats as Ministers Grew and Gibson, Undersecretary Phillips, and Assistant Secretary J. Butler Wright were primarily interested in developing professional diplomats, the best of whom could be sure of rising to ministerial rank. To them the Civil Service Reform League's recommendations for strict application of the merit system, higher salaries, and a pension plan to secure a continuous supply of qualified personnel came as a blessing. In January 1920 Grew revealed to Wright his anxiety that the quality of the young men entering the diplomatic profession would decline in future years unless the service were made economically attractive.[104] According to him, the political leaders of the State Department—Lansing and Polk—were aware of the diplomat's needs, but were powerless to help until the Congress enacted new legislation. The Congress, however, had to be convinced that the diplomatic corps was vital to the nation and not merely the receptacle of gilded youth looking for a gay, exciting, and not-too-demanding lark abroad.[105]

To persuade Congress of the importance of their role, the diplomats carefully chose their tactics. One fact which stood out in the minds of Grew, Gibson, and Phillips was that the consular branch had always received better treatment at the hands of the legislature, because consuls were able to show that the expansion of American commerce was in their interest.[106] Grew was well aware that diplomacy had a far more important political role than increasing overseas trade, but he also knew that "the only element of the Foreign Service that appeals to the public is the ability of the Service to ensure business, better business, bigger business."[107] He therefore begged diplomatic friends to make it known to businessmen who were visiting American embassies for favors that the diplomat would appreciate some kind words for career diplomats if the businessman ever got to Washington.[108]

Congressional hearings on Foreign Service reorganization presented a more direct channel through which the diplomatic career men tried to awaken the public. There were two sets of House Committee hearings on the Rogers bill, one in December 1922, the other in January 1924. Since the bill failed to be called to the floor of the Senate in March 1923, it was reintroduced in the next session of Congress, and another set of House hearings took place in January 1924. No career diplomat testified in the 1922 hearings, but Secretary of State Charles Evans Hughes, former Undersecretary Frank Polk, and former Ambassador to Great Britain John W. Davis outlined the needs of diplomatic secretaries. Hughes described how the new role in international affairs which the United States had played since the First World War made the diplomatic service a first line of defense, as important to the welfare of the country as the armed forces. Only by making the Service more attractive through adequate salaries, post allowances, and pensions could the competent men needed as diplomats be induced to join the Foreign Service.[109] Both Polk and Davis recalled their experiences dealing with the low compensation given diplomatic secretaries.[110] Davis related that whenever a young diplomat asked his advice about staying in the Service, Davis invariably inquired about the young man's private financial resources. If the secretary was fully or mostly dependent on what he earned as a diplomat, Davis recommended a speedy exit from the Foreign Service.[111] Ever since Davis himself had left the embassy, he had believed that the only way to avoid a tremendous labor turnover among diplomatic secretaries was for Congress to pay these men adequately, and to assure them a fair chance that good work would be rewarded by promotion to ministerial rank.[112]

Career diplomats took over the job of presenting their Service's needs in the January 1924 hearings. Assistant Secretary of State Wright explained that the low salary scale not only drove out men already in the diplomatic service, but discouraged applications from capable men of moderate means. A standard procedure of the State Department's personnel office was to chill every prospective applicant who inquired about salaries with the words: "The experience of the department is that at present the remuneration of secretaries in the diplomatic service is unfortunately not such as to enable the department to assure them that they will be able to live on their salaries at all posts to which they may be sent."[113] Needless to say, such words of warning had a depressing effect. Wright reported that in one recent year the State Department had received over three thousand requests for information about diplomatic careers, but that less than twenty men had taken the written qualifying test for the diplomatic service.[114]

Minister to Poland Hugh Gibson also testified, concentrating on the business aspects of diplomacy. It was ironic that Gibson was chosen to represent the diplomats' case, commending the commercial benefits of his service, for of all the diplomats interested in Foreign Service reform, he was the most committed to the idea that the political role was paramount in diplomacy. During the previous three years Gibson had corresponded with other members of the diplomatic branch, expressing his disappointment with the amalgamation provisions of the Rogers bill.[116] Most of the diplomats he questioned were in agreement that interchangeability between the two branches would damage the social prestige of the diplomats.[117] Yet Gibson was in favor of the other provisions of the Rogers Act, and believed that the actual functioning of a new personnel system, which, it was to be hoped, the diplomats would control, was more important than any statutory language in the Rogers Act. He therefore followed the strategy laid down by Grew and explained that since the World War, foreign governments had interested themselves more and more in domestic and foreign commercial relations.[118] Businesses that had once been private were then in government hands, and postwar governments were often dominated by men hostile to the United States. It had become a diplomat's fundamental task to maintain such relations with a foreign government as would allow American business to operate freely abroad. This had been accomplished, Gibson told the Committee, by attempting to prevent the enactment of discriminatory tariff and trade regulations and by gathering information to show how safe a country was for American investment.[119]

To a Congressman who wanted to know why businessmen did not find diplomats who could be of help in seeking out foreign markets, Gibson replied that the career men could indeed help if businessmen would only consult them from the very beginning of their overseas operations. Diplomats on the scene were in the best position to square American business practices with those of a foreign land, thereby preventing the petty irritations which gave rise to complaints from businessmen that the Foreign Service officers paid too much attention to pushing cookies at teas and too little attention to advancing the nation's commerce.[120] Gibson also explained that a system of allowances for entertainment and other diplomatic expenses would greatly aid American businessmen. Unless a diplomat knew a member of the foreign office of the country to which he was accredited personally, it was impossible to go outside channels to comply with a businessman's request. And the only way for an American to establish that sort of personal relationship was to entertain his opposite number. Gibson reminded Congressmen that since they themselves were often the recipients of the American embassy's hospitality, it was only common decency that the embassy personnel be given the funds with which to entertain their foreign and American guests.[121]

Within the State Department, diplomats tried to cooperate with the consular branch in agitating for reform. Both groups were aware that their interests were not identical and that relations between them were never smooth. Nonetheless, they both understood that they could not get a reorganization bill passed unless they presented a united front to the Congress. Since the diplomats did not have a journal of their own, they used the *American Consular Bulletin* to publish their views on reform. When Grew was Minister to Denmark in 1921, he submitted an article describing the recent reorganization of the Danish Foreign Service, describing how the Danes had amalgamated their diplomatic and consular corps, had raised salaries, and had granted post, transfer, and installment allowances all of which supplemented an already existing pension system.[122] Other diplomats send in word to the *Bulletin* that the French, British, Belgian, and Norwegian services had also been amalgamated, and had had their salaries raised in the wake of the war's dislocations.[123] The changes had all been "designed to produce 'business results.' They tend to remove the remaining vestiges of what might be called the monarchial tradition in diplomacy. They emphasize the economic and merge it with the political, so that in a number of foreign service office reorganizations any distinction on this ground has been entirely lost sight of."[124] As I mentioned earlier, the diplomats had had a long-standing fascination with the European services, and owing to a combination of political and bureaucratic circumstances, American career men wanted to ape the Europeans. In some countries where European powers maintained embassies, the United States had only legations, causing the courtly status of American diplomats to be lower than that of the Europeans.[125] In other words, the Americans wanted to be as accomplished as the Europeans, have as secure a job tenure, and play as important a political role.[126]

When the Americans saw the Europeans reorganizing their services to "produce 'business results,' " they took heart. If the European services broke down the wall separating diplomats from consuls, American diplomats would suffer no loss of social status by doing the same thing. The European precedent even held out the prospect that the American Foreign Service might actually surpass those of the other powers in prestige. If all nations agreed that commercial expansion played an important role in the work of diplomats, Americans were in the best position to reap the rewards. Where previously the commercial might of the United States had made Americans seem crass Yankees to foreigners, a new world-wide respect for commerce would obviously boost the prestige of American envoys. Consequently, the model of European reorganization became a powerful argument in convincing career diplomats to drop their objections to joining with consuls in a new amalgamated service.

In Washington the senior career diplomat at the State Department, Undersecretary William Phillips, was always on hand to present his service's views to Wilbur J. Carr's consular office, which was redrafting the Rogers bill. When the bill suffered a temporary setback in the Senate in 1923, Phillips lunched with Carr and his staff to plan strategy to get it through during the next Congressional session.[127]

The men in the consular service with whom Phillips collaborated, Carr and Tracy Holingsworth Lay, did most of the tedious work involved in presenting a serious reorganization proposal to the Congress.[128] To the consular service, higher salaries were not the important issue. The best paid consuls were making $8000 a year in 1920, twice as much as the highest paid diplomatic secretaries.[129] Travel and post allowances were important, however, especially in the lowest ranks. Whenever a consular clerk was appointed, he learned that the State Department could not consider paying his passage from the United States to his post.[130] Such a system had resulted in the appointment of consular clerks who belonged only to the American upper class or were nationals of the country in which they worked.[131] Salaries were also inadequate if there happened to be an inflation, fluctuating rates of exchange, or other conditions of local hardship. Robert P. Skinner, American Consul General in London, explained in 1922 that his salary had been reduced by 20 percent in 1921, when the rate of exchange between pounds and dollars jumped from $3.27 to $4.65 to the pound.[132] In order to assure that the salaries paid to overseas representatives were adequate, Carr insisted that a system of post allowances be established by statute for the new Foreign Service.[133]

The consular service also wished there to be a provision for generous pensions. Carr realized that salaries paid by the government could never compete with those of private business. If, however, a man who liked consular work could be assured of a comfortable old age, he would be unlikely to succumb to the blandishments of high-paying banks and business houses. Carr drove his point home to Congress by having a former consul, Julius Lay, testify as to why he had left the service.[134] Lay stated that he had found consular work the most stimulating and enjoyable he had ever done, but had to leave the government to take a $25,000-a-year post with an international banking firm simply because there was no pension for consuls or diplomats.[134a] If a pension fund were established, he said that he would quickly rejoin the consular corps. Thus a pension system not only would allow the consular service to retain the capable men it had trained, but also, as Carr insisted, would allow the service to humanely retire consuls who had lost their efficiency.[135]

Above all, the consuls desired to have a fused Foreign Service in which they would have the same chance of promotion to ministerial rank as diplomats, and in which diplomats would receive their first training as consuls.[136] In this way consuls hoped to enhance their own status and to stop the real or imagined affronts they suffered at the hands of diplomats.[137] To many diplomats fusion or interchangeability seemed a presumptuous incursion into their domain, and they resolved to resist them both. Since they recognized that the Congress had previously been more amenable to the commercial arguments of the consuls than to the political arguments of the diplomats, they knew that they needed the consuls' support to gain higher salaries and a legally protected career for themselves. However, the consuls would not help them until they agreed to an amalgamation of the two branches.

The Rogers Bill contained an amalgamation provision. Foreign Service officers were to be divided into diplomatic and consular groups, and, on the recommendations of a personnel board, members of one group could be assigned to the other.[138] The number of transfers was not specified, allowing consuls and diplomats to interpret the provision as they would. Robert Skinner summarized the consuls' position on interchangeability in his testimony of December 1922, in which he discussed how modern international relations required highly trained Foreign Service officers who were attuned to the close relationship between economics and international politics. The government could not afford to pay successful businessmen enough to attract them into the Service, nor did the State Department want to hire business failures, dreamers, or expatriots who might be attracted by a career in exotic lands. The only way to get competent Foreign Service officers was to select good men from the colleges and universities and train them in business practice in the consular establishment.[139]

Actually, the diplomats did not believe that the bill would result in many transfers from one branch to the other. Testifying in 1924, Gibson explained that interchangeability ought not be carried to the point where the pride and morale of one branch of the Service could be destroyed. He understood that all transfers would be from the consular to the diplomatic branch, since he knew of no diplomat who wanted to be a consul. Diplomacy, after all, was "a broader field of activity and responsibility" than consular work, so that he was wary lest there be so many transfers that the diplomatic service would get demoralized about the prospect of promotions being usurped by outsiders.[140]

Behind the scenes, diplomatic officers made certain that the idea of fusion did not make much progress. One of J. Butler Wright's subordinates sent a memorandum to his chief in November 1923, criticizing the American Chamber of Commerce in London for giving the Rogers bill an endorsement which called the division between the consular and diplomatic services anachronistic. It was as sensible to let consuls work as diplomats by virtue of the fact that both were engaged in foreign affairs, Wright claimed, as it was to let a sleeping-car porter be an engineer because both were engaged in transportation.[141] Another diplomat, Lewis Einstein, became so alarmed at the prospect of consuls becoming diplomats that he circulated a letter to American embassies in Europe enlisting aid in blocking the amalgamation provisions of the bill.[142] Hugh Gibson also opposed amalgamation, but he believed that diplomats would be able to block the appointment of consuls to diplomatic work by controlling the new personnel system.[143] As for Joseph Grew, he contributed a jocular tone by sending a dreadful limerick to Gibson immediately before he left Warsaw to testify for the Rogers bill:

A Washington feller named Rogers,
Is nuts for old consular codgers,
His pals call him John
But I call him Bill,
For without the Bill, who would be Rogers?[144]

At times, consuls felt that the diplomats were deliberately sabotaging reorganization proposals. "So far as I can see," Carr wrote in his diary on February 5, 1923, "the diplomatic men want to have the service improved without making an effort or admitting the need for improvement."[145] A month later, when the Rogers bill had been lost in the Senate rush to conclude business by March 4, the consuls charged the diplomats with treachery. Carr received word that Assistant Secretary of State William Castle had opposed the bill all along, since higher salaries and amalgamation would lower the class of the diplomatic corps. Tracy Lay told Carr that he regarded Castle as "untrustworthy," and added that Castle "bootlicks, is insincere and has a dangerous tongue."[146] At a strategy-planning session with Congressman Rogers and William Phillips on March 8, Carr and Lay resolved to point out and isolate any diplomatic officer who was disloyal to the idea of reform.[147]

At the next session of Congress the Rogers Bill became law. It provided that diplomats and consuls would be reclassified into nine grades of Foreign Service officers who would be paid salaries ranging from $3000 a year for class nine officers to $9000 a year for class one, thereby ending the discrepancy between consular and diplomatic salaries. Moreover, the new salary was attached to an officer's rank, as in the armed forces, not to a specific job, as in the civil service. In this manner the law acknowledged that the distinct character of the Foreign Service lay in the personal accomplishments of its members, not in the functions implicit in an officer's job.

The Act also established a fund for post allowances and a pension system which would allow men who had served twenty-five years to retire at age sixty-five on half-pay—a pension sizably greater than the one in force for other federal employees. The Act tried to put interchangeability among consuls and diplomats into practice by allowing the president to appoint a Foreign Service officer to either a consular or diplomatic post at any time on the advice of a new personnel board. Executive Order 4022 of June 7 established two more boards to handle the recruitment and training of new members.[148] The Examining Board was to set requirements for entrance to the new Service, while the School Board would draw up the curriculum for the new Foreign Service School, an institution in which future recruits were to absorb the particular outlook that Foreign Service reformers had developed over ten years.

Consuls greeted the Roger's Act with almost hysterical joy. Indeed, the *American Consular Bulletin* devoted its entire July 1924 issue to the Act's history and implications. The issue contained sketches of the help given reform by Representative Rogers, Secretary Hughes, Assistant Secretary Wright, and Director of the Consular Bureau, Carr. It even included a picture of the pen the President had used to sign the bill.[149]

Congratulations from consuls, diplomats, businessmen, and educators poured into Carr's office, and they were richly deserved.[150] It was his office that had received the bill from Rogers in the summer of 1922, and Tracy Lay who had completely redrafted it in the fall.[151] Lay had also written the letter Hughes was to sign, endorsing the bill.[152] Once it had reached the floor of the House early in 1923, Carr suggested to Hughes that its chances would be substantially improved if President Harding could be persuaded to include it in his legislative program.[153] During the furious rush to pass the bill in 1923,

Carr and Tracy Lay had gone to Capitol Hill daily during February and March to buttonhole Senators. Moreover, it was Lay who had discovered that minority Leader Joe Robinson of Arkansas favored the bill, and it was Carr who had reminded Senator Oscar W. Underwood of the promise he had made to support Foreign Service reform after trying to sell pig iron in Mexico and finding the consular corps inefficient.[154]

In the reorganization of the Foreign Service, Congress played only a subsidiary role. The Rogers Act was debated twice in the House, in February 1923 and in April 1924, but it never was in the Senate.[155] Each time, the bill had passed in the House with large majorities.[156] What opposition there was came from the Democrats, led by Tom Connally of Texas, who had objected to the pension plan as being too generous, and to the amalgamation procedures as being inimical to the interests of consuls. Connally had also found the tone adopted by proponents of the bill too commercial and had accused them of forsaking American liberal principles for a Foreign Service that "went forth with a salesman's satchel with dollar marks all over it."[157] Most Congressmen, however, had accepted the argument of John Jacob Rogers that a forward postwar overseas commercial policy was necessary to relieve the plight of American farmers—a policy that could best be served by a reorganized Foreign Service.[158]

On the Senate side, the Rogers bill had encountered little opposition and merely a procedural delay. Senator Henry Cabot Lodge's Committee on Foreign Relations had unanimously approved the bill in February 1923.[159] But when Lodge brought the bill to the floor on February 28, three days before the end of the session, he failed to gain unanimous consent to its passage. The minority leader, Senator Robinson, returned the bill to committee in order to devote more time to a shipping bill.[160] Tracy Lay, upon hearing that the Senate had failed to act, accused Lodge of deliberately allowing the bill fail, in the belief that Lodge was jealous of the prestige the law would give his Massachusetts protégé, John Jacob Rogers.[161] When Lodge brought the bill to the Senate floor the following May, there was no rush to adjourn. Lodge briefly outlined the benefits of a reorganized Foreign Service for American commerce, after which the law was enacted without discussion or dissent.[162]

The consuls' congratulations to Carr were perhaps premature, for although he had worked hardest for the bill, the consular branch was not the one that profited most from its enactment. Not only was the conception of the new Service set-up vague as to its function and methods, but the fact that salaries and allowances were then high enough to attract the superior men who had previously shunned a Foreign Service career meant that the new pension system could keep the new men at their jobs. Moreover, the interchangeability feature did not satisfy the consuls' yearning for social equality, and the Personnel Board created by the Rogers Act decided in favor of the diplomats, so that transfers from consular to diplomatic work were rare indeed in the decade following 1924.[163]

PART TWO

Professional Ways

IV

The Foreign Service School
1924-1931

THE Foreign Service reformers inside the State Department, while agitating for the Rogers bill, enlisted the aid of many private groups and individuals with an interest in foreign affairs.[1] Once the bill became law, placing the Service on a firm career footing, its leadership grew increasingly apprehensive about the attention outsiders paid to the machinery of professional diplomacy. Departmental reformers wanted to retain absolute control over the training for, and admission to, the new diplomacy, fearing that men who received their formal diplomatic training outside the Department might display dual loyalties—to their schools as well as to their Service—in their subsequent diplomatic careers. The diplomats also distrusted the so-called utopian trend which they perceived in the foreign-relations courses that had become popular in American universities after the war. Moreover, they sensed that utopian writers like James T. Shotwell of Columbia, James W. Garner of the University of Illinois, Manley O. Hudson of Harvard, and Charles Seymour of Yale underestimated the competitive nature of world politics and were belittling the need for career diplomats.[2] For both bureaucratic and intellectual reasons, they decided that new recruits should receive their instruction in the art of diplomacy at the State Department's Foreign Service School, which had been created by the Rogers Act.

The first class of recruits entered the school in April 1925, and left after only five months because of the great need overseas for Foreign Service officers. Thereafter, each class spent a nine-month probationary period in the Victorian sprawl of the old State Department. For two hours each day the recruits attended lectures at the school, and during the remaining time worked as clerks, learning the Department's procedures.[3]

The Foreign Service School fulfilled several distinct functions. It provided its students with the fundamental points of diplomatic practice, in the hopes that graduates would be able to discharge full diplomatic duties immediately upon arrival at their first posts. The School's director, William G. Dawson, a career consul, also conceived of the training period as the beginning of a lifetime of study in diplomacy and international relations.[4] But the School had an additional and more important function to perform as a morale-building agency.[5] From his very first days there, a new recruit was persuaded of the need to acquire a professional diplomatic outlook. Reformers hoped that the close association of the recruits in their year at the School would continue throughout their careers, in much the same way as the members of the same class at the military academies thought of themselves as a distinct group within their services. By encouraging each entering group to think of itself collectively, the reformers hoped to create strong bonds of friendship and shared associations among the new men.

In its first years of operation the school provided recruits with a particular outlook on international relations which distinguished them from the amateur American diplomats of an earlier era and the utopian international-relations theorists of the 1920s. The lectures covered a range of subjects, from the personal deportment of Foreign Service officers to accounts of American policies around the world. The purpose of the entire course of study was to encourage young diplomats to develop a "realistic" and professional outlook on world politics—one that differed from that of previous amateur diplomats in being steadier and less impulsive. Indeed, it was completely at odds with the utopianism which some writers have claimed characterized the academic study of international relations in American universities in the twenties.[6] Most of the instructors were public officials who shared the realistic approach to world politics outlined earlier by Paul Reinsch, Archibald Carey Coolidge, and Lewis Einstein.[7] The others were university professors who rejected the schemes for the reform of international relations presented by such utopian scholars as Shotwell, Hudson, Garner, and Seymour.

All the instructors, regardless of background, wanted the diplomatic recruits to develop a hard, yet uncynical, attitude in regard to foreign affairs, so that they were taught to appreciate the contentious nature of politics among nations, and to be skeptical of programs which sought to abolish international conflict by reforming the machinery of world politics. New diplomats were told to reserve their reforming zeal for their own Service. The fundamental lesson they learned was that the patient application of professional diplomacy best guaranteed that the turbulent state system would not erupt into war.

Diplomatic Deportment

The Foreign Service School's curriculum was divided into two broad areas. Introductory lectures included accounts of the personal deportment of a Foreign Service officer and the procedural methods to be used in the field. The second and larger category of lectures consisted in an analysis of political affairs. But what was stressed in all instruction was the theme of "professionalism." Every lecture explicitly or implicitly distinguished the behavior of the new diplomat from that of his predecessors in overseas missions and that of contemporary critics of foreign policies.

The best descriptions of the personal behavior expected of professional diplomats were found in the welcoming speeches delivered by upper echelon State Department officials at the opening sessions of the school. These remarks had all the rhetorical felicity of a university president's greeting to a freshman class, and the recruits paid as little attention to them as would a typical freshman.[8] They were important, however, for what they revealed about the lecturers, for their indications of what the leadership expected of the new recruits, and for the idea they gave of how the speakers conceived of their own institution.

Several of the Department officials who had helped draft the Rogers Act—Joseph C. Grew, J. Butler Wright, Wilbur J. Carr, and Tracy H. Lay—greeted the recruits by telling them of their responsibility for making the new system work.[9] Others, in describing the hopes they entertained for the Service under the Rogers Act, were merely meant to encourage the new men. Some of the speeches, however, had an ominous tone to them. The new men were told that they had to demonstrate publicly the fact that professional diplomacy surpassed the previous system; otherwise, as both Undersecretary Grew and Assistant Secretary Wright explained, the Congress might decide that it had been misled into reorganizing the Foreign Service of the United States. Now, according to Grew and Wright, it was up to the new Foreign Service officers to make honest men out of all the diplomats who had sworn to Congressional committees that trained diplomats with secure job tenure advanced foreign policy more than did political appointees. If the new officers proved no better than the old-style diplomats, the State Department leadership would despair of ever organizing a Foreign Service in which all positions belonged to career men as a matter of right.[10]

A large part of an officer's task was that he support skillfully not only the United States in relation to other governments, but his own Foreign Service within the United States. An officer's job security depended upon how well he sold his Service to the American public and, especially, to its Congress. Grew explained that the main job of a diplomat was that of "smoothing things over," and he candidly admitted that a diplomat had to be more careful of the susceptibilities of Americans than of foreigners. A Congressman who had reason to feel snubbed on a visit to an American embassy could cause trouble for the entire Foreign Service, as well as make life miserable for the offending officer. Indeed, Grew's own career had been jeopardized by a misunderstanding with some junketing Senators who had visited his legation in Copenhagen in 1920, and he did not want the new Foreign Service to be sabotaged by Congressional pique.[11]

Personal experiences with the national legislature were also reflected in the remarks of Assistant Secretary of State Wilbur J. Carr, who for over a decade had been the State Department's principal advocate before Congress. Carr told the young diplomats that each of them had to sell the Service to the American public, reciting with gleeful horror one apocryphal tale of how a group of Congressmen on the loose in Europe had not been able to find a single diplomat or consul in his office at eleven in the morning. He explained how his own work before Congressional appropriations committees was made all the more difficult by dilatory conduct on the part of overseas personnel. If, however, all Foreign Service officers keenly sought to improve the reputation of the Service with the Congress, then the Department would receive all the additional appropriations it needed for higher salaries, representation allowances, and impressive buildings for its overseas missions.[12] All of these exhortations for good relations with the public might have been made, of course, to any civil servants. When they are seen, however, in the context of the campaign for Foreign Service reform which had just been concluded, and of the diplomats' basic distrust of amateurs who interfered with their work, they were an indication that, in the minds of Grew and Carr, the professionalism of their Service was not yet secure.

Departmental leaders also told entering officers of the splendid opportunity they now had for developing an *esprit de corps*. The notion of a close community of diplomats was not new. In the heyday of the old, dynastic diplomacy, foreign envoys of all "civilized" states prided themselves on common membership in an exclusive guild. The Foreign Service reformers had for years stressed the common bonds they hoped would develop among our own career diplomats. In 1916 Henry White, dean of American professionals, had compared diplomats of different lands serving together in the same country to college classmates. For the friendships they formed transcended national boundaries owing to their common interest in the diplomatic craft. Such international friendships, which diplomats often formed at their first posts, could eventually be of profit to their country's foreign policy when they and their colleagues abroad rose to preeminent positions in their respective foreign offices.[13]

When Grew or Assistant Secretary of State Leland Harrison told entering diplomats about the Service spirit, they had in mind something more precise than a vague wish for the future. They wanted new recruits to emulate the camaraderie of their own tightly-knit group. Grew, Harrison, Phillips, Fletcher, Gibson, and several officials in the War and Treasury Departments jointly owned a house at 1718 H Street in Washington, two blocks from the State Department. There, calling themselves the "Family," they resided while on leave or when assigned to the Department,[14] and they took not only their work but their colleagues home with them. While on vacation, they traveled with each others' real families.[15] In other words, they constantly mixed official duties with private enjoyment, so that they lived diplomacy all day, every day. This semiofficial kinship was the kind of *esprit de corps* the first generation of professional diplomats wanted to instill in the men who were to follow them.

The first professionals had developed their own close community partly because they were pioneer professionals who felt threatened by amateurs, and partly because their social and educational backgrounds were similar and congenial.[16] If the new Foreign Service developed as the reformers hoped, with many officers of diverse backgrounds assured of a secure job tenure, none of the conditions which had created the Family would obtain for the new career men. The State Department leadership, therefore, sought to devise new ways to maintain the old spirit.

What distinguished the *esprit de corps* of the New Diplomacy from that of the old was the fact that in the post-Rogers Act period, the State Department had tried to replace informal associations among members with institutionally created solidarity.[17] The Foreign Service School itself was designed to initiate a process of identification with the diplomatic profession. After diplomats had graduated from the school, their teachers wanted them to remain friends. Instead of suggesting the unworkable arrangement of a giant Family, all of whom shared a diplomatic dormitory, or hoping that the new officers would inevitably form close associations like the one centered at 1718 H Street, the older men advocated a professional association.[18] Grew told one entering class that the feeling of belonging to a group of professionals was "one of the finest things you will ever come across," and that the newly formed (1924) Foreign Service Association, with its monthly journal and regular luncheons in Washington, as well as the Department of State Club in the capital, were voluntary groups that molded individuals into a corps of diplomats.[19] Although the Association and the Club were not officially sponsored organizations, Grew explained that the Department had made morale-boosting its permanent policy, which was implemented by thus informing field workers of decisions taken in Washington and circulating reports from other missions around the globe.[20]

Throughout the period of professionalization, American diplomats compared the quality of their Service with that of the European powers and found American diplomacy wanting. Before passage of the Rogers Act, they had used the reorganization of the European foreign services after the war as an example for the United States to follow.[21] Hence, at the Foreign Service School, the reformers told the recruits that a continual part of their job would be to study the organization of other countries' foreign services. Tracy Lay, a consul-general who had a role second only to Carr's in drafting the Rogers Act, instructed new men to keep the Department officially informed of any adjustments in the form of other nations' Foreign Services. Such information would help the Department formulate high policy, since nations gained competitive advantages in world politics by refining their foreign service machinery. Lay also wanted officers in the field to send information on this subject to the *Foreign Service Journal*[22] so that American diplomats would no longer feel personally inferior to their European counterparts.

The Department hoped that the personal quality of the new Service would rise to the level of the Europeans' as soon as the new men conscientiously worked to improve themselves. It also decided to recruit men of broad interests and accomplishments, and hoping that once in the Service, they would continue to stretch their minds. Grew, for example, urged young men to cultivate an intellectual hobby outside their work. "The best kind of rest," he claimed, "is not just letting one's mind grow fallow, but by following some other interest." Intellectual breadth had a utilitarian purpose—that of enabling diplomats to develop social and intellectual contacts with foreigners who could be useful to American foreign policy.[23]

Moreover, there was the question of a diplomat's public image. The lecturers, who recognized that the work of Foreign Service officers was not so arduous as to consume all their time, were concerned about the political consequences of diplomats enjoying themselves often and over long periods of time.[24] William Castle, a former dean at Harvard College who served as Chief of the Division of Western European affairs in the mid-twenties, encouraged recruits to satisfy domestic critics by writing scholarly works on the history and culture of the countries in which they were stationed. Castle admired the European diplomats who did just that. To American Foreign Service officers, diplomatic scholarship was equivalent to a badge which improved the prestige of the Foreign Service and taught diplomats how to polish their prose. In any case, lecturers hoped that, in the end, writing for publication would raise the level of American diplomatic language to that of the British Foreign Service.[25]

The last bit of general advice given to classes at the Foreign Service School concerned the attitude a diplomat ought to assume toward other countries and toward his own while stationed at a foreign post. All the recommendations to young recruits revealed the precarious position of American foreign officers, who were obliged to distrust both foreigners and nonprofessional Americans. One of a diplomat's obvious tasks was to promote a friendly relationship between the United States and the land in which he was stationed. For example, if a diplomat happened to acquire a reputation for unhappiness abroad, his sources of information usually ran dry. Yet it was even more disastrous were he to show too much fondness for his post, for the Department would then question his credibility as an objective political reporter, diminishing his chances for success. On the other hand, uncritical appreciation of a foreign land smoothed the way for friendships abroad, but insidiously changed a diplomat's perspective to that of his host.[26]

Nevertheless, the school's instructors were far more concerned about creating the proper attitude toward the United States than about the dangers of an unbalanced attitude with regard to foreign countries. Opponents of professional diplomacy had often charged that residence abroad over too long a period stripped envoys of their Americanism, and tended to make them hypercritical of their homeland.[27] Either they would sneer at its seeming cultural parochialism or they would resent domestic interest in foreign affairs. The school tried to combat any increase in world-weary snobbery so as to protect the new bureaucracy. For example, Grew warned entrants against succumbing to the blandishments of American expatriates, who would try to get them to join in their carping against the United States. According to Grew, "The only thing you can do when you meet these people is to keep a dignified attitude and allow no remark ever to be made in your presence disparaging to the United States unless it is good constructive criticism." At the same time, he cautioned the young men to be wary of the ardent flag-wavers among overseas Americans. Support for such fellow countrymen would not strengthen American foreign policy, and would make a diplomat appear bumptious in the eyes of his host.[28] For men whose professional standing among their overseas colleagues depended upon their apparent balance and sophistication, projecting the image of a crude Yankee chauvinist could prove ruinous.

Most of the instructors also gave the recruits practical information on the work of the State Department. In a short course of lectures Allen Dulles, Chief of the Division of Near Eastern Affairs, presented a very general overview of political reporting. His remarks covered the aims of political reports, the subjects to be reported on, and the skills and methods necessary for success in the most important of diplomatic tasks.[29] Together, his lectures formed a coherent statement on the standards of professional diplomatic practice that were expected to be upheld by American diplomats. They conveyed Dulles's and the Department's attitude that diplomatic skills came slowly and required constant attention and practice. The most important diplomatic skill, Dulles claimed, was soundness of judgment, which could be acquired over the years through emulation and habit.

Like many other lecturers at the School, Dulles began by telling his listeners that diplomacy was indeed a legitimate profession, the need for which had changed but had not been eliminated by modern communications.[30] Now that an American envoy could receive hourly instructions from Washington and was no longer an independent negotiator, he was most useful as a political reporter. Therefore modern negotiations required not only open channels of communications but also information adequate to the shaping of policy. How well a diplomat provided accurate information was what determined his usefulness to the Department.[31]

Although he had listed in outline form the subject matter and sources of political reports, Dulles was primarily interested in convincing future diplomats that there were no fast rules for turning out good dispatches. Like most diplomatic skills, this one derived from experience and intuition. The criteria he offered for judging the worth of a dispatch—an aptitude for writing, accuracy of information, and above all, soundness of judgment— were neither startling nor particularly helpful; but Dulles's description of the making of a good political report did reveal the arduous process by which young Foreign Service officers were supposed to acquire the "art" of diplomacy.

The best preparation for political reporting, he believed, was a solid grounding in the theory, history, and practice of international relations. Dulles advised young men to learn the diplomatic, political, and economic history of the country to which they would be sent, as well as the history of the diplomatic relations between the United States and that country. Repeating his unfavorable comparison between the style of American diplomats and that of the dynastic diplomats of Europe, Dulles recommended that young men add polish and perspective to their accounts by studying the memoirs and published dispatches of the great European diplomats during the period of crisis before the 1914 war.[32]

Diplomats, said Dulles, had constantly to be aware of the principles of American foreign policy. An officer was obliged at all times to relate the information contained in his reports to relations between the United States and his post. When recounting political developments in a country, he also had to keep in mind the relative importance to the Department of the field in which he was stationed. Special pleading for an improvement in our relations with a particular nation had to be avoided.

Moreover, Dulles suggested specific ways of looking at international questions that would aid a diplomat in writing his dispatches. Coherence and continuity made for the best reporting, and to achieve them, a conscientious officer would, before leaving for his post, list the questions he considered most important. Furthermore, diplomats had to concern themselves with the same problems that were of interest to articulate Americans, so that it was essential that officers keep in contact with the American press, not so much to gain insight as to be aware of how international questions were being presented to the public, one of the diplomat's jobs being to rectify the uninformed misconceptions of American editors.[33]

According to Dulles, the sources most important to a diplomat in compiling a dispatch were personal contacts with other foreign envoys. Given the common bonds among professionals, diplomats of other nations were a primary source of information, and the facts gleaned from colleagues were what officially justified the diplomatic social whirl. However, information received from men in other foreign missions raised rather delicate problems of discretion. To receive information, a diplomat had to part with some of his own, and Dulles advised candor rather than mystery in the sharing of intelligence. Since he thought too much had been made of secrecy in diplomacy, he warned officers against receiving clandestine information which not only risked enraging the authorities, but whose accuracy was difficult to judge.[34] Dulles added that the close personal associations formed at the Foreign Service School would help officers share information with each other later on. He also advised them that overseas functionaries in other American departments could be relied on as sources of information, cautioning them to avoid rivalry with the military, naval, and commercial attachés. Coyness or secrecy among those various bureaus could dam the flow of useful information. He suggested, too, that consuls in different cities of the same country keep in constant touch with one another,[35] for whether they knew each other through the School or through the Foreign Service Association, the work of the Department would be facilitated if they kept in contact.

Like the other lecturers, Dulles encouraged the young men to broaden their horizons. A diplomat could not form an accurate impression of a country by relying on information received only in the capital. He therefore suggested that it would be wise for a man, on his own initiative, to travel widely in the country so that he might better understand its political affairs. If he were a consul, travel would permit him to meet his colleagues in other cities.[36] Travel, however, had to be undertaken at the officer's own expense, for in 1925 the Department did not yet have the money to spare, so that professionalism in that area had to be acquired unofficially.

Dulles, like the other instructors, brought in the notion of the "Service ideal" as a leitmotif. Newcomers were advised to cultivate their personal talents and then devote them to the advancement of the Service as a whole. They could rest assured that the Department learned exactly how a junior man behaved himself through the efficiency reports, Chiefs of Mission, or Inspectors. His advancement through the ranks of the Service depended upon the quality of his work as a sophisticated and critical political observer.[37]

Foreign Policy

The bulk of the instruction received in the school concerned policy. Political issues ranged from general statements on relationships between international commerce and world politics to specific questions regarding the attitude of the United States toward particular areas of the world. Since the diplomats' political outlook was internally inconsistent, the lecturers attempted to point out both the change and the continuity in world politics, as well as the abiding differences and similarities in the behavior of various states. They described the United States as simultaneously a self-seeker of commercial advantage and a disinterested regulator of international rivalry. The nature of the state system, they claimed, was proof of the need for an active overseas policy. The complexity of international relations also demonstrated the need for full-time students of world affairs to direct United States foreign policy.

Professional standards demanded that good diplomats appreciate those subtle distinctions in "national psychology" which made various countries conduct their affairs differently. New officers were told that each nation had a specific way of observing the world, one which remained constant despite changes in government and, more importantly, changes in political systems. A lecturer at the school, Professor Bernadotte E. Schmitt, an historian at the University of Chicago, warned diplomats not to believe that the revolutions of postwar Europe had altered the structure of international politics. Confidential documents of the German and Russian Foreign Offices from 1914 "exhibit the psychology of German and Russian diplomatists and I doubt very much whether, in spite of the changes in government in both Germany and Russia, there have been any fundamental changes in the psychology of Germans and Russians." The constancy in national outlook arose from the immutability of national interests. "We know," said Schmitt, "that the foreign interests of a country remain much the same from year to year, and, one might say, generation to generation."[38]

The struggle for commercial and political preeminence helped a nation define its self-interest. What the lecturers said about the relations between commerce and diplomacy was reminiscent of the agitation for Foreign Service reform, when both diplomats and consuls had insisted (for bureaucratic reasons) that modern international relations consisted in a subtle blending of commerce and politics.[39] Men who truly understood the material foundations of international relations made the best diplomats. One of the disadvantages of the old dynastic system was that the diplomats, for all their personal charm, lacked an awareness of the commercial foundation of foreign policy. Tracy Lay of the old consular branch, who emphasized how the war had shocked all the "civilized" nations into understanding that their Foreign Services existed on an unsound basis, held the old system of great power diplomatic rivalry in Europe responsible for the outbreak of the Great War. The old system's signal fault, he claimed, was its blindness to the interdependence of commercial and political factors in international relations.[40]

The new career Service in the United States, with its amalgamation of the diplomatic and consular branches, was an institutional means of carrying out foreign policy on a commercial basis. Lay warned recruits to eschew all the "altruistic and idealistic" fancies about world politics they might have learned in college. International life was neither a military nor a religious exercise. Rather, it was a "race for production . . . a race for markets. It ha[d] been going on for a long while—long before the war—but it ha[d] been intensified very greatly by the war . . . The basis for competition [was] selfishness, that is self-interest. The principle of nationalism [is] self-interest."[41]

As subtle "realists," diplomats had to adopt a flexible attitude toward economic determinism. Lay indicated that the commercial factor did not completely dominate the politics of a government, that emotion and sentiment often played a part in international relations. He warned, however, that "when the policy of a government is for the moment adverse to the economic interest of that country, that policy is ephemeral."[42] The principle of the commercial basis for all political action was exemplified at the time by the foreign trade policy of the United States. Lay pointed out that in the thirty years since 1894, the United States had produced more goods than it had consumed. American and European industries found themselves in the identical position of being unable to curtail production for fear of business slumps. All industrial nations had engaged in fierce competition for overseas markets, and it was necessary for Foreign Service officers to understand the origins of commercial rivalry, since the job of the Foreign Service was "taking care of our exportable surplus." It had to devise methods of clearing trade channels of the artificial barriers erected by other nations to dam the flow of American goods. On the other hand, diplomats could not be too assertive as nationalists, for "we do not wish to give occasion for any more comment about American imperialism," which could lead to the choking off of American overseas trade by foreigners.[43]

Through an understanding of the commercial underpinning's of international rivalry, professional diplomats distinguished themselves from amateur observers of international relations, who were baffled by international competition or thought state rivalry the result of cynical dynastic maneuvers. That understanding justified the diplomats' claim to be the only men capable of assuring the flow of international commerce. It also provided a framework for looking at certain intractable political questions of the day in a realistic manner. Their firm grasp of the commercial basis of international rivalry was the reason for diplomats being superior both to American amateurs, who were confused by international relations, and European diplomats, who were unable to comprehend the material foundations of world politics because they were blinded by historic national hatreds.

William R. Castle told the future diplomats how an understanding of world commerce would give them a superior moral and intellectual vantage point in relation to the new states of Europe. Most Americans, he claimed, had been misled by their feelings for national self-determination in Europe.

They had, out of sentimentality, lost their good sense and supported the creation of economically unviable states out of the wreckage of the Austrian and Russian empires. The State Department, Castle was happy to report, had not been so naïve as to applaud the dismantling of the splendid economic unity of Central Europe. Indeed, its opposition to the creation of some of the successor states had provoked criticism of the Department from the more ardent backers of European nationalism. Castle dismissed this carping as the kind of ignorance to be expected from nonprofessionals, and hoped that America's new diplomats would pay no attention to the special pleading of the sentimental among the citizenry. Only diplomats had a good enough understanding of world economics to give balanced judgments on territorial questions. Only diplomats understood that "in these modern days" economic considerations "seem more vital and more lasting than any others. They are permanent while other [race, nationality, and political structure] fluctuate."[44]

American diplomats persuaded themselves that they saw all sides of the controversial questions of nationalism. Their knowledge, the prosperity of their country, and its historical development outside the system of European rivalries made them better able to judge the competing claims of European nationalists than the Europeans themselves. Europeans were too close to national rivalries, had suffered too much in the recent war, to see that there was more than one point at issue. All they believed was that the doctrine of self-determination seemed to satisfy their aspirations. Castle claimed that this doctrine "seemed more spendidly right because people wanted it to be right." An economic tragedy had occurred when the magnificent commercial unity of the Habsburg Empire was shattered to satisfy the selfish aspirations of Czech, Slovak, Polish, Magyar, and other nationalists.[45]

Castle played a variation on Wilsonian themes which was common among professional diplomats when he opposed the successor states on economic grounds. Both Wilson and the diplomats of the twenties believed in the exceptionalism of the American nation. Wilson came to that conclusion from his comparison of American and European history.[46] The professional diplomats also implied that the historical development of the New World had diverged from that of the old. They disagreed with Wilson, not over an appreciation of the United States as a redeemer nation, politically superior to the European dynasties, but over differences of method. The professional diplomats contended that only a part of the American public was an instrument for the control of world politics[47]—that part, of course, being the professional student and practitioner of diplomacy.

International law made international commercial conflict controllable. To State Department leaders, international law was not a remote set of principles which idealistic men sought, with little chance of success, to impose upon the world system. The principles of international law regulated, but did not curtail, the competition among states, and all nations recognized law as a substitute for harmful world anarchy. The realistic view of international law was expounded to the school by Ellery C. Stowell, former chairman of the National Civil Service Reform League's Committee on Foreign Service from 1919 to 1924. When he lectured to the school in 1926, he was a professor of government at the American University in Washington. Stowell explained that the main interest of a state was to "get ahead of the other State—to win its way in the world." Idealists like James W. Garner and Manley O. Hudson were wrong in supposing that law was an institution designed to protect the weak from predators. The strong created the law for their own protection, and they enforced it "because it ensures them of possession of what they have at the least possible cost." The weak, too, accepted laws written by the strong, since some kind of predictable justice was preferable to the strong exercising of arbitrary power. International law, said Stowell,

> is the law of the strong States, made to preserve for strong States their possessions and also very carefully made so that it will not interfere with keen competition with their rivals. Made in this way you would expect that State system not to interfere with the very wide power of competition, and that is found to be the case when the facts are examined.[48]

Stowell's stark system of international law offered American Foreign Service officers a justification for advancing it as a fundamental object of American foreign policy by which they could uphold legal principles without succumbing to charges of silly idealism. International law ordered the world on American terms, which could be willingly accepted by other nations. Stowell's system implied that professional diplomats, upholding the law, were to be the means by which national rivalries would be contained.

A belief in the commercial foundations of international life, a skepticism with regard to self-determination, a respect for national psychology, and a belief in the meliorist effects of international law made up the so-called realistic set of assumptions on international affairs. When lecturers discussed specific United States foreign policies, their remarks derived from that view. Nowhere did they give a fuller account of realistic foreign policy than in their lectures on the meaning, fairness, and methods of American policy toward Latin America.

Traditionally, service in Latin American posts had been considered a graveyard for American diplomats. European or Oriental missions seemed to offer glory and the chance to play a major political role. On several occasions after passage of the Rogers Act, the Foreign Service Personnel Board had to discipline officers who refused to serve in Latin America, and yet for Chiefs of Mission there, it recommended men who somehow could not reach a high level of efficiency in their diplomatic work.[49]

The professional ideal was a means of overcoming this distaste for Latin American duty. It demanded that an officer accept assignment wherever the Department chose to send him.[50] The Chief of the Division of Latin American Affairs, Francis White, told recruits that the Department no longer regarded Latin American officers as stepchildren. Only able, experienced, and enthusiastic officers could direct operations in that hemisphere and advance the new State Department policy of "helping the Latin Americans help themselves."[51]

The permanent staff of the Latin and Central American divisions of the State Department—Francis White, Dana Munro, and Stokely Morgan—all explained Latin American policy to the school. The United States, they said, wished, in a disinterested manner, to help the people of Latin America achieve political stability and economic well-being. Toward the Latin Americans, they all exhibited an uninhibited and unembarrassed paternalism, whereas toward domestic critics of American policies in the Western hemisphere, they displayed the expert diplomat's contempt for the uninformed meddler.

White told the students that the governments in Latin America looked upon American diplomats as guides for the proper conduct of their own affairs, and advised them to show the same balance and coolness in Latin America that they exhibited elsewhere. They were not to expect a swift development of modern political institutions in Latin America, because the "Latin temperament and climate" worked against political progress, while in Central America, "low racial quality" contributed to the general backwardness. Experts in Latin American affairs, however, had an excellent opportunity to improve conditions among the Latins, who were "very easy people to deal with if properly managed." They were people who "responded well to patience."[52]

Prosperity, intelligence, and expertise gave American diplomats the opportunity to protect the Latin Americans from the fruits of their own ignorance and folly. Foreign Service officers were staunchly to deny any suggestion that American policy was imperialistic. White, Munro, and Morgan all believed that charges of imperialism were made by ignorant American sentimentalists who knew nothing of conditions in Latin America, or out of the malice caused by domestic malcontents.[53] Munro stated that the charge of imperialism had often been raised because of the occasional intervention of American troops in Central America. Constant revolution and financial chaos had forced the United States to send troops to restore order. "Radical elements and political opponents in this country" often made political capital out of those occasional interventions without regard to the merit of the cases,[54] whereas American diplomats were convinced that the basis for such actions had been the protection of American lives and property, the enforcement of international agreements, and the forestalling of military action by European powers.

Diplomats had a ready reply to domestic critics who complained that the United States government should take no interest in the fate of its citizens who were trapped in Central America during times of upheaval. Although opponents did not say that American business had no right to be in those tumultuous lands, they did contend that if a man was foolish enough to leave his home, he should be prepared to protect himself. To Morgan such critics seemed blind to the role diplomats played in making international commerce regular and predictable. Their advice seemed at once cowardly and illegal. They seemed to be saying that a foreign investor "should manage his business interests in foreign lands on the principle of a clever gambler, by trying to make large profits as quickly as possible, and get away before they are taken from him." The critics of investment made no mention of the regulative force of contractual obligations, and their arguments were "not the way to encourage the spread of American commerce and industry throughout the world, and if the Department subscribed to that view there would soon be very little American business and few American businessmen abroad."[55]

Their moral influence and even their moral superiority were readily accepted by Latin American experts, but imperialism, as it was practiced by the Europeans, was anathema to American policy. The United States had always acted with "extreme reluctance," even in situations in which she was "clearly compelled to intervene." She had withdrawn her troops with dispatch, and her goal for the past twenty years had been "to help these nations reach a point where they can manage their affairs in a manner which will leave no pretext for interference by ourselves or anyone else."[56]

Although offended by the suggestion that the United States was an imperial power in this hemisphere, the directors of American foreign policy did have a clear vision of the desired political structure of Central America. Stokely Morgan defined it as a system of "independent, orderly, constitutional governments, enabling these countries to stand as equals among the nations of the earth, with political peace and economic prosperity."[57] To achieve that goal, the State Department had collaborated with the Central American republics in drafting a treaty which would deny diplomatic recognition to revolutionary regimes.

While assessing the nonrecognition doctrine, diplomats were supposed to remember the realistic lessons of international law, and were not to apply the principle of nonrecognition in an obtuse, legalistic manner. Morgan even objected to the Article of the Central American Treaty of 1925, prohibiting diplomatic recognition of revolutionary regimes as the result of blindness to certain basic facts of Central American political life: "The framers of Article 2, actuated undoubtedly by the highest motives in the world, lost sight, as idealists are apt to do, of some of the practical considerations of the case." They missed the point that under the nonrecognition doctrine, changes of regime were virtually precluded, since coups d'état and revolutions seemed to be the only way opposition politicians could gain power in Central America. Morgan further suggested that Americans had been duped by cynical Central American negotiators who had drawn up the clause to "assure the party then in power a never-ending term in office."[58]

Despite the fact that Americans had met with "woefully little success" in persuading the constitutional authorities to hold fair and free elections, Morgan told them not to abandon hope. The comic-opera nature of Central American elections should encourage skepticism, but not cynicism. When a dictatorial regime felt compelled to adhere to the forms of constitutional practice, "that alone is a great step towards the achievement of a real democratic government." As applied in Honduras and Nicaragua, the nonrecognition doctrine was already making steady progress toward "universal and unquestioning acceptance of the doctrine that law and order must prevail."[59] Intelligent, learned, realistic, and self-confident American Foreign Service officers were to be the agents who made the Central Americans understand that their own best interests demanded the creation of sound law and order in that hemisphere.

Other experts in the school gave courses on American policy in the Far East, disarmament, political revolution, and such commercial questions as agreements concerning rubber, petroleum, and cables. None of the courses requires detailed analysis here, for they all displayed the same "realistic" outlook that characterized the other courses at the school. All the experts advised the recruits to look below the surface in order to see the material bases of American policies, and contended that diplomats were better able to judge political questions than uninformed politicians. On all those issues, they believed that the United States was more disinterested than any of the other Great Powers. Regarding the Far East and the economic issues of the day, the lecturers were actively suspicious of the motives of the diplomats of the European powers, whom they suspected of conspiring to gull Americans into yielding their rights to equal treatment. The future American diplomats were enjoined to place their faith in their own skills and the soothing effects of international law. And it was suggested that those states which put themselves beyond the pale of international law, particularly Bolshevik Russia, should be isolated by those nations which wanted to make the international system work in a predictable fashion.[60]

The instructors were particularly careful to make certain that the future diplomats entertained no false "idealistic" hopes in the new international machinery resolving long-standing international disputes. To avoid disillusionment, they would have to accept the constancy of human strife, and understand that their job was to regulate, not eradicate, such contentions. In a lecture on disarmament policy in 1926, Alanson Houghton, our Ambassador to Great Britain, speculated that it would take a century to abolish world armaments, explaining that the French view of disarmament, with its insistence of security guarantees and multilateral reductions of general war-making power, was more realistic than the British plan of merely reducing standing armies. The popular American conception of disarmament entertained by such idealists as James Garner, James Shotwell, Edward Bok, or Salmon Levinson was more off-base than the British. The United States in its splendid isolation, with no neighbors to fear or to hate, considered disarmament merely as a sensible way to take men from a nonproductive army and put them to work. To uninformed Americans disarmament was a moral question. To the Europeans it was a vital matter of security. A proper resolution of the question demanded expert knowledge of the relative economic and military strength of all the states of the world. When military reductions were put into effect, they had to be based upon a nation's entire war-making potential. The scrapping of weapons and machinery would doubtless take decades.

Although Houghton cautioned against glib optimism regarding disarmament, he indicated that the relative military security of the United States enabled its representatives to act as disinterested mediators between nations at the forthcoming League of Nations Preliminary Disarmament Conference at Geneva. If American delegates properly understood the difficulties inherent in disarmament, they could provide the good offices to reduce arms and at the same time assure the security needs of the Europeans.[61]

The view American diplomats held of the new democracies of Europe also squelched hopes for immediate and automatic improvement in world politics. William R. Castle, who was in charge of the Department's Western European Affairs Division, was not notable either for his idealism or his optimism.[62] His unhappy projection of the economic chances of the Habsburg successor states has been explained. He also had harsh words for the new democracy in Germany, claiming that the German Republic had emerged not through a political or social revolution, but only because the cowardly Kaiser had fled his country in 1918. The continuation of the Empire would not, he said, have been a bad idea, for while William II may have been a nincompoop, he had surrounded himself with "very keen and clever people to tell him what to do."[63] The Kaiser had provided the German people with a political center of gravity which they now lacked.

Since the Armistice, Germany's government had suffered from a lack of central authority. In all nations where it existed, the parliamentary system was vulnerable to votes of no-confidence, and in the multiparty system of the German Republic, instability was certain. In the welter of weak parties, individuals had come to count for more and more in German affairs. Despite its democratic constitution, the Republic stood in danger of being captured by strong men. How much better the system would be, Castle lamented, if the Germans still had the real spirit of unity which the Emperor had provided, instead of their present noble-sounding but jejune constitution.

Castle implied that in observing new political developments, diplomats had to look beyond the façade of artificial declarations and laws to the reality of a nation's social, economic, and political arrangements. Only a professional diplomat, devoting himself full-time to the study of international affairs, had the means to understand how nations worked. Such an understanding would lead him to appreciate how little easy schemes of political reform could improve politics, and how, if impressed upon the public, it would make diplomatic jobs more secure.

Castle's conservative, organic view of politics was common among the State Department leaders. The professional ideal they sought to impress upon the diplomatic neophyte was that foreign affairs required a singular form of expertise which most articulate Americans did not possess. Diplomatic skill was intuitive rather than technical. It developed only in time and only if diplomats were in close association with other men whose habits of thought were similar. The best diplomats were not experts trained in one narrow field, but men of broad culture who comprehended vast amounts of information regarding political and international affairs—men who believed that they understood the meaning of international developments better than amateurs because they understood "human nature." The smooth and steady methods they wished to employ in negotiations were designed to show their colleagues in other, older diplomatic services how well they had grasped the psychology of nations.

While their view of mankind was conservative, it was hardly cynical, for they believed that men were not irremediably evil. Rather, political man in his natural state of ignorance, both at home and abroad, was crude, but his intellectual betters could edify him. In domestic political debate, professional diplomats could, if their career were secure, teach the uninitiated the truth about world politics. Trained Americans overseas, with their intelligence, prosperity, and disinterest, believed they could help benighted foreign peoples learn how to conduct their affairs properly. In the diplomats' view, such reformers as Shotwell, Levinson, Garner, Hudson, or Bok, with their schemes for reordering the world, were doomed to disillusionment and were courting international disaster by undermining the authority of the professional diplomats, who truly understood politics among nations.

By depicting international relations as an arcane subject, comprehensible only to a few men who invested energy and skill in their studies of world politics, the leadership of the school provided an intellectual justification for a professional corps of Foreign Service officers. At home, diplomatic expertise was intended to protect the newly-won job security of American Foreign Service officers and accord them the deference due respected teachers. Overseas, the officers would combine their honest disinterest as Americans with their sound judgment as diplomats in an effort to diminish international strife. Given the work involved, American diplomats hoped to win full acceptance, and even admiration, from the members of the diplomatic guild throughout the world.

V

The Professional Mystique, 1924-1931

DIPLOMATS and consuls throughout the period of reform never did settle upon a precise definition of the job of a Foreign Service officer, nor on its requirements. The reformers explained to businessmen, educators, and politicians that the professional practice of diplomacy differed sharply from the methods employed by amateurs. What the Foreign Service of the post-Rogers Act period considered ideal was a corps of foreign affairs experts who combined mental flexibility, balance, tact, and something called "sound judgment" with a thorough general education and adequate technical knowledge. *Esprit de corps* was more important to the efficient exercise of foreign policy than any personal qualities an officer might possess. Foreign Service officers were supposed to submit dutifully to the discipline of their superiors.[1] The reformers not only expected each officer to perform his assignment cheerfully and to proceed willingly to any part of the world to which he was ordered,[2] but they predicted that new recruits would be animated more by a desire to improve the quality of their service than by selfish career ambitions.[3]

The amalgamated Service created by the Rogers Act did not live up to this ideal. Perhaps no Foreign Service could have overcome the personal, careerist aims of its members. Modern research into the functions of complex organizations shows that bureaucracies seldom operate as their formal organizational charts might indicate. Cliques, quasi-legal but tacitly accepted administrative practices, and informal lines of communication abound, and while such informal arrangements often divert a bureaucracy from its stated goal, they do satisfy the real psychological and career needs of a bureaucracy's officials.[4] However, a large part of the Foreign Service's internal difficulties and political travail was the result of more serious tensions than the conflict between personal ambition and collective welfare, which is inherent in complex organizations.

One problem was that the diplomats' ambiguous view of their own careers made it impossible for them to state precisely the type of officers they wanted. What they conceived of as an ideal diplomat was at once an imitation of the English and French professionals and a frank, uncynical American who conducted negotiations in an open and disinterested fashion. The reformers wanted the new diplomats to conduct foreign policy with the skill of the practitioners of the Old Diplomacy, but expected their aims to be those of the new.[5]

Secondly, the expertise concept of diplomacy presented a dilemma. While diplomats believed that some type of special education was necessary to make a man into a diplomat, they rejected the argument that technical knowledge formed a major part of a Foreign Service officer's intellectual equipment. Judgment, presence of mind, and "soundness" were all deemed more important than any technical knowledge.[6] To have allowed technical skill to be the principal measure of diplomatic effectiveness would have provided an opening for other agencies, such as the Commerce Department, to assume a predominant role in international affairs.[7] Further, a primary reliance on technical performance would have meant that the former consular branch, which was far more "technical," could dominate the former diplomatic branch in the new Foreign Service.

The idea of service discipline and *esprit de corps*—self-abasement for the good of the Foreign Service—was countered, of course, by the hard facts of personal ambition and unofficial cliques. The older diplomats felt obliged to two corps. The older and stronger of these was the private group of first-generation diplomats who had created the new Service; the newer and weaker was the recent amalgamated bureau. While the older men sought to impart some of their "clubbiness" to the larger Service as a whole, they looked for institutional means to do so. Inevitably, the easy conviviality of the older group could not be automatically transferred to men who had not shared the experiences of the reforming generation. Jealousies and mistrust between members of the club—the Family, plus new recruits and lateral entrants—became common in the years following passage of the Rogers Act.

The most ambiguous area in the definition of the new diplomatic career was the extent to which diplomacy was to achieve rigorous professional status in the post-Rogers Act years. Although reformers talked repeatedly about assuring new entrants a career in a diplomatic "profession," the job they had in mind was more similar to a Victorian calling than to a twentieth-century scientific profession. Like the Victorian vocations of Church and civil service, American diplomacy was to show its social mettle by providing an environment in which practitioners could learn their craft by assimilating the teachings of their superiors and predecessors.[8] New recruits differed from the amateurs who preceded them not by being technical experts whose knowledge could be rationally verified,[9] but by committing themselves to a life-time career in the Service, combined with their certainty of job security.[10] This tenure guaranteed them the time and the appropriate professional environment in which to develop their diplomatic skills—skills that could be acquired only by patiently applying the style and wisdom of the new diplomat's superiors.

Since experience and socializing in the Service were as important as formal instruction in the universities or the Foreign Service School, full professional status could not be granted a graduate merely because he had completed a prescribed course. Since diplomacy was a calling, a true understanding of it unfolded only gradually, as a man made his way up in the career.[11] This organic conception of diplomacy differed greatly from the amateur notion that any political campaign-contributor was capable of doing diplomatic work. But it was, at the same time, at odds with the outlook of those commercial attachés and congressmen, who, enamored of technical prowess, held that diplomats ought to be technical experts.[12] In the seven years following the passage of the Rogers Act, the equivocal notion of diplomacy as a vocation and a career, portrayed as the New Diplomacy when in fact it resembled the old, triumphed over the simpler conception of rigorous professionalism.[13]

Politics, Friendship, and Professional Diplomacy

It was during the reform years that diplomats and consuls formed their attitudes toward the political overseers of foreign policy. The professional ideal required that Foreign Service officers be the loyal civil servants of politicians.[14] In actual practice, diplomats had political ideas of their own. They expected politicians to pursue an active foreign policy, and demanded that they respect the Foreign Service officers' professional autonomy. The professionals, however, distrusted officials who took an active interest in foreign affairs without deferring to the expert opinions of the Foreign Service. In fact, they worked particularly well with presidents who actually professed ignorance of international relations.

Thus the professionals clearly disliked Woodrow Wilson's diplomacy. They grew impatient with his policies,[15] resented the influence of his confidant, Colonel Edward M. House,[16] scorned his first Secretary of State,[17] found the second a cold and aloof lawyer,[18] and considered the third a genial incompetent.[19] Diplomats believed that Wilson intentionally sought to exclude them from political work, with the result that, in the election of 1920, several of them supported Warren G. Harding.[20]

During the administrations of Harding and Calvin Coolidge, the State Department gained influence and self-confidence. While not blind to the intellectual deficiencies of President Harding, the professionals found him a sincere admirer of the career Foreign Service. Since the President, too, was well aware of his incapacity for sustained thought in the realm of foreign affairs of or anything else for that matter, he left foreign policy to the men who called themselves experts.[21] In actual fact, he chose some notoriously poor advisors, but his selection of Charles Evans Hughes as Secretary of State partially redeemed the reputation of his cabinet. Harding liked to surround himself with diplomats.[22] For their part, the diplomats used their social access to the President to explain to him the value of assigning professional diplomats, rather than political cronies, to important overseas posts. After his first year in office, the National Civil Service League reported that Harding had done more for the Foreign Service than any president since Theodore Roosevelt.[23] Similarly, Coolidge, who also professed ignorance of foreign affairs, also won the respect of career officers.[24]

Career men enjoyed good relations with Secretaries of State Hughes and Frank B. Kellogg, but for widely different reasons. Since Hughes impressed diplomats with his intelligent grasp of foreign affairs,[25] the diplomats supported his foreign policies.[26] He was also convinced by the diplomats' arguments for the value of professional diplomacy,[27] and believed that professional diplomats were useful not only as a substitute for membership in international organizations, but could replace military forces in areas of disarmament.[28] Thus Hughes actively supported Foreign Service officers in political maneuvers, and the Foreign Service accepted Kellogg because he continued to promote career men to high ranks.

Another factor in setting the diplomatic outlook was that diplomats and consuls developed strong bonds of friendship among themselves. Since the two groups had organized themselves independently of one another, relations between them were never good in the period from 1914 to 1931. The tension caused by their differing conceptions of professionalism was responsible for the inconsistent definition of professional diplomacy which emerged in the State Department practice during the years following passage of the Rogers Act. Each group had its own ideal of what a good diplomat or consul should be,[29] but each failed to live up to it because of the intervention of personal ambitions and jealousies. In the diplomatic branch the supposed aim of a smoothly working organization in which unquestioning members carried out their assignments was frustrated by the development of cliques of insiders who seemed to control appointments. At the same time, the leadership of the consular branch actively discouraged the development of an inner club, but found itself outside the locus of power in the amalgamated service. The consuls grew jealous of the prestige enjoyed by the diplomats and tried to enlist the help of powerful political allies to redress the imbalance.[30] In the end, however, the ties of friendship at the core of the former diplomatic branch prevailed over the opposition based on bureaucratic principles which had been advanced by the consuls. In other words, the gentlemanly aspirations of the diplomatic branch became the professional code of the Foreign Service.

Consuls not only used a rhetoric of scientific procedure in personnel administration, but seemed to have abjured personal connections and friendships as a method of organization.[31] Unfortunately, Wilbur Carr's attitude toward in-service friendship was confused. He wanted the Department to rely increasingly upon objective testing to select the best Foreign Service officers, yet the qualities he thought could be measured scientifically defied objective analysis. Having found the diplomats undemocratic and clubby, he wanted new officers to be selected for their congeniality. He, in agreement with the diplomats, thought technical expertise less important than personal readiness, but, since he wanted the Service as a whole to resemble a club,[32] he objected to the conflict between the insiders and outsiders within the diplomatic branch.

In 1914 Carr had complained that the consular oral exams were no help in eliminating incompetent candidates. Many frivolous or dull young men had passed the test, partly because only a very few well-qualified candidates bothered to take it. One corrective had been to make the Service more attractive—a task taken up by the reformers who had agitated for the Rogers bill. A more serious difficulty was the oral examination itself, which, as Carr believed, was "not sufficiently scientific to develop whether the qualities desired actually exist in the applicant."[33]

After putting in a great deal of effort immediately after World War I, Carr developed a system for evaluating the consular orals on an "objective" basis.[34] Examiners rated candidates who took the half-hour exam on a scale of zero to a hundred in each of four categories:

1) *Character-disposition*.
   a) Character.
      1) Moral excellence.
      2) Strength or weakness.
      3) Courage.
      4) Forcefulness.
      5) Seriousness.
      6) Maturity.
   b) Disposition.
      1) Amiability.
2) *Personality*.
   a) Address.
      1) Bearing.
      2) Charm.
      3) Attention.
   b) Manners.
      1) Social conduct.
   c) Health.
   d) Personal appearance.
3) *General Intelligence*.
   a) Readiness.
   b) Judgment.
   c) Discretion.
   d) Resourcefulness.
   e) Command of English.
   f) Accuracy of Information.
4) *Experience and business capacity*.
   a) Experience.
   b) Business capacity.[35]

These categories show how difficult it was for the Department to establish a scientific standard for judging candidates. In the first place, a half-hour interview was hardly enough to make accurate assessments of a candidate's qualities.[36] This problem was, of course, inevitable whenever the Department's hopes for a large pool of applicants were realized. More significant difficulties arose from the misuse of the notion of "scientific" measurement of character.[37] The first two categories, "character-disposition" and "personality," were not amenable to scientific scaling.[38] The examiners could and did indicate their reactions to a candidate's traits of character, but their judgments were necessarily personal and based upon shared assumptions as to what constituted good consular behavior.[39] By setting up a supposedly scientific guide for grading the oral examination, Carr had merely deceived himself into believing that he had discovered "objective" criteria for determining that which precisely went into making a good Foreign Service officer.[40]

The criteria used by the examining board brought cautious and congenial men to the Service, for they forced the examiners to be more careful in eliminating objectionable individuals than they were in selecting extremely quick or intelligent men. The board was to judge an applicant's character from his answers to a series of factual questions on American politics, economics, foreign affairs, and current cultural events. [41] The method used by the board to arrive at an estimate of a man's "general intelligence" was indicative of the premium it placed on cautious statement. "Accuracy of information" and "command of English," two qualities that could be determined by "objective" standards, were last on the list. Preceding them were four traits—readiness, resourcefulness, judgment, and discretion—which were carefully designed to neutralize one another. [42]

Clearly, Carr had designed his "scientific" selection process more in order to recruit congenial men than to discover the finest technical experts in the field of international relations and commerce. Consuls, for example, resented the diplomatic branch's tendency to allow friendships formed outside the Department to dominate the social habits or professional outlook of new recruits. [43] Carr had wanted to make certain that the Foreign Service officers' primary, and perhaps even exclusive, loyalty was to their Service. Indeed, his objection to the close ties made among some of the higher diplomatic officers had obviously nothing to do with their technical knowledge, but was based on their loyalty to the good of the Service as a whole. [44]

Although the public regarded the diplomatic service as less technically minded than the consular, [45] the leadership of the consular branch placed no simplistic faith in the value of expertise. It, too, was concerned with finding an intelligent group of men who could be molded into a highly spirited corps of Foreign Service officers. Indeed, the leadership of both branches was equally devoted to the relative claims of expertise and loyalty. Finally, the problem concerning congeniality and merit was subtly resolved. Both diplomats and consuls advocated formal, impartial recruitment: no one was considered for admission to the Foreign Service who did not receive a score of eighty on a two-day series of rigorous written tests. [46] And both retained their authority over recruitment by personally selecting those who had adequately passed the oral examinations. [47]

During the reform period the Service was officially democratized. The pay raise, the pension plan, and the travel and representation allowances required by the Rogers Act made the Department more attractive to men without private income. [48] After 1924 the Department dropped its warning to applicants regarding low pay, [49] so that during the decade after the act was passed, the social backgrounds of applicants broadened somewhat. The proportion of applicants who listed their fathers' occupation as "professional" or "white collar" dropped slightly from 54.1 percent to 48.1,[50] with 74.9 percent having attended public schools in 1936, and 17.8 percent, private schools.[51] The proportions were similar to those of the pre-Rogers-Act consular branch, 73.2 percent of whose members had gone to public schools, and 23 percent, private schools. Yet the proportion of applicants from public-school backgrounds in the thirties differed substantially from the pre-Rogers-Act figures of the diplomatic branch. In 1924, 72.3 percent of all diplomats had attended private schools, and only 16 percent, public school.[52] Moreover, applicants to the amalgamated Service came from a broader range of universities. Whereas, in 1924, 32.4 percent of all diplomats and only 5.4 percent of all consuls had attended Harvard, in 1936, 5.4 percent of *all* recruits for both branches came from Harvard. In the later period it was the applicants from Georgetown, George Washington, Stanford, and the City College of New York who did best on the Foreign Service exams.[53]

Two important exceptions to the democratic principles of the Service leadership were women and blacks, who presented the most serious challenge to the diplomats' conception of their own Service. Before the First World War, diplomats stated explicitly that the civil-service principle could not be applied so broadly as to permit women to enter the Foreign Service on the same basis as men. In 1909 Assistant Secretary of State Frederick Van Dyne warned against admitting women to the Foreign Service on the grounds that "the greatest obstacle to the employment of women as diplomatic agents is their well known inability to keep a secret"[54] [55]—an attitude that persisted in the State Department well after passage of the Rogers Act. By that time, however, the leaders were more circumspect in expressing their antifeminism. They responded in a flustered, embarrassed manner to the general question of women's rights, and in a surreptitious manner to attempts by women to gain diplomatic posts. One of the questions of the Examining Boards that used to tax applicants on the Foreign Service oral in 1924 was: "What are the principle reasons, in your judgment, for granting the right to vote to women?"[56] Diplomats did not categorically oppose women's suffrage, but they did find it a curious, novel notion which required much reflection.

When Joseph C. Grew became Chairman of the Foreign Service Personnel Board in July 1924, he decided to exclude women from the Service without violating the letter of the merit principle. He feared that women would interfere with the convivial atmosphere of the Foreign Service,[57] that they would ruin morale by demanding special treatment, and that they would not be competent for South American duty, since the sexual attitudes of Latin Americans would make it impossible for them to do their work. He could see the reputation of a woman diplomat being shattered one night in South America were she called upon to deliver an official note to a bachelor colleague. In other words, if the State Department was not free to send women to Latin America, "it would be manifestly unfair and inconsistent to send women to our more desirable posts in Europe, leaving the men to fill the undesirable ones."[58]

Grew devised several subtle strategies for excluding women. Since he was afraid that a public statement barring women from the Foreign Service would raise opposition "from Maine to California,"[59] he favored direct, personal appeals to mothers of women who contemplated a diplomatic career in the hopes that they would stop their daughters from sitting for the written tests. This method had the advantage of being strictly private, but Grew realized that some women would be unmoved by parental pressure and that the best qualified of them would pass the written exams. He therefore recommended privately to the Personnel Board that "we shall have to fail [women] on their oral examinations on the grounds that they do not possess the necessary qualifications for the Service."[60]

The oral examinations were also intended to be a barrier to those blacks who passed the written tests. Comparing well-qualified women with well-qualified blacks, Grew concluded that blacks, too, would have to be failed on their orals without explanation. He realized that the Department could not state publicly its racial or sexual biases, for it had to maintain the appearance of the merit system for admission and promotion.[61]

Consequently, few women or Negroes received Foreign Service commissions during the reform years. In 1925 the Department, under pressure from President Calvin Coolidge, dropped its explicit policy of discrimination on the orals,[62] but no flood of women or blacks swelled the Foreign Service ranks. When Grew learned that the President objected to prejudice on the orals, he asked the Board to raise the standards for all applicants[63] on the presumption that few women or blacks would meet the higher qualifications.

During the first six years of the Rogers Act, very few women or blacks entered the Service. Of the sixty women who took the Foreign Service examinations, six passed and were declared eligible for appointment, and their record of success was slightly lower than the men's.[64]

Lucille Atcherson, the first woman to pass both exams and to be appointed to the Service after passage of the Rogers Act, was sent by the Board to Switzerland, where Hugh Gibson was Minister. Since Gibson had been just as opposed to the admission of women to the Service as Grew, the two men exchanged sorrowful letters about the sad state of affairs which permitted women to enter the Foreign Service. Gibson resented having Atcherson at the Legation in Berne. He wondered where he would have to seat her at dinner and how she would dress, and whether she would ever make a good diplomat, regretting that Grew had inflicted her upon him. Grew, for his part, replied that he was as miserable as Gibson at seeing women in the Service, offering some rather silly suggestions for a unisex diplomatic outfit to be worn by both male and female diplomats, and trying to soothe Gibson by suggesting that he keep his eye on Atcherson to prevent mischief. The two men squeezed what forlorn humor they could from Atcherson's appointment, with Gibson signing his dispatch "Michael J. O'Prune" and Grew calling himself "Wee Willie Winkie."[65]

As for the blacks, the Department did not record how many of them took the exams, but few gained appointments during the reform period. From 1914 to 1930, seven blacks were appointed to Foreign Service positions. Of these, however, three were noncareer appointments as Minister to Liberia.[66] While the Wilson administration was criticized for denying diplomatic appointments to Negroes,[67] the record of the succeeding Republican administrations was no better.[68] Since the Foreign Service staff realized that a Republican administration was thought to be more favorably disposed to the demands of blacks, diplomats were cautious in discouraging them. Once, when William Phillips was Assistant Secretary of State in 1919, he received Archibald Grimke, a black leader in Washington, who pressed him to admit more blacks into the Foreign Service in the future. However, Phillips not only put him off with generalities, but turned the encounter to his own advantage by emphasizing the work his own great-uncle, Wendell Phillips, had done for blacks.[69]

Nevertheless, as I mentioned earlier, the social background of applicants was broader than in the past, but the leadership of the Foreign Service wanted recruits to share straightaway, or to soon acquire, its own outlook on world politics and professional diplomacy.[70] Whenever a young man who shared the diplomats' views came to the attention of the Department, the leadership went out of its way to encourage his interest in professional diplomacy,[71] following the new recruit's career closely, and grooming him to take over departmental work. The men of the first generation had easy and informal relations with their protégés,[72] and tried to make the accession to power of those who were to follow them easier and more predictable than their own had been, using institutional means to increase the prestige of their careers. They also carefully retained a personal responsibility for the type of men who entered the new Service and for the quality of the Service itself.

What distinguished the professional performance of diplomats from that of consuls was the fact that an influential clique had existed within the diplomatic branch of the Foreign Service since 1915. The web of relationships woven at 1718 H Street N.W. in Washington was responsible for the outlook and style of diplomatic secretaries for years after passage of the Rogers Act. The house itself, one block from the State Department, was purchased in 1915 by several diplomats, as well as Treasury and War Department officials, to offer them a *pied à terre* while in the capital.[73] The "Family"[74] included not only the first three professional diplomats to hold the post of Undersecretary of State—Fletcher, Phillips, and Grew—but also Leland Harrison, Basil Miles, James Sterling, and their close friends. Whenever one of them returned from a foreign assignment for a brief visit to Washington, he would stay at 1718 H Street, and for a while during the twenties, when neither Fletcher nor Harrison was married, they lived together in the house.[75] Although several members of the Family—Phillips, Grew, Harrison, Miles, and Wadsworth—had attended Harvard from 1900 to 1905, Fletcher had never even gone to college, but his connection to Theodore Roosevelt made him feel almost like a Harvard alumnus.[76] Ever since they had entered the State Department in the Roosevelt Administration, many of them had served together in China, and even when separated, they had kept in touch, so that when they assumed preeminent professional positions in the twenties, they had been friends for years.[77]

The Family was officially only the corporate name for those with a stake in the 1718 H Street house, but in fact it included many of the first generation of professionals. The correspondence between the house and the overseas missions directed by Lewis Einstein, Joseph Grew, Hugh Gibson, or Fred Morris Dearing made the Family headquarters virtually a second foreign office.[78] Since the letters were friendly, not official, they were a way for those in the field to unburden themselves with regard to foreign problems. The tone of those private letters revealed that many of the "Family" members were of two minds when it came to foreign affairs.[79] In their official dispatches they would follow the instructions of the political chiefs conscientiously, but in their letters to friends, they often bristled at what they considered the blindness of politicians.[80] It would appear, then, that the Family members considered themselves wiser than the political directors of foreign policy, and more honest than the officials of other foreign offices or than the diplomats of other countries.

Occasionally, they directed overseas missions on their own during the twenties. In such cases they tried to run their offices as independent fiefs, choosing as junior secretaries men of whom they were especially fond and training them in their own way. Officers like Franklin Mott Gunther, Norman Armour, J. Pierpont Moffat, and George Summerlin were all eagerly sought by Gibson, Grew, Phillips, and Fletcher when they accepted missions in Europe.[81]

However, the creation of diplomacy as a professional career made it increasingly difficult for the Family to keep all of its protégés together. Once the new personnel system of promotion and transfer for merit went into effect, the Personnel Board consciously strove to disperse the recruits who had served under Family members. The Board wanted to send competent junior men to the posts in the Orient or Latin America, which were coming to be controlled by professional ministers and ambassadors. These career ambassadors were supposed to teach diplomacy to the most recent graduates of the Foreign Service School. Although that process of dispersal occasionally brought the Personnel Board into conflict with the wishes of the Family members, who wanted to keep their protégés, the Board did not want any one mission to become top-heavy with talent.[82]

Another reason for breaking up the coteries attached to the Family was the Board's desire to establish the principle of professional obedience to its assignment policies. Its official position on transfers was that "Secretaries are expected to take their turn in whatever part of the world their services may be required, and every secretary, whether married or unmarried, must be prepared to go to the post to which he may be assigned."[83] In actual practice, however, the Board pursued a far more flexible and less professional policy, for it feared offending Family members who did not want their best men taken from them. It also had to overcome the distaste of many diplomats for duty outside the glamourous capitals of Europe. Although fond of describing the Foreign Service as the "first line of defense" of the Republic,[84] the personnel directors were reluctant to impose a military type of discipline on the junior secretaries. Morale and the clublike atmosphere of the Foreign Service would suffer if the Personnel Board were too insistent in demanding men to accept transfers to uncongenial posts. It therefore consciously distinguished its assignment procedure from that of the armed forces, and allowed secretaries a greater choice as to where they would be stationed than did the military.[85]

The Personnel Board did not have a clear policy for assigning secretaries because of the ambiguous nature of the professional ideal. In practice, the Board accepted the diplomats' low opinion of certain stations, and sent men to posts as rewards or punishments for their behavior. Undersecretary Grew, the Board's first chairman, had grown up as a diplomat in Europe, and was thus fully committed to the view that relations with the Great Powers was the most important aspect of American foreign policy. He considered Latin America a backwater to which very young, or inferior, or recalcitrant officers should be sent.[86] On several occasions after passage of the Rogers Act, the Board required secretaries to serve some time in Latin America to atone for insubordination or incompetence. The practice of exiling, as it were, men in bad favor, had the undesired effect of reinforcing the common opinion among members that the Service did not consider all posts to be of equal importance, and was not trying to improve the quality of diplomacy in all areas of the world.[87] The results of this transfer policy were deleterious from the standpoint of both friendship and professionalism, since it not only increased competition for the favor of one's chief, but damaged the professional ideal that every man serve willingly and to the best of his ability at any post whatever.[88]

Moreover, ideally, a diplomat was not meant to participate in politics and policy. As disinterested and nonpartisan experts, Foreign Service officers were supposed to be primarily the transmitters of information to the Department. If a diplomat held political opinions, he was to keep quiet about them unless asked, and he was surely out of order if he allied himself with a political party or faction.[89] The strictures against political activity worked well enough for the young recruits coming into a professionalized Service, but not for the older generation, who had built up friendships with political figures in the years during which they fought for the new Service. Since most of the men who had come into the Service before passage of the Rogers Act had needed a political benefactor to survive, it was only natural that certain senior civil servants overlook the professional ethic in order to retain the favor such political friends.

Henry P. Fletcher was perhaps the greatest offender when it came to the code of political neutrality. He was a committed Republican from the time of his experience with Colonel Roosevelt's Rough Riders until the day of his death. After leaving the Foreign Service in 1929, he devoted himself to his Philadelphia business interests and Republican politics, and then became, in the unhappy year of 1936, the Republican National Chairman.[90] During the time he was an undersecretary or an ambassador in Europe, he supported Republican candidates with sizable contributions or statements of endorsement.[91] Indeed, Fletcher counted among his most intimate friends such Republican giants as Joseph Grundy, Pennsylvania Senators David Reed and George W. Pepper, House Speaker Frank Gillette, and President Warren Harding, with whom he constantly exchanged letters and gifts, and played interminable rounds of golf and poker.[92] The running correspondence he kept up with his political friends revealed his attitudes toward the major foreign policy events of the day. For example, he greeted the defeat of the Democrats in 1920 as the "end of our international joy ride." The next two elections, however, gave him pause. The Democratic success in the Congressional elections of 1922 alarmed him, and the Progressive campaign of 1924 convinced him that socialism was stalking America.[93]

Fletcher used his carefully cultivated relations with the great and powerful to enhance his own career, even though his own advancement was a mockery of the Foreign Service's professional integrity. Immediately upon leaving Washington for Brussels in 1922 as Ambassador, he looked for a promotion to a more exciting capital,[94] bombarding his friends in the Congress with requests to sound out the Secretary of State on prospects for the post of Ambassador to Paris or London.[95] Occasionally during 1923 he even transmitted rumors to friends to the effect that Myron T. Herrick in Paris or John Davis in London was intending to give up his post, and asked his patrons to lobby for him.[96]

Having been informed by Senator Reed that there would be no Paris post for him in the immediate future, and that the new President, Coolidge, could not appoint an Easterner to Great Britain,[97] Fletcher switched his attention to the Embassy in Rome, from which Richard W. Child was soon expected to retire,[98] and his political friends brought his request for a change to the attention of Secretary Hughes.[99] Certain of Fletcher's benefactors believed that he had a competitor for the Rome job in the person of another career diplomat, William Phillips,[100] but Phillips specifically denied the charge in a personal letter to Fletcher.[101] Finally, when Child resigned, Fletcher's political maneuverings did pay off: he was named Ambassador to Rome on February 17, 1924.[102] Foreign Service officers all over the world showered their congratulations upon him in the belief that he had enhanced their careers. But, in fact, the methods he had employed had undermined the career principle itself.[103]

Fletcher's success and the advancement of the diplomatic branch it represented brought cheers from the diplomatic secretaries, but provoked Wilbur Carr's resentment.[104] The fact that Fletcher had an important position at the center of the Family provoked even more frustration. The consuls' distress applied as well to other diplomats who seemed to gain the lion's share of departmental perquisites.[105] Carr had formed a bitter opinion of Fletcher as early as 1921. Having disclosed the qualities he deemed necessary in a consular official—commitment to the missionary purpose of the Department of State, combined with humility carried to the point of self-righteousness—he went on to condemn Fletcher as

> . . . clearly vain, only fairly penetrating, no command of language and yet wants to be the whole circus. He cannot rise high because he lacks idealism and vision. He can't lead for the same reasons, and because he would drive rather than try to lead, and his manner creates obstinacy and suppresses enthusiasm on the part of the driven. But suppose he seems disagreeably vain, unctious, what harm does it do me, for example? Unpleasant, of course, but harmful—hardly. The little dignity of independent authority I may lose will soon be forgotten, and I shall learn many things which otherwise I should miss. Again Emerson is right.[106]

Diplomats and Consuls Confront Each Other

Carr's feelings toward Fletcher reflected the bitterness of many other consuls, who distrusted aspects of the diplomatic branch's outlook and style. They resented its clubbiness when it excluded consuls, its condescending to those who advocated the commercial functions of a foreign office, its aping of Europeans, and above all, its disregard for efficient and stylized forms of organization.[107]

During the drafting of the Rogers Act, Carr had complained that the diplomatic branch was trying to sabotage the amalgamation provisions of the new law.[108] He unjustly accused the highest levels of the diplomatic branch of duplicity, but correctly suspected diplomats of wanting to maintain social superiority over consuls, claiming that the leaders of the diplomatic service supported the amalgamation provisions for purely political reasons, not in order that they might mingle with consuls. Realizing that the consular service had closer relations with the Congress than they did, the diplomats had joined up with their consular counterparts, and used the rhetoric of commercial expansion primarily for the benefit of Congressmen they believed incapable of appreciating the larger political role of a Foreign Service. Despite all their political maneuvering, the diplomats never believed that the consuls were their social equals, nor did they believe that the functions of consuls were interchangeable with those of diplomats. In fact, they did not even expect consuls to be capable of doing political work in the amalgamated Service.[109]

In the four years following passage of the Rogers Act, diplomats denied former consuls an equitable share in promotions. Having learned from their study of world politics that the actions of government were far more important than any stated goals of international law, they applied that principle when competing with the consuls. Before the Rogers Act became law, diplomats had assured one another that the administration of the personnel system, not the language of the statute, was their primary concern.[110] But after 1924, they succeeded in dominating the new personnel system, thereby making the professional ethic of the new Foreign Service conform to their expectations.

As soon as the Rogers bill was enacted, Carr, who became an assistant secretary under the Act, and Undersecretary Grew had set to work to organize the Personnel Board of the new Service. The Act was vague on personnel organization, stating only that the secretary of state was to report on the efficiency of officers.[111] Although in the plans they presented for the new Board, Carr and Grew had differed over how much discretion the Board ought to exercise over the daily workings of the Service, their differences in fact represented the more fundamental clash over whether consuls or diplomats should control the new Service.

Carr's plan for the personnel organization extended the system used in the consular bureau to the entire Foreign Service. He wanted the Personnel Board to be a consultative body, meeting only once or twice a year. The daily administration of the Foreign Service would thus be in the hands of a personnel bureau made up of representatives of the two branches and headed by the chief of the consular bureau's Personnel Office. In sum, the new bureau would be an expansion of the Personnel Office of the consular service, which had been supervising admission and promotion in that branch since 1921.[112]

The diplomats' plan, on the other hand, sought to diminish the power of the consular branch. Diplomats wanted the Personnel Board to have full control over the daily operations of the Foreign Service, and suggested that there be two representatives from each branch and a chairman who was to be an impartial outsider, chosen by the Secretary of State.[113] They also wanted a revised system of personnel management, since they feared that the elevation of Carr's Personnel Office would force diplomats to conform to the consular mode of behavior. Grew assessed Carr's plan warily, admitting that it was "based upon his long experience in managing the Consular Service, and from the point of view of machinery, it approaches perfection." He complained, however, that it "would tend to bureaucratize the whole Foreign Service, which would tend to take much of the spirit and morale out of the Diplomatic Branch, at least."[114] The Undersecretary feared that the consuls had laid too much stress upon "objective" measurements of an official's ability and too little upon the "soundness" of judgment of junior members of the diplomatic corps.[115] For the diplomats had supported the Rogers Act to make their own position more secure, not to allow professional rivals to dilute their privileges.

When the diplomats finally presented their plan to Secretary Hughes, Carr angrily defended his own suggestions as a matter of personal pride. He had proprietary feelings toward personnel administration and resented diplomats invading his personal territory by suggesting a plan of their own.[116] Repeating his charges to them in person, he railed that the "diplomats had contributed nothing to this work [of creating a personnel system] and had no experience to justify their submitting a separate plan themselves."[117]

True, the diplomats had had little experience in personnel administration, but they had had a great deal in conducting negotiations. Grew used subtle persuasion to convince the Secretary that Carr's scheme was unacceptable. First he told Carr that the diplomatic secretaries would like all Foreign Service officers polled to see if they approved of Carr's plan. Since Carr considered a formal poll an affront to his experience in personnel matters, Grew agreed that perhaps it was unnecessary, but insisted that there had to be some way of determining the attitudes of the men in the field toward any new system. Carr again assured him that his plan had the support of his men. Armed with that instance of Carr's intransigence, Grew told Hughes that Carr had been too secretive in drawing up his plan. The proposal Grew then submitted called for a single director of personnel, "who shall be a member of neither branch of the service but can command the confidence of both branches." Having thus removed the possibility of Carr or one of his men being the power behind personnel administration, Grew conceded that "with this one exception, the Carr plan would be acceptable, and all its other machinery, including a School Board and an Examinations Board would be adopted."[118]

After reviewing both plans, the Secretary worked out a compromise which satisfied most of the objections presented by the diplomats. Since Hughes had decided that an outsider in charge of personnel could easily thrust the Foreign Service out into the political arena, and splitting the difference between the two plans, he set up a five-member Personnel Board which was to meet monthly. Daily operations were to be in the hands of an executive committee of the Board, made up of three Foreign Service officers, each of whom would be "members of the Personnel Board and vote thereon."[119]

The Secretary's compromise satisfied the diplomats but annoyed Carr, since it stripped him of direct authority over personnel. First Hughes tried unsuccessfully to get Carr's agreement; then Grew and Wright spoke to him, but they, too, could not budge him. Finally, Grew gave up trying to persuade, and instructed Carr to incorporate the Secretary's plan into an Executive Order.[120] "He seemed much distressed and prophesied its failure, but drew up the order as instructed." Satisfied that the interests of the diplomatic branch had been maintained, Grew reported that "Hugh Wilson, Butler Wright, and I think that most of the diplomatic sec'ies [sic] in the Department felt that the best possible plan had been evolved."[121]

Just how successful Grew, Wright, and Wilson had been was borne out in the policies the Personnel Board pursued during the next three years. The five-member Board consisted of Grew as chairman, Carr, Wright, Consul-General Charles Eberhardt as chairman of the Executive Committee, and Consul-General Edward Norton.[122] As soon as the Board assumed authority in July 1924, Grew sent a Circular Instruction to all Foreign Service officers explaining the cautious policy it was to follow in transferring men.[123] For purposes of upholding career spirit, all officers were supposed to consider themselves part of a single Service, though their duties were to remain separate, following a distinction between consuls and diplomats "well established by international law and practice." If they performed their duties zealously, they stood to be promoted to the rank of minister. And although new recruits would receive instruction in both diplomatic and consular work in their first years in the Service, Grew quickly scotched the consuls' hopes for constant transfers from branch to branch:

> If an officer is particularly adapted and fitted to one branch of the service he will be expected to serve in that branch, regardless of his own preferences; if on the other hand the qualifications of an officer should appear to render him almost equally valuable for either branch, he will be permitted to remain in the branch of his choice, so far as that course may be consistent with the best interests of the service.

Grew envisioned that most transfers would occur during the first years of a recruit's career. During that time, the Board would decide where it could best use his talents. It would avoid "indiscriminate transfers," but "whenever it is apparent . . . that an officer in one branch can render better service to the Government, with consequent increased advantage to himself, or meet an existing need in the other branch, the Department will feel free to transfer him and it will expect him to accept cheerfully the changed status."[124]

Grew's circular relieved diplomats, but alarmed consuls. From the highest levels of the diplomatic service to the lowliest protégé of the Family, diplomats were happy to hear that their ranks would not be permeated by socially inferior former consuls.[125] If, in fact, the system worked as planned, the amalgamation provisions of the Rogers Act would not at all lower the diplomats' social prestige. Consuls, on the other hand, greeted Grew's circular with apprehension. As the system began to work, with few transfers and the bulk of promotions going to former diplomats, the consuls began to feel that they were being cheated and persecuted.[126]

During its first two years in operation, the Personnel Board confirmed both the hopes of the diplomats and the fears of the consuls. The first time a consul was nominated to the post of minister, the Board indicated its reluctance to appoint consuls to high diplomatic posts. In September 1924 Carr suggested that Robert Skinner, Consul-General in London and the highest ranking official in the consular service, be sent to replace Rabbi Joseph Kornfeld as Minister to Iran. Since the professionals had found Kornfeld, a personal friend of Warren Harding, untrustworthy for having argued too strongly and sentimentally for more American aid to the Armenian refugees in Iran, they were pleased when he submitted his resignation.[127] Moreover, Coolidge had agreed with Hughes to replace the political appointee Kornfeld with a professional, and Skinner was the highest ranking consular officer. But when Carr presented Skinner's name to the Board, Grew demurred, questioning the Consul-General's diplomatic finesse. Grew had not only heard rumors from the Family that Skinner had offended many English officials by his brusque manner, but was skeptical as to the consuls' competence in diplomatic work. "I do feel," he allowed, "that consuls who have demonstrated diplomatic ability should be given their chance to become Ministers, but the qualities that go to make up a successful consular officer are not always those which tend to make a successful diplomat; and from my knowledge of Skinner I think he is an example of this principle."[128]

One year after Grew had managed to wrest the Teheran post from Skinner, the Consul-General wrote the Personnel Board to protest about the preferential treatment it was granting diplomats. He spoke for most consuls when he complained that diplomats were being promoted faster than consuls, and, more importantly, that too few consuls were being given the opportunity to do diplomatic work.[129] Grew considered the discontent serious enough to explain that the framers of the Rogers Act had never intended free transfer between the two branches. Invoking the aid of a dead man, he told Wright and Carr that John Jacob Rogers, "shortly before his death in January, 1925 told me that he thought that the Act was being carried out in the only wise manner, and he felt that transfer between the two branches of the Service in the upper classes should be effected with great discrimination. He hoped that at least a few such transfers could be made, and that has been done."[130] Grew believed that Rogers had accepted the diplomats' argument about the separate development of the two branches, and that most of the present members of either branch would stay where they had received their training.

Skinner's letter was only one of fifty-eight received from the hundred Foreign Service officers Grew had asked for an opinion as to the first year of the Personnel Board's operation. On a whole, the replies from the field revealed great disaffection with the Board's motives and policies. Since the consuls expressed their belief that they were being passed over for promotions in favor of younger, less experienced men whose only qualifications seemed to be diplomatic standing, the Board decided that a stronger public relations effort had to be made to uplift morale.[131]

Despite the Personnel Board's explanations and Grew's appeal to the memory of John Jacob Rogers, morale among consuls continued to worsen. Indeed, for three years after the Rogers Act had become law, visitors to America's overseas missions reported that, since 1924, the consuls had become increasingly depressed about the fact that diplomats were receiving promotions with unseemly haste, while they languished in menial and inglorious posts. Curiously enough, even the diplomats were not completely satisfied with the new personnel system.[132] One high-ranking State Department official, William Castle, who aligned himself with the diplomats, was anxious lest the Personnel Board promote so many secretaries that a vacuum would be left which would have to be filled by consuls. "That is a situation," Castle told Moffat, "which I want to avoid at all hazards."[133]

As the morale of the consular officers continued to ebb throughout 1925 and 1926, the Board sent one of its members, Consul-General Edward Norton, on a tour of inspection. To begin with, he found that most consuls were angry at the fact that five diplomats, but no consuls, had advanced two grades in the two years since the Act. ''The question seems to be,'' one irate consul wrote Norton in January of 1927, ''whether all the brains are in the diplomatic branch? I have done my best to arrive at some explanation but have racked my brains in vain . . . Are the two branches considered as separate entities in making the promotions? If so, what system is used to arrive at the percentage of men to be promoted in the two branches?''[134] Another disgruntled consul put the case against the Board even more harshly. He asked:

> Are we to assume that diplomatic secretaries of ½ or $^3/_5$ the foreign service experience of consular officers surpass them in efficiency so that they may logically pass them in promotion? . . . If efficiency alone governs advancement, if the wall has been broken down between the two branches of the service, then we are forced to believe either that the consuls in the cases cited were only ½ as intelligent and capable as their diplomatic colleagues, or that one year in the diplomatic career is equal to two years of consular activity.[135]

The general picture of promotions had indeed revealed that, proportionately, nearly twice the number of diplomats had received promotions as had consuls. For example, by December 1926, only 37% of the 365 consular officers had been promoted. Consuls also complained that, class by class, diplomats had to serve less time before being promoted. Norton found this charge particularly well founded for classes I, II, and III.

TABLE I

Average *age* seniority, consuls over diplomats, by class	I	II	III	IV	V	VI	VII	VIII
	10.2	6.7	10.9	8.1	10.5	6.2	9.5	8.0
Average *service* seniority, consuls over diplomats, by class	8.7	6.6	8.1	4.9	7.1	5.9	5.7	4.0

Norton concluded that the reason for the more rapid advancement of diplomats over consuls was that the two services were being evaluated differently. The Personnel Board assigned promotions on the basis of how far a diplomat or consul was from the top of his respective service, not on his relative position in it. Since there were approximately half the number of diplomats as there were consuls, the diplomats did twice as well when the lists were amalgamated. Norton suggested that the Personnel Board rectify the disparity by immediately promoting six additional consuls in each of the first three classes.[137]

He did not suggest, however, that the Board cease distinguishing between the branches. So long as that attitude persisted, diplomats and consuls would continue to fight to gain preeminence for the specific work they did and for their outlooks on international affairs. Moreover, the consuls continued to assert that "the duties of a diplomatic secretary are not more important than those of a consul in the same relative class, nor is the performance of secretarial duties more efficient. Rather the contrary has been observed in the past."[138]

On top of these revelations came a full-blown scandal in the form of a promotion list prepared for Congressional approval in February 1927. To the consuls' friends in Congress, the list gave the impression of having systematically excluded former consuls from promotion, whereas former diplomats and friends of the family had been promoted. As a result, although State Department investigation later concluded that the Personnel Board had prepared the February list properly, the former diplomats were stripped of their authority on the Board. The most significant casualty of the "diplomatic smashup" was Grew, who in 1928 was forced to relinquish the undersecretaryship and accept the post of Ambassador to Turkey.[139]

After the troubles of 1927-28 had blown over, the consuls enlisted the aid of Senator George Moses of New Hampshire to reduce further the power of the former diplomats.[140] Moses had held hearings on Foreign Service administration in 1928, but it was not until 1931 that any new legislation regulating Foreign Service personnel was passed. A variety of reform schemes were presented, but no one suggested that the Rogers Act be revoked or that the old system be revived. The Moses-Linthicum bill, which passed in 1931, was a very mild corrective in the opinion of the consuls.[141] To begin with, the new Act provided for post allowances in especially expensive cities, which for long had been a goal of reformers wishing to democratize the Service. But the law's major reforms did revise the practice of personnel administration. It suggested tenure in consular posts before new officers could receive diplomatic assignments, and revised the personnel system. It set up a single personnel list and a Division of Foreign Service Personnel, directed by Carr, which was to handle the routine chores of administration.[142] Thus the Act not only stripped the former diplomats of their power of favoritism, but ensured that any new recruits would be members of a fused Foreign Service. By 1934, 42.3 percent of Foreign Service officers had held commissions in both branches of the Service,[143] and less than a third of the officers who had entered the consular service before the passage of the Rogers Act had received diplomatic commissions.[144] In the higher ranks, however, there were few transfers. Most consuls who would in the future receive diplomatic assignments were recruited after 1924. And not only were they members of the fused Foreign Service, to which they gave their professional allegiance, but graduates of the Foreign Service School who did not bear the old consuls' grudge against the diplomats.

The Moses-Linthicum Act ended the administrative but not the intellectual dominance of the Foreign Service by former diplomats, whose idea of world politics and the career of diplomacy became the code of the Foreign Service. There was great solidarity among the recruits who entered the Service from 1924 through 1931, and who had adopted the diplomats' conception of a Foreign Service career. Moreover, the diplomats restricted former consuls from entering diplomatic work in the four crucial years after passage of the Rogers Act. During those years the former diplomats held out to the new recruits, who had absorbed their mentors' outlook at the Foreign Service School, the prospect of performing significant diplomatic tasks after fulfilling a consular apprenticeship. Thus the diplomats succeeded in transforming their Victorian idea of a calling into the career outlook of the new self-regulating Foreign Service.

VI

The Diplomatic Mind at Work,
1919-1931

BY 1931, Foreign Service officers had created a structure of beliefs concerning world politics and their mission in international relations as well as American diplomacy, and they retained almost those same beliefs through a depression, a world war, and a cold war. What effect did the diplomats' career code have upon the aims and conduct of American foreign policy? Admittedly, it is hard to isolate the impact of a single group from the many which helped shape foreign policy in the twenties. The bulk of the work done by diplomats during those years consisted largely in the filing of routine dispatches. At no time did Foreign Service officers demand that they be given complete freedom to plan and direct America's foreign relations. At least since the Spanish-American War, foreign policy in the United States had been made by politicians, the executive departments, the military, and articulate members of the general public interested in international law, commerce, and conciliation. The First World War had provoked in the general public a passionate interest in international relations and America's role in the post-war world—an interest that had not diminished by the defeat of the Treaty of Versailles in 1920. As for the career diplomats, their effect on foreign policy in the twenties was reflected by the influence they exerted on the aims, assumptions, and actions of noncareer men. Since the Foreign Service officer's role was that of a teacher, he found himself attending to routine matters in large foreign policy questions in a way he hoped would instruct his political superiors and the articulate public in the proper course of action overseas.

It is pointless to recount each and every contribution the diplomats made to foreign affairs in the twenties. Yet for an understanding of the political consequences of their views, it is worth taking a brief *tour d' horison,* as the diplomats might have said, of those administrative questions in which Foreign Service officers actively gave political advice rather than prepare simple technical reports on political questions. The diplomats' political style and influence is most clearly discernible in matters of immigration, commerce, and disarmament—at those times when they placed their foreign policy judgments in the framework of their grand conception of world politics and American society.

Foreign Service officers made a distinction, in their own minds at least, between the statement of the general foreign policy aims of their country, which they claimed to be the duty of democratically elected politicians, and the methods of organizing and applying that policy effectively, which they considered their mission.[1] At the Foreign Service School, in their public statements, and in their private correspondence, the career men pledged the loyalty of their Service to the objectives of their political superiors. In return, they expected the politicians and the public to form their overseas policies in accordance with the professional diplomats' interpretation of world events. Diplomats further demanded that they be permitted to draw up long-term plans for foreign policy, for only then could politicians be certain that they were pursuing policies which had realistic prospects of success.[2] If politicians chose to ignore the advice of professional diplomats while setting political objectives, the career men were not to be blamed; but diplomats took the responsibility for their interpretation of instructions, the advice they gave, and the manner in which they conducted negotiations.[3]

Diplomats continually insisted that administration was more important for the success of a nation's foreign policy than the specific political objectives of its leaders. If they were good administrators, their explanation of the likely consequences of certain actions defined the limits of the choices available to politicians, who ostensibly were responsible for stating the overseas intentions of the United States. Believing that they possessed a clearer insight into the dynamics of world politics, Foreign Service officers in the twenties asked their political superiors to permit them to advance American overseas interests by shrewdly administering negotiations. Actually, the diplomats' advocacy of the methods rather than the aims of diplomacy was a result of the bureaucratic structure of the new Foreign Service, and resembled similar arguments put forth by members of other professional civil services in Europe and America. Two of the foremost theorists of bureaucracy, Karl Mannheim and Robert Merton, have observed that it is characteristic of the bureaucratic mind to turn political problems into questions of administration, thereby providing civil servants with a legitimate reason for offering advice on burning contemporary issues.[4]

The traditional view of the State Department's influence in the twenties is that career officers within the Department were effectively prohibited from conducting foreign policy by constraints imposed by an isolationist public. Dexter Perkins, writing in 1953, at a time when American scholars observed and condemned what they considered an isolationist tendency in American thinking, concluded that public opinion prevented the State Department from taking a firm stand in favor of American participation in the League of Nations or the World Court, and caused it to lose interest in the political consequences of the First World War.[5] By concentrating his attention upon formal American accession to international organizations, Perkins overlooked the forward policy pursued by the government in those areas of foreign affairs outside the "high policy" concerns of war and peace.[6] Diplomats turned their attention to commercial matters and questions of immigration partly because the public had questioned American participation in European politics, but also because they themselves considered any formal participation of the United States in the League of Nations as irrelevant to America's position as a world power. Moreover, Perkins paid no heed to the professional diplomats' attitude of scorn and condescension toward a public they believed to be uninformed. In fact, rather than abandon the position they had held for twenty years regarding the United States as a world power, they encouraged the government to forego an unpopular adherence to the League, to concentrate upon strengthening American commerce, and to make certain that American immigration legislation was respected.

In other words, professional diplomats adopted a strategy of influencing high policy by conducting routine immigration and commercial matters in their own way. In assessing those issues, they came to the conclusion that they were intimately bound up with issues of national security as well as world peace and order. Naturally, the diplomats did not become the actual spokesmen for high policy, but they did affect those most particularly political areas of foreign policy through the advice they gave and the style in which they gave it. Indeed, the Foreign Service officers charted an active political course by establishing themselves as the directors of an active "low policy."

Immigration and American Society

Diplomats demonstrated their belief in the indissoluble union between politics and administration, their fears regarding the fragility of American domestic social institutions, and their conception of their profession as the agency for orderly change by the manner in which they handled the question of immigration into the United States after the First World War. Immigration restriction became an explosive issue in American politics twice during the interwar period. The argument over how best to limit it was resolved by the establishment of a national-quota system during the five years following the First World War. Later, in the years immediately before and after America's entry into the Second World War, thousands of refugees from Nazism severely strained the quota system by demanding visas. In both periods, however, professional diplomats played a prominent role in constructing, administering, and explaining the restrictionist policy.[7]

During the twenties their attitude toward immigration combined the nativist principles of American society and their bureaucratic rivalry with other branches of the government. On the one hand, they supported the restrictionists' nativist assumptions that the American democracy had to be protected from the taint of undesirable ''anarchists,'' ''paupers,'' ''reds,'' and ''criminals.''[8] How else could the United States remain free from the noisome class conflicts that had made the European nations unfit for the world leadership America sought? Diplomats accepted the nativist argument that Orientals, southern and eastern Europeans, and Jews would depress the wages of native labor, lower the intelligence of voters, and incite domestic insurrection.[9] They also believed that the immigrants from southern and eastern Europe in the thirty years after 1890 had not been as acceptable for American citizenship as the earlier western European immigrants had been. DeWitt Clinton Poole later described the new immigration's baleful effect upon American institutions:

> They [the Poles and Hungarians who immigrated between 1890 and 1920] have brought to the United States a different way of life which is probably being absorbed into our own.
> As far as you can characterize it, this different way of life is Hegelian. It's George Wilhelm Frederick Hegel's idea of the fathership or mothership . . . of the state—that the state is responsible . . . it's completely un-American . . . you'll find Roosevelt was re-elected in 1940, which to me was a calamity, not because it broke the tradition— by about five or six big cities, and it is those cities where there is this newer immigration. They were city dwellers. They didn't go out into the country the way the Germans and Scandanavians did.[10]

Yet while diplomats supported such sentiments as those, Foreign Service officers recognized that the invidious national-quota system could poison relations between the United States and the countries least favored by the quotas. To ensure good relations was their job, so that diplomats deeply resented the interference of politicians, the press, and the public, for they believed that meddling of that type could ruin the effectiveness of United States foreign policy.

The heavy demand for entrance into the United States after the First World War had placed an enormous burden of work on American consulates, which acted as the courts of first instance in the granting of visas to prospective immigrants.[11] Consequently, career men within the Department of State had welcomed this new work as positive proof that the United States needed a larger and more professional Foreign Service, and in the end, it had been partly responsible for passage of the Rogers bill.

At the 1921 House Foreign Affairs Committee hearing on the bill to establish national quotas for admission to the United States, the State Department had prepared an elaborate request for more discretion in the handling of immigration work. Arguing the case for the Foreign Service, Wilbur Carr complained to the Committee that the result of "the visa work [of American consuls in Eastern Europe] has been to stop almost completely the commercial work of the consular service." He pleaded for more consuls and more power so that his officials might reject applicants they considered unsuitable for admission. Although he thought the provisions of visa regulation which banned "radicals, reds, and anarchists" were splendid, he wanted consuls to have the authority to reject applicants they believed were apt to become threats to the social as well as the political institutions of the United States.[12] In other words, he wished both to protect the United States from bad characters and to shield consuls from domestic outcry were aliens to be granted visas in their home countries and later barred from the United States at the port of entry. If consuls were to receive more authority from Congress, fewer aliens would arrive in the United States who were unable to pass the Immigration Service's physical, moral, and mental tests. There would also be fewer heart-rending cases of foreigners being turned back at the pier, which would mean less adverse publicity for federal officials. In sum, Carr hoped that consuls would be enabled to exercise enough discretion abroad as to eliminate largely the need for deportation proceedings.[13]

Although he strongly urged complete consular discretion in the 1921 Immigration Act, the Foreign Service did not receive the authority it demanded until the quota law passed in 1924. Under the former Act, consuls had administered quotas, rejecting only those applicants who were politically unsuitable for entry into the United States. After 1924 the monthly quota changed to a yearly one, reducing from twelve to one the annual number of scenes made by disappointed rejects milling about outside the doors of United States consulates. The 1924 Act also gave consuls power to refuse a visa to anyone unlikely to gain admission to the United States at port of entry,[14] the purpose of which was to protect the Foreign and Immigration Services from adverse domestic publicity. In other words, the Foreign Service would gain in a negative sense by not alienating any other federal agency. By rejecting unfit applicants, consuls would be following the wishes of the majority of the public who wanted to exclude aliens, and by rejecting them at a good distance from the United States, consuls would not risk offending that minority of the public who was in favor of continuing a free flow of immigrants. Thus both constituencies would be satisfied.

The restriction of immigration was greatly expounded and justified at the Foreign Service School. During the five years after passage of the Rogers Act, diplomats and other government officials lectured at length to Foreign Service recruits on immigration. The lecturer's views regarding foreigners, domestic politics, and international relations provided an intellectual framework for new consuls to work within when they had to administer visa regulations. Of the 282 recruits who went through the school in its first five years of operation, 93 (or 33 percent) of them later held consular or diplomatic positions in those European cities where refugees applied for United States visas in the late thirties.[15] The Foreign Service officers' unsympathetic responses during the refugee crisis was fully consistent with the method and outlook presented to recruits at the Foreign Service School. Lecturers at the school freely offered unkind opinions of both the politicians and those members of the public who competed with professional Foreign Service officers for control of United States foreign policy. Diplomats and representatives from other executive agencies explained to the recruits precisely why restrictions had been imposed and how officers were intended to enforce visa regulations, combining their contempt for aliens with their fear of politicians, their scorn for the American public, and the mutual respect that existed among themselves.

In fact, the lectures were permeated with a nativist social outlook, offering a militant justification for the strict enforcement of the quota system.[16] Nelson Truslow Johnson, a sixteen-year veteran of the Foreign Service who had been appointed Ambassador to China in 1925, explained to the recruits the baleful social consequences of immigration to the United States.[17] According to his biographer, Johnson was a lover of Chinese civilization and a steadfast advocate of the Chinese cause in the United States from 1925 to 1941.[18] Yet while he undoubtedly believed he was a sincere friend of the Chinese, his attitude toward them at the Foreign Service School revealed that his admiration of Orientals was actually more paternalistic than fraternal. Johnson explained with grim satisfaction how immigration restriction had been transformed from a West Coast movement, scorned by the best men of the East in the nineteenth century, into a national insistence upon the exclusion of aliens in the twentieth.[19] Since the 1890s, he said, the East had learned how European immigrants had depressed the wages of the natives and put a strain on their institutions, just as the Chinese and Japanese immigrants had done in California in the decades after the Civil War. Following the nativist argument, which, as I repeat, suggested that the quality of the new immigrants from southern and eastern Europe was lower than that of the older, northern immigrants, he claimed that the new immigrants' motives for coming to the United States were cruder than those of former immigrants. No longer was America the haven for hard-pressed religious or political refugees like the Puritans or the German ''Forty-eighters.'' Instead, as he explained, base and selfish economic gain now lured aliens to the New World, and it had become apparent not only to Johnson but to the public who had demanded immigration restriction that ''we were getting unfit people from Europe.''[20]

The newer immigration from southern and eastern Europe proved to Johnson's satisfaction that the ''idealists,'' who held that democracy could flourish in an ethnically heterogeneous America, were misguided. Johnson insisted that the United States had to turn away the new immigrants in order to preserve the American democracy, having been convinced by domestic politics during the First World War that ''the so-called melting pot of the United States was a myth.''[21] As advocates of the Allied cause, diplomats had been outraged by the anti-Allied ''hyphenates,'' especially Irishmen, Germans, and Jews, who had opposed American support for Britain, France, or Russia. In Johnson's opinion, the ''hyphenated Americans'' contributed to what Madison Grant had called in 1915 ''the passing of the Great Race'' of Anglo-Saxons,[22] and he considered the history of race relations in the United States to have been an unmitigated disaster and further proof of the undesirability of free admission for aliens. While he hoped the United States would emulate Australia and try to establish racial homogeneity, he feared that a sizable black minority was already challenging the purity of the white race, and was certain that the attempt during Reconstruction to grant citizenship to freedmen had been a blunder. Perhaps, he mused, the radical spirit of vengeance in the North had made it inevitable that former slaves be granted suffrage after the Civil War, but ''it is somewhat doubtful if it would be settled that way now . . . I think if we had to do it all over again we would not admit Negroes to citizenship. We do not propose at present to grant that right to yellow people.''[23]

Since the professional diplomats saw the Bolshevik regime in Russia as a political threat, they considered it one more justification for rigorously scrutinizing applications for admissions to the United States. Several instructors at the Foreign Service School explained to the recruits that the Soviet government was a pariah regime whose aim was the subversion of the institutions of all other states.[24] One student of Soviet policy in particular, Robert F. Kelley, Chief of the Department's Division of East European Affairs, informed recruits that it was not necessary for the United States to recognize the Soviet regime in order to enjoy the benefits of commerce with the Bolsheviks.[25] While wishing to trade with the Soviet Union, Foreign Service officers feared that the Soviet government was tampering with the machinery of United States immigration requirements by way of their trade agents. Franklin DuBois, Chief of the Department's visa office, claimed that the Soviet trade office, Amtorg, occasionally sent representatives illegally into the States as spies, and saw Amtorg's sharp practice's as a nefarious conspiracy between Jews recently arrived in the United States and Bolsheviks in Russia, intended to shatter domestic harmony in America. He claimed that between 1922 and 1924 Amtorg had employed ''low class Jew lawyers to represent them,'' but that pressure from the State Department in 1925 had induced Amtorg to retain ''a reputable firm of lawyers'' to assume responsibility for the conduct of Soviet commercial agents in the United States.[26]

DuBois's jibe was characteristic of an attitude of genteel anti-Semitism among Foreign Service officers. William Phillips, when Undersecretary of State in 1923, had recorded in his diary, in May, that his opposite number, the Soviet Undersecretary for Foreign Affairs, a man named Weinstein, was ''a perfect little rat of a Jew, born in Buffalo, and utterly vile.''[27] Other diplomats did not believe in the idea of a Bolshevik-Jewish conspiracy, but did resent the aggressive efforts of eastern European Jews to enter the United States. Hugh Gibson, when he was Minister to Poland immediately after the First World War, often complained that American Jews, acting on behalf of their coreligionists in Poland, had been meddling in the delicate work of professional diplomacy.[28] As he wrote the Department in June 1920, regarding the Hebrew Immigrant Aid Society, an American group trying to help Jews reach the United States:

> Those people [the H. I. A. S. representatives in Warsaw] have been getting altogether too high-handed and the patience of the Department is not going to last much longer. I have recommended that the people

there [in Washington] be told that their representatives at Warsaw have either got to behave themselves or get out. It's no use fooling around with people of that sort.[29]

One consul, Richard Cameron Beer, who had been in charge of visa work in Budapest in 1922, kept his mother and sister informed of how disreputable the Jews he saw were and how they gave his chancery office an "aroma no zoo in the world can equal."[30] Beer had detested the *nouveaux riches* he encountered at the opera and heaped scorn upon the poorer Jews who sought to emigrate. After filling one monthly quota in 1922, he asked his sister,

> Well, what are you doing with your Yids? I sent you a whole new flock of them this year. There must have been at least sixteen rabbis and cantors among em. I held up a couple of cantors. I don't like cantors. Theyre hair is too long and their beards is all full of soup and they generally smell and theyre fingernails is wonderful. [sic][31]

Although diplomats embraced nativist notions of American society, they understood that immigration restriction could create animosity toward the United States overseas. They therefore wanted any explanation of American immigration laws to be entrusted to Foreign Service officers, who were skilled in the gentle art of persuasion, rather than to blunt and belligerent restrictionist Congressmen. Lecturers instructed recruits to persuade foreign governments of the wisdom and correctness of the American immigration policy, and suggested that they show less sympathy for the ruffled feelings of excluded foreigners than for the restrictionist sentiments of American Congressmen. Franklin DuBois told recruits that they were patiently to explain to foreign governments the racial reasons behind America's immigration restriction, specifying that the regulation was strictly an internal matter, and discouraging false hopes that the United States would revise the invidious quota system.[32] He also suggested that they adapt their arguments to the susceptibilities of their hosts. For example, Japan, whose citizens had been virtually excluded from the United States barely a year before DuBois spoke, was the country most sensitive to the effects of the new immigration statute.[33] During the Senate debate in 1924 over the abrogation of the famous Gentleman's Agreement between the United States and Japan (1907-08), the State Department had objected to the United States canceling that understanding. Secretary of State Hughes supported the Japanese argument that unilateral action on the agreement by the United States could sour relations between Washington and Tokyo. Rather than discourage the Congress from abrogating the Agreement, the apparent collusion between the State Department and the Japanese Embassy in

Washington only inflamed the Congress's jealousy of its legislative prerogative. The Senate then passed the suspension of the Agreement to prove to the
Japanese that the United States would permit no meddling in the internal
matter of immigration.[34] Recalling the hostility with which the Senate and
the press greeted the State Department's advocacy of the Japanese cause,
DuBois urged that, in the future, diplomats posted to Japan persuade the
Japanese to accept American notions of the incompatibility of different
races. History, he said, proved the incapacity of different races to live
together in the same land unless they were compelled to intermarry or unless
one racial group dominated all the others, and he suggested that Foreign
Service officers impress that point upon their Oriental hosts when stationed
in Japan or China.[35]

The desire to promote good relations with other agencies of the Federal
government was another reason for strong bureaucratic pressure being
exerted upon the Foreign Service officers to enforce the quota regulations
strictly. Recruits learned that officers should protect other agencies, especially the Immigration Service, from the adverse publicity that accrued when
"sob sister" reporters, writing for that minority of Americans who favored
free immigration, told of the deportation of aliens. W. W. Husband, the
Commissioner-General of Immigration, told the school that the safest way
of preventing that sort of bad publicity was to reject visa applications
overseas,[36] thus avoiding the meddlesome views of the sensationalist
American press, as well as earning the gratitude of the Labor Department's
Immigration Service. Husband claimed that when consuls rejected applicants in foreign cities, they also spared Immigration Service the rage of irate
politicians and prominent private citizens who wanted particular visas is-
sued. In conclusion, Husband explained that Foreign Service officers, being
physically remote from the United States, were better able than Immigration
officers to withstand the delegations of misguided and meddling Americans
who "swoop down on us [Immigration Service officers] to admit some
derelict who has arrived at some United States port."[37]

During the twenties, diplomats enforced the quota system because it
was their job as civil servants to carry out the wishes of a restrictionist
Congress. They were nevertheless opposed to it even in the thirties, in the
face of growing demands for visas from religious and political refugees from
Germany.[38] No matter how sympathetic they may have been to the plight of
Hitler's victims, diplomats in Europe continued to be reluctant to issue
visas. When two professionals, Lewis D. Einstein and George F. Kennan,
were asked to help refugees, their reactions were indicative of how suspicious our Foreign Service was of German refugees and their American

friends. Einstein, retired United States Minister to Czechoslovakia and a foe of the Nazi regime, refused to join a League of Nations Commission on Refugees when asked to do so by James McDonald in 1933,[39] because of his feeling that the group's appeal to admit refugees was expressed in terms which suggested that only Jews were the victims of Hitler. He was also doubtful that Jewish refugees, being conscious of their ethnic distinctiveness, would be easily assimilated into American social life, adding that he was convinced the American public would never endorse a relief plan designed to comfort Jews alone.[40] As for George Kennan, Second Secretary at the American Embassy in Berlin, it was bureaucratic rivalry that contributed to his reluctance to protest the German treatment of Jews in 1939. Kennan resented the interference of Congressmen in all negotiations, and believed that their pleas for more Embassy aid to refugees seeking admission to the United States were rooted in mean personal ambitions and an attempt to curry favor with a few of their constituents. In his opinion, any protest to the German government from American diplomats would only poison relations between the United States and Germany and do nothing to alleviate the hardships of Germany's persecuted minorities.[41]

The Strategy of ''Low Policy''

Diplomats hoped their political superiors would pursue an active ''high policy'' worthy of a great power, but since the role of Foreign Service officers was advisory and administrative, they lacked direct control over the high-policy conduct of the government. Therefore they developed a strategy of low policy which consisted in directing commercial and immigration questions in a way likely to convince their political superiors to make the high-policy choices they themselves approved. For example, the advice diplomats gave regarding the United States' foreign commercial policy helped them effect their plan of setting the high policy of the United States on a firm foundation of superior administration. They also played a prominent role in influencing the State Department's views on private overseas loans, international cable-landing rights, and raw material concessions overseas. When diplomats offered commercial advice, they put into practice their long-standing views on the interdependence of commerce and politics. Since American security, unlike that of the older European powers, was based upon her commercial power, the overseas commercial policy of the United States was too important to be left in the invisible hands of the free market. Faced with restrictive trade policies after the First World War,

American businessmen needed the assistance of the government in maintaining what they considered a competitive position in world trade. The diplomats, for their part, insisted upon the government creating its own commercial policy, for they doubted that businessmen would be able to grasp the larger political implications of their overseas commerce.

In the aftermath of the First World War, the State Department for the first time enunciated a general policy with regard to loans made by private American citizens to foreign governments. Until the war, the government had had no coherent policy on private investment abroad. During the Taft Administration, for example, the phrase "dollar diplomacy" became a slogan for American interference in the financial affairs of the Caribbean government. President Wilson, during his first administration, muted the government's interest in private investment overseas; by the end of his presidency, however, the State, Treasury, and Commerce Departments were advocating American overseas investment as a means of restoring and enlarging the international trading system wrecked by the First World War. By the time of the Harding Administration, the State Department considered private loans a means of relieving suffering overseas and expanding the world market without the United States having to participate in an unpopular League of Nations. [42]

Interested as it was in the fate of private loans overseas, the State Department in the years after the First World War wrestled with the problems of defining precisely the role the government would play in regulating the outflow of private capital. On the one hand, the State Department wished to be kept informed of all prospective loans, since it found certain types unacceptable and wished to proscribe five of them: (1) loans to governments for balancing of budgets with deficiencies due to insufficient taxation; (2) loans for armaments; (3) loans for foreign monopolies which engaged in restrictive practices against American businesses; (4) loans to governments not recognized by the United States; and (5) loans to governments in arrears in their public debt to the United States government. [43] At the same time, officials in the State Department were more cautious about the prospects of repayment of many foreign debts to private lenders than were the lenders themselves or officials in the Commerce Department, so that Secretary of State Hughes and Arthur Young, the economic advisor of the State Department, wanted to be sure that the United States government did not even give the appearance of acting as the guarantor of loans made to dubious credit risks.

Herbert Feis, who, in the 1930s, became the economic advisor to the

State Department, later told how the Department had developed a statement on loans in March 1922.[44] After much consultation within the Department, in which two Foreign Service officers, Leland Harrison and Fred Morris Dearing, played an active part, it demanded in March 1922 the right to review all foreign loans contemplated by American banking houses. The Department proclaimed that it was not passing on the merits of various loan proposals, but that it had to be kept informed of on-going negotiations. If a prospective borrower were recognized by the United States, not in arrears to the United States government, and did not intend to use the loan to purchase armaments, the American banker would be informed that the Department had "no objections" to the loan. In dubious cases, the banker would receive a note to the effect that the Department was "not in a position" to agree to the proposed transaction.[45] Such bureaucratic locutions were carefully formulated by the State Department to absolve the Department from any responsibility to the lenders, should the borrower prove incapable of payment. Hughes wanted bankers to realize that while the government approved of the flow of capital outside the United States, and while diplomats might wish to delay loans as a counter in delicate negotiations, the Department was not underwriting them. To have given the impression that the government agreed to guarantee the loans of private citizens would have meant that outsiders—namely, bankers, rather than politicians and the State Department—were responsible for the political goals of United States foreign policy.

Career Foreign Service officers were not only instrumental in advising Hughes with regard to the policy on loans, but exercised wide discretion in administering it. When, in the twenties, Leland Harrison was Assistant Secretary of State, he was the man in charge of reviewing loans proposed by American bankers. Since he lived at the Family residence at 1718 H Street, he would query Family members stationed in Latin America or Europe as to the status of loan negotiations.[46] Assistant Secretary of the Treasury Eliot Wadsworth, another Family member who also resided at 1718 H Street in the year immediately following the March 1922 declaration, shared the other members' contempt for political hacks, and scorned several of the officials who had come into the Treasury under Secretary Andrew Mellon. Wadsworth handled foreign loans for the Treasury Department and, together with Harrison, decided that the Treasury Department would follow the State Department's lead in ruling on loan proposals.[47] Indeed, he reflected the career diplomat's characteristic views on the relationship between foreign commerce and international politics in his handling of loan policy. For example, he believed that overseas commerce was crucial to American foreign policy, but that foreign policy consisted in more than trade expansion. He had no use for those American bankers who, in his opinion, lacked perspective when it came to strategy and international politics. He suspected the veracity of the foreign officials seeking loans, as well as their capacity to pay, and he feared the subtlety of foreign—especially British—bankers and diplomats. Harrison, along with the other Foreign Service officers, explained his position officially to the Foreign Service School and, in memoranda, to the Secretary of State.[48]

During the twenties, Foreign Service officers extended their commercial work beyond financial matters to cable-landing negotiations and raw material decisions. As in the case of exportation of capital, they pursued both strategic and commercial objectives when conducting negotiations concerned with communications and raw materials. Their aim was to assure the United States adequate sources of vital raw materials, such as rubber, petroleum, and metals, which could not be interrupted by the diplomacy of any European power.[49] The communications and raw materials policy was supposed to gain (in the mid-East, Latin America and the Orient) the secure footholds which would permit the United States, without joining the League of Nations, to behave like a predominant world power. In Latin America, and to a lesser degree in the Middle East, commercial-strategic decisions on loans, cables, and raw materials made up the bulk of American policy with regard to those regions.[50] Foreign Service officers, particularly Family men and their protégés, were instrumental in carrying out that policy, which was intended to secure strategic advantages for the United States as well as commercial rights for American firms.

But professional diplomats were not the only government officials concerned with overseas trade in the twenties. The Department of Commerce under Herbert Hoover pursued an aggressive overseas economic policy and encouraged American businessmen to invest abroad and tried to break the restrictive trade policies of other governments that placed the United States at a competitive disadvantage.[51] However, the Commerce Department's interest in the strategic implications of an aggressive commercial policy provoked intense resentment in the State Department. Consequently, in the case of loans, diplomats inside the State Department had successfully excluded the Commerce Department from ruling on the merits of private loans in 1922.[52] Later, during the agitation for passage of the Rogers Act, the Bureau of Foreign Commerce under the direction of Julius Klein, a personal friend of Hoover, and Wilbur Carr's opposite number in the Commerce Department, lobbied in the Congress for the establishment of an independent overseas jurisdiction for a proposed Commerce Department Foreign Service. Carr strenuously objected to a rival Foreign Service and, through masterful Congressional lobbying in 1924, managed to suppress a bill giving the Commerce Department the right to supervise its attachés directly, without going through the channel of the United States Chief of Mission in any given country.[53]

Carr's arguments, which had the full support of both diplomats and consuls, misrepresented the Commerce Department as neglecting the connections between an active commercial policy and the larger strategic interests of the United States. Indeed, the fact that the Foreign Service was vying with the Commerce Department reflected the diplomats' conviction, reiterated so many times in the years after 1919, that American strength and international order in the twenties rested upon diplomats as guarantors of a stable system of international commerce. The argument ran as follows: only career diplomats, with their generalist training, understood the political implications of commerce and the commercial implications of political decisions; therefore only diplomats were capable of directing American business and strategic affairs.[54]

The advice given by the Foreign Service officers regarding immigration and commerce was subtly bound up with recommendations on the high-policy areas of American military posture and plans for disarmament and world peace. In fact, their advice with respect to the various disarmament negotiations and schemes for world peace reflected their deep skepticism as to the ability of the machinery of international organizations to eliminate conflict from world politics. At the same time, they pursued their meliorist course, believing that professional diplomats, fully aware of the genuine reason for disagreement among nations, were the most suitable agents for achieving any effective reduction in armaments. Alanson Houghton explained to the Foreign Service School the dangers of entertaining hopes about the immediate success of disarmament negotiations. He told the recruits to be wary of domestic visionaries like Edward Bok, whose dreams of achieving universal peace were merely illusory.[55] If, however, Foreign Service officers maintained a healthy skepticism about an immediate end to the European arms race, the American diplomats who were negotiators and observers at disarmament conferences could play an effective role as mediators.

Hugh Gibson, while Minister to Switzerland from 1924 until 1927, pursued the same meliorist goal of professional diplomacy in his work at the continuing Geneva disarmament conference. Privately, he doubted whether armaments could ever be completely scrapped, professing to understand the motives behind the French desire for a strong land force and the British insistence on naval parity with the United States. He saw his role as that of a mediator among the great foreign powers, whose fear of their neighbors made them less secure than the United States and hence less amenable to a reduction in armaments. He doubted that armaments would ever be eliminated, and considered that the purpose of the continuing effort at disarmament was to make certain that nations could confidently expect military balances to be maintained.[56]

Perhaps the best example of the professional diplomats' attempts to restrain what they believed to be the optimistic illusions of their amateur political superiors came in 1927, when Secretary of State Frank B. Kellogg joined with French Foreign Minister Aristide Briand to write a treaty outlawing war—a pact that was derived from the Edward Bok and Salmon Levinson peace scheme that gained wide public support during the late twenties and early thirties. Kellogg was not as highly regarded by the professionals in the Department as had been Charles Evans Hughes, who had shared the diplomats' belief in the slow improvement of international affairs through the agency of skilled diplomats. In contrast, Kellogg was more impressed by the machinery of international law, and thus occasionally disregarded the advice of the Foreign Service.[57]

At the time of its inception, the Kellogg-Briand pact was applauded, by everyone except the professional diplomats in the State Department, who were convinced that mere clauses in a treaty would never be able to eliminate the conflicts endemic in international politics. William R. Castle and his staff in the Division of Western European Affairs warned Kellogg that the treaty would not end war and that, moreoever, it was a ploy on the part of the subtle French to get the United States to protect them in the future. Indeed, Castle preferred that the treaty not be signed at all, since it might lull Americans into a false sense of security. Castle did try to restrain his boss from offering American aid to the French, and he succeeded in changing a bilateral treaty into a meaningless multilateral statement of good intentions.[58]

The Kellogg-Briand treaty was an example of how professional diplomats failed to set policy, but contented themselves with influencing a decision by the manner in which they offered advice. In other words, Foreign Service officers had an advisory function, which was the closest they ever came in the twenties to playing a dominant role in the policy-making process. Obviously, foreign policy in the twenties, as throughout

American history, was the product of the aims and actions of far more people and groups inside and outside the government than a few hundred Foreign Service officers. Yet their new professional outlook did profoundly shape political action. Diplomats saw themselves as teachers and mediators, explaining to their political superiors the contentious nature of international relations, the character of other countries, and the virtues of long-term planning. They welcomed public interest in foreign affairs so long as that interest was remote from action and supportive of professional Foreign Service officers. They tried to ensure that the actual conduct of diplomacy was in the hands of officials who recognized the delicacy of relations among sovereign states and who claimed insight into the complex connections among society, law, commerce, and politics, thus restraining politicians from actions diplomats considered hasty, quixotic, or likely to give offense overseas. The diplomats sometimes admired the fundamental aims of their countrymen, but feared that untutored men could spoil America's reputation abroad. In the case of immigration they mediated between blunt Americans who wanted to exclude aliens and the foreign-visa applicants or their governments. In the case of disarmament and plans for world peace they mediated between what they perceived as the naiveté of their fellow Americans and the cynicism or belligerence of other great powers. By pursuing that meliorist course, Foreign Service officers finally set boundaries for the conduct of an active foreign policy which would convince politicians, the American public, and foreign diplomats that the United States was a preeminent world power.

Epilogue

The Professionals' Dilemma, 1945-1974

THE career diplomat's tortured outlook on world politics and professional diplomacy had sustained implications for subsequent foreign policies and attempts at State Department reorganization. Several leaders of the reform movement of the twenties remained in the State Department throughout the thirties,[1] and some throughout the Second World War.[2] Moreover, two-thirds of the younger officers recruited during the six years after passage of the Rogers Act helped shape foreign policy during the Cold War.[3] As young recruits, they had assimilated the view that the United States was as self-interested as any other nation and, simultaneously, the disinterested regulator of the world system. They had learned that professional diplomats were an embattled and misunderstood elite who functioned as political reporters and policy planners. They had discovered that the security of their career demanded that they teach American politicians the contentious nature of world politics and persuade them to grant Foreign Service officers greater political authority. The public was to be educated to admire those personal qualities in diplomats which enabled them to succeed in the brutal international world.[4]

What the recruits had learned from their older colleagues was similar to the political advice the younger men offered their political superiors after 1945. In short, career diplomats in the fifteen years after the Second World War advised their superiors to lead a group of Western powers in a "realistic" fashion, containing the Soviet Union, whose aims they believed to be expansionary. A successful confrontation with Soviet power demanded the use of flexible political, commercial, organizational, and military methods, devised and supervised by full-time professionals. The diplomats distrusted any popular zeal for a crusade to "roll back" Soviet successes.[5] While they appreciated and often tried to arouse the patriotic fervor of outsiders, they believed that if the public were to direct the conflict with the Soviet Union, the success of American foreign policy would be imperiled. Foreign affairs required too special a competence and too much patience to be entrusted to people whom the diplomats considered as "primitives."[6]

Foreign Service officers contended also with other federal agencies for control of foreign policy in those years. While claiming that work in foreign affairs required knowledge too specialized to be available to the general public, they added that the direction of foreign policy would be insufficiently flexible if entrusted to technical experts in the Defense Department or in the many special economic, commercial, intelligence, or propaganda agencies that had been established to wage the Cold War. For example, during the early years of the Cold War, State Department professionals feared that the Defense Department wanted to challenge the Soviet Union in an inflexibly belligerent manner. George Kennan, author of the famous article "The Sources of Soviet Conduct," which became the basis for our containment policy, later admitted in his memoirs that his plans for opposing Soviet foreign policy quickly hardened into military dogma.[7] In the councils of the Truman Administration, Kennan and his assistant in the State Department's policy planning staff, Charles Bohlen, often found themselves in the anomalous position of opposing attempts to codify long-range objectives for American foreign policy. In 1950 both Bohlen and Kennan criticized the draft of NSC 68, a National Security Council document which projected Soviet behavior for the decade after 1950, because they considered it too precise and inflexible. They warned that professional diplomats, keenly sensitive to changes in the international environment, might have their hands tied by such dogmatic statements as NSC 68. Despite the obvious intelligence of their argument, it failed to influence the political directors of foreign policy, because Kennan and Bohlen were unable to enumerate precisely the skills of generalist Foreign Service officers.[8] Dean Acheson, in many ways an admirer of the general readiness and *savoir faire* of diplomats, complained in his memoirs that he often felt uneasy when they explained their special skills to him, for they seemed to be expounding a type of mysterious wisdom too arcane for the layman. Acheson also explained that he often relied upon military advice because it seemed more rigorous and testable than that of the diplomats.[9]

In the late fifties and early sixties, after the State Department had instituted reforms to make the Foreign Service more amenable to the skills of specialists in law, economics, or science, the professional diplomats continued to doubt the ability of members of other government agencies to grasp the subtleties of international relations. During the political and scientific negotiations between the Western powers and the Soviet Union, which took place from 1957 to 1963 and culminated in the signing of the Limited Test Ban Treaty of Moscow, the professional diplomats who were involved scorned the scientific experts as politically useless, as incapable of properly conducting negotiations.[10] Similarly, in the early sixties, the State Department led the fight against the attempt of the members of the National Academy of Sciences to set down a precise law for international uses of outer space. The Department again argued that a precise international law for outer space at too early a date would interfere with the future flexibility of the directors of United States policy.[11]

In the decades after the Second World War, professional diplomats continued to assert that they, with their combination of special political acumen, grasp of international relations, and skill at negotiating, should be in charge of directing foreign policy. Their desire to exclude the general public from foreign affairs leadership and simultaneously to ensure their position against the inroads of the technical specialists of other agencies deepened their commitment to their inconsistent notions of their own profession. As a result of the tension between politicians and career men, the informal diplomatic club and the bureaucratic Foreign Service made several further efforts at achieving Foreign Service reforms in the years after 1929—reforms which followed the pattern set in the Rogers Act era, and which confirmed the uneasy position of the Foreign Service officer when it came to creating foreign policy.

During the late thirties and the Second World War, President Franklin D. Roosevelt deliberately ignored the career men within the State Department,[12] which provoked a reaction very like the diplomats' hostility to Woodrow Wilson during the First World War. Their sense of isolation was greater, however, since they had come to believe they possessed a Service that deserved public respect.[13] In 1944 Seldin Chapin, the Director of the Foreign Service during the war, began work on a bill to strengthen the Service by increasing its technical capacity. What he had in mind was a model of Wilbur Carr's activity on behalf of the Rogers Act when he testified to the needs of the Foreign Service. The resulting Foreign Service Act of 1946 established a Foreign Service Institute to train recruits in Washington and a corps of Foreign Service Reserve officers to provide technical skills on special assignments, thus reforming the Foreign Service School as instituted by the Rogers Act: the new school had a permanent staff, whereas the former had only visiting lecturers; and students were not only enabled to devote themselves full-time to their academic courses, but had the opportunity to receive instruction in languages and specialized areas.[14] However, officers in mid-career could return to the Institute for advanced instruction, and the Institute as a whole was meant to serve as a focal point for Service morale.

The act both recognized the tension between technical and general knowledge, permitting recruits to pursue either a general or an area course, and made a distinction between regular and reserve officers, confirming the diplomats' uncertainty as to technical expertise. They knew that technical knowledge would help them to play an active role in complicated negotiations, but were reluctant to think of their entire Service as technical, for to have done so would have excluded Foreign Service officers from discussions on the principles of American foreign policy.[15]

The next period of reform occurred during the Eisenhower Administration. In 1953 and 1954 Henry M. Wriston, President of Brown University, chaired a public committee on foreign affairs personnel administration. The Committee recommended in 1954 that the staffs of the Foreign Service and the State Department be amalgamated.[16] The Department's response that year was the elimination of the separate personnel administrations for overseas and Washington-based officers, in the hopes of giving greater continuity to foreign policy. The Wriston commission also expected that amalgamation would finally end the persistent complaints to the effect that diplomats overseas adopted an alien perspective and that desk officers in Washington became parochial.[17]

The post-World-War-Two years saw a vast expansion in the number and kinds of foreign affairs agencies and personnel. To begin with, there was a greater number of career diplomats and an increase in other foreign affairs agencies that far outstripped the growth of the Foreign Service.[18] Old reformers like Phillips and recruits of the twenties like Kennan greeted the proliferation of specialized agencies and the growth of the Foreign Service with skepticism. In part, their unhappiness with the impersonality of the new foreign affairs bureaucracy was rooted in nostalgia for the *esprit de corps* of the pioneer days of the Rogers Act period.[19] Phillips complained that the old Department, in which diplomats personally knew all the other members of the Foreign Service, was a thing of the past by 1950.[20] The old, informal conviviality of the twenties had been replaced by institutions. Even the old Family headquarters at 1718 H Street Northwest had become the property of a bureaucratic organization, the National Association of Retired Diplomats and Consuls. The veterans' misgivings about the Foreign Service of the fifties was, according to students of bureaucracy, common among founders of new organizations. Once the initial pioneering period is past, the control of new organizations ceases to be the exclusive property of a single group. Rules become routines; impersonality and organizational conservatism become the symptoms of a mature bureaucracy.[21]

In one sense, the veterans' longing for the twenties was proof of the success of their reforms, but the old reformers' uneasiness at the size and quality of the Service reflected more than simple nostalgia. Officers who had entered professional diplomacy after the Act of 1946 and who had never known the intimacy of the old Service also complained about certain failings of the new.[22] For example, the years following there forms of the Wriston Commission witnessed another period of intensive examination of the Foreign Service by diplomats and outsiders who were unhappy with the administration of United States foreign relations. Academics, the Carnegie Endowment for International Peace, the Brookings Institution, the State Department, and the Foreign Service Association all studied the problem and proposed changes.[23] While recommendations differed in nearly every report, and few of the suggested reforms ever came to fruition, all the studies agreed on three continuing areas of discontent: the competing claims of generalists and specialists in conducting foreign affairs; the internal "living system" of the Department of State; and a sense of isolation from the centers of political authority.

The attempt to resolve the first of those problems resembled the battles of the twenties between diplomats and consuls, but with one important difference: the fifties and sixties saw a range of special skills applied to foreign affairs—skills which were unknown or irrelevant to foreign policy in the twenties. The growth of American overseas aid programs created the need for more and different economic experts, whereas the development of scientific technology in aviation, atomic energy, and outer space had immediate implications for international relations. Also, the application of the mathematical game theory radically altered the practice of professional economists and military strategists, and had definite implications with regard to the conduct of international relations. Even international political relations, the traditional preserve of the professional diplomat, underwent qualitative changes in the late fifties and early sixties, given the final deterioration of colonialism and the independence of states in Africa and Asia. Academic observers of international politics outside the State Department called the development of techniques to deal with a radically altered international environment the New Diplomacy. The New Diplomacy of the sixties had no relation to the open negotiations proposed by Woodrow Wilson; rather, for such scholars as James McCamy, the members of the Brookings Institution, and Zara Steiner, it came to mean the employment of specialists, whether experts on specific continents, development economists, specialists in scientific work, or systems analysts.[24]

Due to the demands of outsiders in favor of the New Diplomacy, the Congress insisted in the 1959 revision of Foreign Service Act of 1946 that the technical experts attached to the Foreign Service Reserve Corps be promoted at the same rate as men who followed the generalist path. Within the Service, the demand for more specialists was greeted with misgivings. On the one hand, Foreign Service officers welcomed the opportunity to include specialists within their ranks, for in this way they were in a better position to control foreign policy when it dealt with technically recondite subjects. But on the other hand, the diplomats feared the incursion of experts who had been trained differently, so that they strongly resisted the lateral entry of technical experts in the early sixties, and scorned the Congressional stipulations that the specialists be promoted as fast as the generalists. For its part, *The Foreign Service Journal* repeatedly questioned the amalgamation provisions of the Wriston commission, which had placed the Reserve officers on the same footing as the regular Foreign Service. The Senate Committee on Foreign Relations, which polled over fifty returned Foreign Service officers in 1959, discovered that they greatly objected to the augmentation of the position of technical experts. The regular Foreign Service officers also voiced strenuous objection to the attempt to establish a Foreign Service Academy.[25] Arguing in much the same way as Wilbur J. Carr had when he opposed the scholarship provisions of the Rogers bill, the Foreign Service in 1960 objected that the proposal to establish a special academy to train diplomats would create a clique of technical experts unable to direct high policy.

The Service's subordination of technical knowledge to general readiness offended the technical experts, just as the diplomats' elevation of their branch had embittered the consuls in the late twenties. One study of the State Department organization in the middle sixties discovered that the diplomats' inability or reluctance to define their profession precisely interfered with the Foreign Service's achieving its stated goals of political reporting and policy planning. The political reporting of the junior officers in the Service became wooden and uninteresting, because they told their superiors what they wanted to hear, rather than explaining the real world.[26] Communications within the Department were misdirected, proceeding from the top down rather than from the bottom up. Many junior officers were unhappy with the way promotions were made, claiming that there were no "scientific" standards for advancement within the Service. Diplomats believed that their own reluctance to set scientific standards for judging diplomatic work would make the Foreign Service a generalist directory of foreign policy; instead, the Service often became the home of inadequate political reporters.[27]

Several retired Foreign Service officers and State Department officials echoed that indictment. For example, one former diplomat, Gordon Tullock, expounded a general theory of the behavior of bureaucrats, based in part on his experience in the Department, in his book *The Politics of Bureaucracy*. Tullock did not deal directly with the problems of the Foreign Service, but his explicit comments about professional diplomats were damning: he claimed not only that knowledge of foreign cultures was of "limited usefulness" in securing diplomatic promotion, but that it was generalism which was the road to success. He also noted that a diplomat's primary constituents were his superiors, who were told what they wanted to hear. "Influencing foreigners," he said, "is, of course, one object of the American Foreign Service,"

> but there is not one simple way of determining how successful any particular individual has been in this task. As a result, the Department of State tends to overlook this factor in deciding on promotions. The ambitious diplomat will, if he is wise, confine himself to influencing Americans. His reports should be based on an analysis of the Department of State, not upon the country he is obstensibly reporting. Quite naturally, as a polished diplomat, he will not admit all this, probably not even to himself.[28]

Tullock's book was one of a spate of works by former State Department employees critical of the organization. Charles Frankel left the office of Assistant Secretary of State for Cultural Affairs with a blast entitled *High on Foggy Bottom*.[29] Smith Simpson reached conclusions similar to Tullock's in *Anatomy of the State Department*.[30] Moreover, in 1970 John F. Campbell, a young Foreign Service officer, published a caustic memoir of his years as a junior officer in the State Department called *The Foreign Affairs Fudge Factory*.[31]

While planning foreign policy for the sixties, the State Department, the Congress, and Presidents Eisenhower and Kennedy all ostensibly agreed with the State Department's desire to coordinate foreign affairs, asserting that the State Department should occupy the central position in coordinating the overseas activities of the American government. Just how the Department was to gain control of the vast proliferation of agencies and personnel which dealt with the new problems of ideological competition with the Soviets, with development problems of the newly-independent states, and with issues raised by the rapid changes in scientific technique was a central concern of the planners of the early sixties. Yet most of the solutions offered were more pious wishes than workable plans. A research team of the Brookings Institution under the direction of H. Field Haviland prepared its proposal for the coordination of overseas activities for the Senate Committee on Foreign Relations in 1959. The Brookings report noted that during the previous fifteen years there had been an apparent loosening of central focus in the administration of foreign affairs. It recommended the eventual establishment of a Department of Foreign Affairs to coordinate the work then being done by the State Department, the information agency, the aid agencies, and any new office which might be set up in the future to deal with overseas work. The model for this scheme was the amalgamation of the various armed services into the Department of Defense in 1948. The Brookings report coupled this recommendation with another proposal which gave far less comfort to Foreign Service officers, who had hopes of regaining a preeminent position to foreign affairs leadership—namely, that before a special Foreign Affairs Department be set up, the Congress should create, for the intelligence, information, and aid administrations, personnel systems as removed from the civil service as was the Foreign Service. Thus the Brookings report delayed until some utopian future the time when all foreign affairs would be controlled by men in the State Department.[32]

When John F. Kennedy became President in 1961, he lent moral support to the movement for the recognition of the State Department as the central focus of foreign affairs activity. Shortly after he took office, Kennedy ordered the Chief of Mission in each country to coordinate all American activities there, and to exercise ultimate authority over the personnel and activities of every federal agency which sent officers abroad. This directive bolstered diplomatic morale in the early sixties, much as similar statements from President Harding and Secretary of State Hughes had encouraged the career men in the early twenties.[33] However, during both periods the diplomats were faced early on with the question of how to realize the authority offered them by their president.

During the sixties, Foreign Service officers rejected the idea of relying on the technical knowledge of functional or area specialists to provide them with the political dominance they sought. Not only did the lateral entry of specialists dim the spirit of the Service, but veteran diplomats doubted whether such specialists had a good enough grasp of the broad complexities of world politics to offer advice concerning high policy. Instead of area specialization, the Foreign Service flirted for a while with two modern techniques that could be applied to the broadest possible range of issues of administration and international politics. The two innovative methods, which fired the imaginations of some Foreign Service officers, were the ideas gaming and strategy developed by the mathematical economists John Von Neumann, Oskar Morgenstern, and their followers, and system analysis, which was developed by economists in the fifties and applied in the Defense Department by Robert McNamara and Charles Hitch during the sixties. While the State Department's fascination with these techniques was no stronger than its earlier interest in area specialization, the persistent attempts to reform the Department through the use of such techniques revealed the diplomats' desire to gain political authority, while at the same time retaining their conception of themselves as gentlemanly generalists capable of dealing with every unexpected aspect of foreign policy. If diplomats retained their professional ideal of men who conveyed a mystique of general ability, they were ignored by politicians who wanted answers they could test. If, however, the professionals were to offer advice in a precise, scientific fashion, they feared that they would be reduced to the level of clerks and consultants, while the interesting political work would go to incompetent politicians. Although certain diplomats hoped that the introduction of the techniques of gaming and systems analysis might be a way for generalists to make high policy in a scientific fashion, the ultimate failure of the attempted reforms was due largely to the skepticism of the majority of diplomats. The memory of the attempts to employ techniques of gaming and systems analysis, however, left a legacy of aspirations for young reformers to follow in the seventies.

From 1959 to 1961, Foreign Service officers had a brief romance with the theories of Oskar Morgenstern. In 1959 Morgenstern, who had spent the previous few years studying the institutions of American national security, wrote a book in which he compared the quality of Foreign Service officers unfavorably with American military officers,[34] concluding that the State Department had lost the ear of the political directors of foreign policy, because professional diplomats could not present their arguments as logically, coherently, and testably as could military officers. Morgenstern stated that, as a mathematician, he found he could test the military men's claims to having devised winning strategies in world politics, but that he was baffled by those of professional Foreign Service officers, who relied upon wisdom, soundness, and good judgment to carry them in political debate. Morgenstern suggested that diplomats were incapable of handling the business of the sixties precisely because they sought to draw a cloak of mysterious wisdom around their activities. As a result, politicians had entrusted more and more foreign policy business to technicians and to military and academic strategists, who clearly stated their assumptions and were willing to be judged by precisely defined canons of results. Morgenstern suggested that one way for Foreign Service officers to gain additional political authority was to adopt the techniques of strategy and gaming to their work, recommending that they attempt to state explicitly the scale of utilities in American foreign policy and those obtaining in the foreign policy of other powers. He urged American diplomats to make, insofar as possible, their assumptions about the world explicit, to operate with strictly rational means, and to try to make quantitative statements about events which they had previously said were amenable only to their special wisdom.[35]

Not surprisingly, Morgenstern's criticism of the behavior of diplomats ignited a raging argument within the Foreign Service. The *Foreign Service Journal* excerpted portions of his book and criticized it for misunderstanding the work of diplomats. It also carried a rebuttal by Morgenstern and counter-rebuttals by several Foreign Service officers in the letters column.[36] The diplomats objected to Morgenstern's insistence that their work lacked a solid intellectual core. Undaunted by his charges that they drew a priestly mantle around their jobs, the diplomats replied that the techniques of strategy and gaming were inapplicable to diplomatic work because the world was too complicated to be reduced to numbers or equations. Morgenstern regarded such arguments as proof of the point they were seeking to refute. Out of kindness perhaps, he allowed that world events were very difficult to reduce to equations, but he insisted that the job of diplomacy in the sixties was to try to make those equations.

The diplomats did not follow Morgenstern's advice, largely because Foreign Service officers were loath to discard notions of the complex, evolving nature of world politics they had developed in the twenties. In one case, however, a group of State Department reformers came close to applying to diplomacy the intellectual child of strategy and game theory—namely, the techniques of systems analysis. In other words, from 1962 to 1967 certain diplomats waged an ultimately unsuccessful campaign to use techniques of systems analysis in the State Department. Their abortive attempt to establish within the Department of State an office of planning, programming, and budgeting, similar to the one created in the Department of Defense by Charles Hitch, was the most ambitious attempt in the sixties to implement President Kennedy's directive that the Chief of Mission assume ultimate control of the foreign activities of the United States government. This proposed innovation was the subject of a case study, *Programming Systems and Foreign Affairs Leadership,* by two of the participants in the proposal, John E. Harr and Frederick C. Mosher.[37] Harr and Mosher described how the system analysts within the Department of State sought to establish budgeting systems for each overseas mission of the government, and hoped that this would exert the real control over the personnel of the other agencies implied by the President's directive. They also intended it to be a means whereby the Secretary of State could tell, by a glance at the daily computer printout, which overseas projects were effectively using the precise quantity of men, money, and energy that were allotted to them. In effect, the innovation sought to impose upon foreign affairs a rational procedure for judging the effectiveness of the personnel and programs of the Foreign Service and the Department of State. As a climax of the attempts to make the innovation a permanent part of foreign-policy-making, the Department of State decided to employ as head of the project Thomas Schelling, a professor of government at Harvard and one of the principal academic proponents of applying the mathematical theory of games to the problems of conflict, cooperation, and bargaining in international relations. Schelling received the offer in early 1967, but refused in May, fearing that there was insufficient time to do the job he wanted within the year's academic leave he was planning to take.[38]

However, Mosher and Harr claimed that bureaucratic and structural objections to the establishment of a systems analytic office, not Schelling's refusal, were the real cause of the scheme's failure. Within a year the systems analysts within the Department of State were resented by the members of the Foreign Service, who were not at all convinced that techniques designed to manage profit-making ventures could be applied to foreign affairs.[39] Their opposition was a repetition of the objection raised to Oskar Morgenstern's ideas, for professional diplomats were skeptical of the outcome of assigning numerical and financial values to questions of world politics. Whereas to the systems analysts the Foreign Service outlook rejected any possibility of a rational approach to international affairs, to the Foreign Service officers imbued with the old view of their career, the systems analysts challenged the primacy of the individual diplomat, who was supposedly capable of understanding the entire range of international relations.

The opposition of the Foreign Service officers alone, however, would not have been enough to reject systems analysis. The innovators were also handicapped by the fact that the political directors of the Department of State, who had initially supported their efforts in 1963, were otherwise occupied in 1966 with the war in Viet Nam and did not offer material support to the embattled reformers when the final decisions on the project had to be made. The most important factor in preventing the fruition of the plan was the opposition of another government agency, the Bureau of the Budget. Since 1961 the Bureau had been incorporating systems analytic techniques in its work. In 1966 President Lyndon Johnson ordered all government agencies to follow a year-round system of Programming, Planning, and Budgeting in their future budget requests. Systems analysts within the Bureau of the Budget clashed with those within the Department of State over who would control the budgeting for overseas operations. The Bureau claimed that it exercised ultimate authority for budgeting and that the innovators within the Department of State were encroaching upon their domain when they tried to oversee the budgets of other federal agencies that operated abroad. Without political support, and whipsawed between the generalists within the Foreign Service, who saw no need for rational budgeting, and the technicians of the Bureau, who feared that the State Department systems analysts were violating their authority, the budget innovations was never put into effect, and its advocates resigned with bitterness. [40]

However, the budgeting plan did raise some hopes as to reforming the profession of diplomacy. One of its by-products was a study by Chris Argyris that was strongly critical of the living system of the Department of State. Another wide-ranging aftermath was a change in the leadership of the Foreign Service Association. During the height of the argument over the budgeting system, a group of young Foreign Service officers had organized themselves into a faction within the Foreign Service Association and had won most of the elective positions in the body in 1967. Styling themselves Young Turks, the new leadership of the Association quickly moved to change the group from the preserve of the old clique into an active organ for reform of the Service. In 1968 the Association published *Toward a Modern Diplomacy,* a book that recognized the widespread dissatisfaction with the Department caused by the denial of political authority to Foreign Service officers. [41] It recommended retaining the old notion of a diplomat as a generalist capable of understanding the complexities of world politics, but suggested that diplomats be able to explain their conclusions to their political superiors, other government agencies, and the wider public in ways that were testable and rational. In short, the Foreign Service Association argued for better "management" of diplomacy.

The unofficial suggestions made by the Association in 1968 became official State Department policy in 1970 with the publication of *Diplomacy for the Seventies: A Proposal of Management Reforms for the Department of State*.[42] Based on the work of over a hundred Foreign Service officers organized into eighteen task forces, the proposals were the fulfillment of the continual desire for self-definition which diplomats had been working at since the Wriston Commission reforms were adopted. The 605-page report argued that diplomats were correct in asserting that the Department of State should be the central coordinating body for foreign affairs, and their claim that generalists were the only officers capable of understanding all of foreign affairs was also supported, but they simply had to present their case as rationally as possible to their superiors and the politicians. What was needed in the Foreign Service, therefore, were officers who could manage the program and the personnel system in such a way as to use most effectively the creativity of the talented diplomats within the Department of State.[43] The career officers who drafted the report argued, in much the same way as their predecessors had in the twenties, that foreign affairs were complex and evolving. The proper administration of foreign affairs required men that had special knowledge and broad-ranging minds. Untutored amateurs obviously lacked insight into world politics, while technical specialists lack the flexibility necessary to meet unexpected situations. Only career diplomats had both the proper knowledge and deportment, that *certaine habitude du monde*, which, as George Kennan said, quoting Jules Jusserand, was necessary to the direction of American foreign policy.[44]

In the months after the report was published, the State Department found that, bit by bit, it was losing its role as coordinator of foreign policy to the National Security Council under the direction of the President's Advisor for National Security Affairs, Henry A. Kissinger. While Kissinger scurried around the world secretly negotiating in Moscow, Peking, and Paris, the Secretary of State, William P. Rogers, found himself merely a cipher, and professional diplomats became profoundly demoralized. Estrangement from the centers of political power proved to be especially bitter to the career diplomats, for Kissinger was a generalist par excellence. A professor of government at Harvard before joining Nixon's Administration, his early work had been an approving study of Metternich's diplomacy, followed by books on the problems of strategy in the modern age.[45] Thus in both his academic and his government careers he had praised the shrewd techniques of secret bargaining typical of the old nineteenth-century diplomats.

Kissinger's closeness to President Nixon seemed to confirm what the diplomats had been insisting upon for a long time: that generalism, imbued with a classical appreciation of world conflict and collaboration, is imperative in the direction of foreign policy. Ironically, however, the diplomats lost rather than profited from the situation, for Nixon's neglect of the State Department in favor of one trusted advisor was perhaps more threatening to the Foreign Service in the 1970s than earlier presidential disregard had been during the First and Second World Wars. During the Nixon Administration some observers suggested that Kissinger's staff had usurped the functions of the Foreign Service, while others denied that the National Security Council was sufficiently staffed to direct foreign policy.[46] The latter opinion seemed to be confirmed by events, for in September 1973 Kissinger left the National Security Council to become Secretary of State in title as well as function. And while his accession to the State Department represented a triumph of the professional diplomats' intellectual outlook, it also confirmed their bureaucratic or institutional failure. Kissinger seemed to demonstrate that general diplomatic ability was necessary to the direction of foreign policy, but his career also showed that a Foreign Service background was not the only way to learn the diplomatic craft. When Kissinger took over the State Department, he brought with him several of his former subordinates on the National Security Council staff. These men, some of whom—Helmut Sonnenfeld and Viron P. Vaky, for example—had previously been Foreign Service officers— formed the nucleus of Kissinger's advisors in the State Department.

Kissinger's relations with career diplomats represented only one more episode in the problematic career of professional diplomats. During both the twenties and the seventies, diplomats were torn between the public's demands for technical knowledge and their own realization that the direction of high policy required a general competence. The diplomats of the twenties had already been generalists who occasionally helped set high policy, and the former consuls had quickly learned the dangers of too great specialization, so that both diplomats and consuls had tried to reconcile the competing demands of technical and general knowledge by telling themselves that the diplomatic insights of a Foreign Service officer developed slowly over the course of a lifetime career. While Kissinger's rise gave the lie to this bureaucratic argument, his success with Nixon, and with the public after

Nixon's disgrace, seemed to confirm the notion that breadth of vision was indeed the essence of diplomacy.

After 1945, Foreign Service officers had tried to gain additional political authority by contriving to be specialists, yet as they became more technical, their Service became more difuse and no longer resembled a congenial club. Thus the diplomats learned to their dismay that too great specialization rendered them vulnerable to the lateral entry of technicians who did not share their *esprit de corps*. Specialization also provoked heated controversies with non-State Department agencies, and, cruelest of all, technical competence was no guarantee of eventual political authority. Therefore, in the sixties and seventies, reformers again sought, and again with limited success, to solve the dilemma of general readiness as against functional specialization by becoming proficient in the use of generalized management skills. On the whole, the reforming officers of the sixties and seventies owed a profound debt to the professional outlook developed by their predecessors during the first period of Foreign Service reform. Although that outlook was so confused and inconsistent that it baffled outsiders, it did serve the bureaucratic, political, and psychological needs of America's career diplomats for over fifty years.

Notes

Introduction

1. Lawrence S. Kaplan, "The Brahmin as Diplomat in Nineteenth Century America: Everett, Bancroft, Motley, Lowell," *Civil War History,* 19, No. 1 (March 1973), pp. 5-28.

2. Henry James, *Nathaniel Hawthorne* (London: Macmillan,1879), pp.110-15.

3. The best description of the differences in diplomatic and consular work in the 19th century is in Warren Frederick Ilchman, *Professional Diplomacy in the United States, 1779-1939: A Study in Administrative History* (Chicago: University of Chicago Press, 1959), chap. 2.

4. Richard Hofstadter, *The Age of Reform* (New York: Vintage Books, 1955), pp. 148-68; A. M. Carr-Saunders and P. A. Wilson, *The Professions* (Oxford: Oxford University Press, 1953), pp. 1-7, 294-97; Kenneth Boulding, *The Organizational Revolution* (New York: Harper, 1953), pp. 3-33.

5. Samuel Haber, *Efficiency and Uplift: Scientific Management in the Progressive Era, 1890-1920* (Chicago: University of Chicago Press, 1964), p. ix.

6. For the tenuous relations between the Foreign Service and the academy, see below, Chap. 2. For an account of relations between the State Department and the Commerce Department, see Tracy H. Lay, *The Foreign Service of the United States* (New York: Prentice-Hall, 1925) pp. 190-222; Joseph C. Brandes, *Herbert Hoover and Economic Diplomacy: Commerce Department Foreign Economic Policy, 1929-39* (Pittsburgh: University of Pittsburgh Press, 1962), pp. 53-72.

7. A subtle philsophical discussion of the relations between "technical" or "rational" knowledge and "general" or "political" knowledge may be found in Michael Oakeshott, *Rationalism in Politics* (London: Metheun, 1962), pp.1-36, 111-36.

8. George F. Kennan, "The Needs of the Foreign Service," in Joseph E. McLean, ed., *The Public Service and University Education* (Princeton: Princeton University Press, 1949), p. 97.

9. For a discussion of the theory of American exceptionalism, see Louis Hartz, *The Liberal Tradition in America: An Interpretation of American Political Thought since the Revolution* (New York: Harcourt, Brace, 1955), *passim;* David Noble, *The*

Progressive Mind, 1890-1917 (Chicago: Rand-McNally, 1970), pp. 23-36; N. Gordon Levin, *Woodrow Wilson and World Politics* (New York: Oxford University Press, 1968), pp. 1-49; Charles Forcey, *The Crossroads of Liberalism: Croly, Weyle, Lippmann and the Progressive Era* (New York: Oxford University Press, 1961), pp. ix-xxv, 221-73. For one diplomat's statement on the implications for foreign policy given America's lack of a feudal tradition, see John W. Foster, *The Practice of Diplomacy as Illustrated in the Foreign Relations of the United States* (Boston: Houghton-Mifflin, 1906), pp. 3-5.

10. See below, Chap. 3.

11. Frederick C. Mosher, "Careers and Career Services in the Public Service," *Public Personnel Review*, XXIII, No. 1 (January 1963), pp. 46-51; Talcott Parsons, "Professions," *The International Encyclopedia of the Social Sciences*, XII (New York: Macmillan and The Free Press, 1968), pp. 336-46.

12. For the best discussion of the "core criteria" for judging whether or not an occupation is a profession, see Parsons, "Professions," pp. 336-39.

13. See *ibid*.

14. Howard K. Beale, *Theodore Roosevelt and the Rise to World Power* (Baltimore: Johns Hopkins Press, 1956), pp. 19-62; John Morton Blum, *The Republican Roosevelt* (Cambridge: Harvard University Press, 1954), pp. 124-41; Forcey, *Crossroads of Liberalism*, pp. 41-52; Lewis D. Einstein, *Roosevelt, His Mind in Action* (New York: Houghton-Mifflin, 1930) pp. 1-9.

15. Wilbur J. Carr, "Reasons Why the Department of State Should Be Reorganized," December 4, 1919 (Carr Papers, Manuscript Division, Library of Congress).

16. See below, Chap. 3. See also, William A. Williams, *The Roots of the Modern American Empire: A Study of the Growth and Shaping of Social Consciousness in a Marketplace Society* (New York: Random House, 1969), pp. 4-49, 432-48.

17. Perry Belmont, "The First Line of National Defense," *North American Review*, CC1, No. 6 (June 1915), p. 886.

18. Gordon Craig, "The Professional Diplomat and His Problems, 1919-1939," *World Politics*, IV, No. 2 (January 1952), pp. 145-58.

19. Sir Ernest Satow, *A Guide to Diplomatic Practice* (2 vols. London, N.Y.: Longmans Green, 1917), Vol. 1, p. 1. See also, the review of Satow's masterpiece by John Bassett Moore, in *American Historical Review*, XXIII, No. 4 (December 1918), pp. 634-38.

Chapter I

1. Arthur M. Schlesinger, Jr., *The Vital Center: The Politics of Freedom* (rev. ed., Boston: Houghton-Mifflin Co., 1962), p. 166. Cf. Smith Simpson, *The Anatomy of the State Department* (Boston: Houghton-Mifflin, 1967), pp. 3-4. See the *New York Times* (April 29, 1900), p. 8.

2. Hugh Wilson, *The Education of a Diplomat* (New York: Longmans, Green, 1941), p. 8; and his *Diplomacy as a Career* (Cambridge: The Riverside Press, 1941), pp. 16-17; William Phillips, *Ventures in Diplomacy* (North Beverly, Mass.: pri-

vately printed, 1952), p. 39; Perrin Galpin, *Hugh Gibson, 1983-1954: Extracts from His Letters and Anecdotes from His Friends*. Introduction by Herbert Hoover. (New York: Belgian-American Educational Federation, 1956), pp. 159-60; Lloyd C. Griscom, *Diplomatically Speaking* (Boston: Little, Brown, 1940), pp. 69-70.

3. See statistics in Ilchman, *Professional Diplomacy in the United States, 1779-1939*, pp. 95, 115; Selden Chapin, "The United States Foreign Service," *Fortune Magazine*, XXXIV (July 1946), p. 198; Secretary of State Philander C. Knox to Rep. Cordell Hull, March 12, 1910 (State Department File 120. 11/22, Record Group 59, National Archives of the United States, Washington, D.C. [hereafter cited as N.A.]).

4. Such a claim was made by diplomatic reformers themselves to account for the low caliber of men in the late 19th-century Foreign Service. See [Lewis D. Einstein], *American Foreign Policy: By a Diplomatist* (Boston and New York: Houghton-Mifflin, 1909), p. 157; the statement by Wilbur J. Carr is in Glenn Levin Swigert, ed., "The Conference on Training for Foreign Service, United States Bureau of Education *Bulletin*, No. 37 (1917), p. 16.

5. I give these two examples of reactions to unhappiness at home because they were typical of some wealthy and dissatisfied late 19th-century Easterners. See Edward White, *The Eastern Establishment and the Western Experience: The West of Theodore Roosevelt, Frederic Remington, and Owen Wister* (New Haven: Yale University Press, 1968), pp. 5-31; cf. Henry Adams, *The Education of Henry Adams* (Boston: Houghton-Mifflin, 1918), *passim*.

6. Henry White, *Diplomacy and Politics*–an address delivered before the American Historical Association, Washington, D.C., December 30, 1915— (Washington: American Historical Association, 1916), p. 2; White to Nicholas Murray Butler, January 27, 1921 (Butler Papers, Butler Library, Columbia University); Carr, "Diary," August 5, 1924 (Carr Papers); Joseph C. Grew, "Diary," August 7, 1924 (Grew Papers, Houghton Library, Harvard University).

7. Allan Nevins, *Henry White, Thirty Years of American Diplomacy* (New York: Harper Bros., 1931), p. 31.

8. *Ibid.*, p. 32.

9. *Ibid.*, pp. 35-36.

10. Henry Kittridge Norton, "Foreign Office Organization: A Comparison of the British, French, German and Italian Foreign Offices with that of the Department of State of the United States of America," *Annals of the American Academy of Political and Social Sciences*, CXLIII, Supplement (May 1929), pp. 21-24; "How Other Nations Do It," *Century*, LVII (February 1968), p. 605.

11. Wilson, *The Education of a Diplomat*, p. 10.

12. Phillips, *Ventures in Diplomacy*, p. 35.

13. Nevins, *Henry White*, pp. 38-41.

14. *Ibid.*, p. 55.

15. Buckler is notable for his later career as a Mediterranean archaeologist, an advisor on Balkan problems attached to the American mission in London during the First World War, and an intermediary between the American government and British liberals and leftists in 1917 and 1918. See William Dunning, "The Diplomatic Career of William H. Buckler," unpublished Master's thesis, George Washington

University (1957), pp. 7-50; Laurence W. Martin, *Peace without Victory: Woodrow Wilson and the British Liberals* (New Haven: Yale University Press, 1958), pp. 115-20, 137-39, 166; Ronald Radosh, *American Labor and United States Foreign Policy* (New York: Random House, 1919), pp. 152-53, 173-74, 275, 282-83.

16. H. L. Mencken, *Happy Days* (New York: Knopf, 1940), pp. 29-33; Dunning, "Buckler," p. 2.

17. Dunning, "Buckler," pp. 6-7.

18. Griscom's father's most intimate business associates were Alex Cassatt, a financier of Westinghouse; George Roberts and Franklin Thomson, two of the founders of the Pennsylvania Railroad; H. H. Houstan, an oil man; P. A. B. Widener, builder of the Philadelphia Street Railroad; Thomas A. Dolan, President of the United Gas Importing Company; Rudolph Ellis and Effingham Morris, Philadelphia bankers. (Griscom, *Diplomatically Speaking*, pp. 12-13.)

19. *Ibid.*, pp.7-8, 15-16.

20. Lloyd Carpenter Griscom, "Reminiscences," *Columbia Oral History Collection* [hereafter cited as *COHC*], (1951), p. 6.

21. Griscom was not the only young man with an interest in diplomacy whom Henry Adams "adopted." When William Phillips, future under-secretary of state took charge of the newly created Far-Eastern Division of the Department of State in 1907, he was lionized by Adams. See William Phillips, "Reminiscences," *COHC* (1951), pp. 30, 39-40.

22. Griscom, *Diplomatically Speaking*, pp. 18-19.

23. *Ibid.*, pp. 25-26.

24. *Ibid.*, pp. 68-69; Griscom, "Reminiscences," pp. 14-17.

25. Griscom, *Diplomatically Speaking*, pp. 69-73.

26. Griscom, "Reminiscences," pp. 15-22.

27. Lawrence Gelfand, *The Inquiry: American Preparations for Peace, 1917-1919* (New Haven: Yale University Press, 1961), p. 35.

28. William T. R. Fox and Annette Baker Fox, "Interwar International Relations Research: The American Experience," *World Politics,* No. 1 (1949), pp. 67-79.

29. The new schools were Georgetown University School of Foreign Service, 1919; the Williamstown Summer Institute of World Politics, 1921; the Johns Hopkins University School of International Affairs, 1925; and the Fletcher School of Law and Diplomacy of Tufts University, 1932. By 1931 there were also 70 universities offering special courses applicable to careers overseas. See below, Chap. 2. See also Grayson Kirk, *The Study of International Relations in the United States* (New York: Council on Foreign Relations, 1948) pp. 3-15.

30. Noel H. Pugach, "Progress, Prosperity and the Open Door: The Ideas and Career of Paul S. Reinsch," Ph.D. dissertation, University of Wisconsin, 1965 (Ann Arbor: University Microfilms, 1967), pp. 17-21.

31. Merle Curti and Vernon Carstenson, *The University of Wisconsin: A History, 1848-1925* (Madison: University of Wisconsin, 1949), Vol. 11, pp. 3-4.

32. Paul S. Reinsch, *American Legislatures and Legislative Methods* (New York, Century, 1920), pp. 205-06. Pugach, "Progress, Prosperity and the Open Door," p. 69.

33. His most important works dealing with international politics or the role of the trained expert are: *World Politics at the End of the Nineteenth Century: As Influenced by the Oriental Situation* (New York: MacMillan, 1900); *Colonial Government: An Introduction to the Study of Colonial Institutions* (New York: MacMillan, 1902); *American Legislatures and Legislative Methods* (New York: Harcourt, Brace, 1922).

34. Pugach, "Progress, Prosperity and the Open Door," pp. 65-71.

35. See testimonial of Stanley Kuhl Hornbeck, "Biography" (Box 89, Hornbeck Papers, Hoover Institution Archives, Stanford University).

36. Reinsch, *Secret Diplomacy,* pp. 218-20.

37. Reinsch, *World Politics,* pp. 3-5.

38. *Ibid.,* pp. 6-11.

39. *Ibid.,* pp. 347-56.

40. *Ibid.,* pp. 420-35.

41. Reinsch, *Colonial Administration,* p. 60.

42. Reinsch, *Colonial Government,* pp. 83-84; *World Politics,* p. 435.

43. Reinsch, *American Legislatures,* pp. 228-30, 240, 261.

44. Haber, *Efficiency and Uplift,* pp. ix-xii, 67, 103-04; Max Lerner, ed., *The Portable Veblen* (New York: Viking, 1948), pp. 19-49; Noble, *The Progressive Mind,* pp. 1-52.

45. Reinsch, *Secret Diplomacy,* pp. 13, 218-22.

46. A. C. Coolidge, *The United States as a World Power* (New York: Macmillan, 1910). This book was based on lectures delivered in 1905 at the Sorbonne in Paris. See also, [Einstein], *American Foreign Policy.*

47. Harold J. Coolidge and Robert H. Lord, *The Life and Letters of Archibald Carey Coolidge* (Boston: Houghton-Mifflin, 1940), pp. 14-39.

48. *Ibid.,* p. 17.

49. *Ibid.,* p. 140.

50. For an account of Coolidge's work on the Inquiry from 1917 to 1919, see Gelfand, *The Inquiry,* pp. 122-30.

51. Coolidge and Lord, *Life and Letters,* p. 139. See William Phillips, "Diary," February 5-6, 1923 (Phillips Papers, Houghton Library, Harvard University); Joseph C. Grew to Archibald Carey Coolidge, April 30, 1920 (Grew Papers).

Edward Morgan was a professional diplomat who served as United States Ambassador to Brazil from 1913 to 1933. Ellis Dresel was a professional diplomat who served as United States Commissioner to Germany from November 1919 to August 1921, and was Chargé d'Affairs at Berlin from 1921 to 1922. Hiram Bingham was an explorer, scholar, and Republican politician. He was a U.S. Senator from Connecticut, 1925-33. Julius Klein was Director of the U.S. Bureau of Foreign and Domestic Commerce under Herbert Hoover, 1921-29.

52. Coolidge and Lord, *Life and Letters,* p. 94.

53. Coolidge, *United States as a World Power,* p. 7.

54. *Ibid.,* pp. 1-40, 134-38, 172-84.

55. He was particularly alarmed by the anti-imperialism of David Starr Jordan's *Imperial Democracy* (New York: Macmillan, 1899). See Coolidge, *The United States as a World Power,* p. 40.

56. Coolidge, *The United States as a World Power,* p. 1.

57. *Ibid.,* pp. 107, 121.

58. *Ibid.,* p. 183.

59. *Ibid.,* p. 183.

60. *Ibid.,* pp. 25-40.

61. *Ibid.,* p. 184.

62. Lewis D. Einstein, *A Diplomat Looks Back,* edited by Lawrence Gelfand, foreword by George Kennan (New Haven: Yale University Press, 1968), pp. xv-xxx. See "A Bibliography of Lewis Einstein's Published Writings," *ibid.,* 251-56. See also, James Bishop Peabody, ed., *The Holmes-Einstein Letters: Correspondence of Mr. Justice Holmes and Lewis Einstein, 1903-1935* (New York: Macmillan, 1964), *passim;* and the voluminous correspondence between Einstein and Roosevelt, Spingarn, John Hay, and French Ambassador Jules Jusserand, in the Lewis D. Einstein Papers, Coe Library, University of Wyoming.

63. [Einstein], *American Foreign Policy,* p. v.

64. *Ibid.,* pp. 3, 7-8.

65. Einstein wrote in 1923: "If our foreign intercourse were exclusively commercial it would be desirable to close up the Department of State and turn it over to the Department of Commerce. But our international relations cover many other fields as well and are continually increasing in complexity. The question of emigration, for instance, or our missionary establishments in Turkey and China, have nothing to do with commerce. Our political interests which made us send two million American boys to Europe were not commercial. In spite of the growing importance of American trade abroad one can never make the part greater than the whole. The day we subordinate our foreign policy exclusively to commercial considerations, we make the government the agent of special interests and not of the whole American people." (Lewis Einstein to Assistant Secretary of State Leland Harrison, September 3, 1923 [Box 4, Harrison Papers, Manuscript Division, Library of Congress]).

66. Einstein, *American Foreign Policy,* pp. 11-12.

67. *Ibid.*

68. *Ibid.,* p. 14.

69. *Ibid.,* pp. 11-12.

70. *Ibid.,* p. 14.

71. *Ibid.,* p. 33.

72. *Ibid.,* pp. 26, 45-51.

73. Gelfand, Introduction to Einstein, *A Diplomat Looks Back,* pp. xv-xvi; Lewis D. Einstein, *Roosevelt: His Mind in Action,* p. 10; and his *American Foreign Policy,* pp. 46-50, 162. For the personal interest Roosevelt took in Einstein's career, see Theodore Roosevelt to Mrs. David L. Einstein (Lewis's mother), February 17, 1903; Lewis Einstein's *aide memoire* of an interview with President Roosevelt, February 19, 1903; Representative A. M. Littauer to Lewis Einstein, January 26, 1905, in which Littauer says that T.R. "has taken great interest in you and your work"; Roosevelt to Mrs. Caroline N. Einstein (Lewis's mother), June 8, 1905; Roosevelt to Lewis Einstein, June 14, 1905; Roosevelt to Lewis Einstein, January 19, 1907; same to same, August 20, 1908. (All in the Einstein Papers.)

74. Alfred Thayer Mahan, *The Influence of Sea Power upon History* (Boston: Little, Brown, 1890); his *Interest of America in Sea Power, Past and Present* (Boston: Little, Brown, 1898); his *Problem of Asia and Its Effect upon International*

Policies (Boston: Little, Brown, 1900); and his *Interest of American International Conditions* (Boston, Little, Brown, 1910).

75. Mahan, *Interest of America in Sea Power,* p. 156.

76. Adams, *Education of Henry Adams,* pp. 423-27; Brook Adams, *America's Economic Supremacy* (New York: Macmillan, 1900); and his *New Empire* (New York: Macmillan, 1902); William Appleman Williams, "Brooks Adams and American Expansion," *New England Quarterly,* XXV (June 1952), pp. 217-32; Robert E. Osgood, *Ideals and Self-Interest in America's Foreign Relations* (Chicago: University of Chicago Press, 1953), pp. 63-65.

77. Einstein, *American Foreign Policy,* p. 162.

78. See Frank M. Stewart, *History of the National Civil Service Reform League* (Austin: University of Texas Press, 1929), Chaps. I, II, III; John G. Sproat, *"The Best Men:" Liberal Reformers in the Gilded Age* (New York: Oxford University Press, 1968), pp. 45-204.

79. Einstein, *American Foreign Policy,* p. 157.

80. *Ibid.,* pp. 162-65.

81. *Ibid.,* pp. 165-70.

82. Einstein, *American Diplomacy,* pp. 28-29.

83. Einstein, "The United States and Anglo-German Rivalry," *National Review,* LX (January 1913), pp. 736-50.

84. Einstein, "The War and American National Policy," *National Review,* LXIV (November, 1914), pp. 257-76; and his "Contraband Difficulty: An American Difficulty," Letter to the Editor, *The Times* (London), December 31, 1914.

85. Einstein, "American Peace Dreams," *National Review,* LXIII (January 1915), pp. 837-50; his "Great Danger," Letter to the Editor, *The Spectator,* No. 114 (January 30, 1915), pp. 152-55; his "Origin of the War," Letter to the Editor, *The Times* (London), August 4, 1917; and his *Prophecy of the War, 1913-1914,* Foreword by Theodore Roosevelt (New York: Columbia University Press, 1917).

For Theodore Roosevelt's attitude toward Wilson's war policy, see the various articles he published during the war years, collected as *America and the World War* in Vol. XVIII of *The Works of Theodore Roosevelt* (National edition; New York: Charles Scribner's Sons, 1923). See also Roosevelt's letters to various Englishmen on American war policy in Elting Morison, ed., *The Letters of Theodore Roosevelt,* Vol. VIII (Cambridge: Harvard University Press, 1954): Roosevelt to Rudyard Kipling (November 4, 1914), p. 831; T.R. to Cecil Spring-Rice (November 11, 1914), p. 841; T.R. to Edward Grey (January 22, 1915), p. 879; T.R. to Cecil Spring-Rice (February 5, 1915), p. 889; T.R. to Edward Grey (November 24, 1915), p. 987; T.R. to Arthur Hamilton Lee (June 7, 1916), p. 1053; T.R. to Cecil Spring-Rice (April 16, 1917), p. 1174.

For Grew's growing belief that American interests were identical to Britain's, see Waldo Heinrichs, Jr., *American Ambassador: Joseph C. Grew and the Development of the United States Diplomatic Tradition* (Boston: Little, Brown, 1966), pp. 20-35.

For Phillips's criticism of Wilson's timidity in dealing with Germany, see Phillips, "Diary," December 1-20, 1916; March 1, 3, 4, and April 1, 3, 4, 1917 (Phillips Papers).

86. See Herbert Croly, *The Promise of American Life* (New York: Macmillan, 1909), pp. 293-313. See also Forcey, *The Crossroads of Liberalism,* pp. ix-xxv, 3-52.

87. Harold Stearns, *The Street I Knew* (New York: Furman, 1935), pp. 170-89; his *Liberalism in America: Its Origin, Its Temporary Collapse, Its Future* (New York: Boni and Liveright, 1919), *passim;* Harry Elmer Barnes, *The Genesis of the World War* (New York: Macmillan, 1926), *passim.* For the post-war disillusionment of the *New Republic* editors, see Forcey, *The Crossroads of Liberalism,* pp. 273-315.

88. James W. Garner, *International Law and the World War* (2 vols. New York: Longmans, Green, 1920), *passim;* William E. Dodd, *Woodrow Wilson and His Work* (Garden City, N.Y.: Doubleday, Page, 1921), *passim;* Charles Seymour, *The Diplomatic Background of the World War* (New Haven: Yale University Press, 1919), *passim;* James T. Shotwell, *Autobiography* (Indianapolis: Bobbs-Merrill, 1960), pp. 156-219; and his "Reminiscences," *COHC* (1962), pp. 73-150.

89. Siegfied Sassoon, *Collected Poems* (New York: Viking, 1949), p. 130.

90. Carr, "Diary," February 6, 1919 (Carr Papers); Robert Lansing to Representative Stephen Porter, January 21, 1920 (State Department File 111/52a. RG 59, N.A.); Wilbur J. Carr, "Reasons Why the Department of State Should Be Reorganized," December 4, 1919 (Carr Papers); Lewis Einstein to Leland Harrison, September 3, 1923 (Box 4, Harrison Papers).

91. Henry P. Fletcher to Senator George Wharton Pepper, November 13, 1922; Fletcher to Senator David A. Reed, November 14, 1922 (Box 9, Fletcher Papers, Manuscript Division, Library of Congress); Lewis Einstein to Leland Harrison, September 3, 1924 (Harrison Papers).

92. Joseph C. Grew, Address to American Manufacturers Export Association, November 12, 1925 (Grew Papers).

93. John Bassett Moore, *International Law and Some Current Illusions* (New York: Macmillan, 1923), pp. 1-5.

94. *Ibid.,* pp. 10-17.

95. *Ibid.,* pp. 30-37.

96. Phillips, "Diary," October 14, 1923 (Phillips Papers).

97. See the following articles in the *American Journal of International Law:* "The Conference of Teachers of International Law," XIX, No. 3 (July 1925), pp. 542-47; "The Foreign Service School," XIX, No. 4 (October 1925), pp. 763-68; "Reforms in the State Department and Foreign Service," XXII, No. 3 (July 1928), pp. 606-10; "Examinations for the American Foreign Service," XXIX, No. 2 (April 1935), pp. 314-17; "The Ban on Alien Marriages in The Foreign Service," XXXI, No. 1 (January 1937), pp. 91-94.

98. Ellery C. Stowell, *International Law: A Restatement of Principles in Conformity with Actual Practice* (New York: Macmillan, 1931), p. ii.

99. *Ibid.,* p. 10.

100. *Ibid.,* p. x.

101. *Ibid.,* p. xi.

102. See Wilbur J. Carr, "The Diplomatic and Consular Service," Address to the National Foreign Trade Convention, Washington, May 28, 1914, in the *Official*

Report of the National Foreign Trade Convention (New York: National Foreign Trade Convention, 1914), pp. 418-33; Lay, *The Foreign Service of the United States,* pp. 3-15; Joseph C. Grew to American Manufacturers Export Association, November 12, 1925 (Grew Papers); Hugh Gibson, "Diplomacy" (unpublished manuscript, Box 3, Hugh Gibson Papers, Archives of the Hoover Institution, Stanford University). Cf. below, Chap. 4, for an account of the theory of international relations taught at the Foreign Service School. See also DeWitt Clinton Poole, "Reminiscences," *COHC* (1952), pp. 103-40.

103. DeWitt Clinton Poole, *The Conduct of Diplomacy under Modern Democratic Conditions* (New Haven: Yale University Press, 1924); and his "Reminiscences," pp. 98-102.

The institute was organized by Arthur Buffington, President of Williams College in 1921. Every August for 10 years after 1921, teachers, interested members of the public, high-ranking naval officers, and State Department officials attended a 2-week session devoted to various topics on international affairs at Williams. See Stanley K. Hornbeck to William Phillips, September 3, 1922 (Box 2, Hornbeck Papers). See also, Arthur H. Buffington, *The Institute of Politics: Its First Decade* (Williamstown: Institute of Politics, 1931), *passim.*

104. Poole, *The Conduct of Diplomacy,* p. 9.

105. *Ibid.,* p. 10.

106. *Ibid.,* pp. 14-15. Cf. the similar conclusion reached by another lecturer at the Williamstown Institute, James Bryce, in his *International Relations: Eight Lectures Delivered in the United States in August, 1921* (New York: Macmillan, 1922), pp. 143-80. See also Hugh Gibson's suggestion to Nicholas Butler that the Carnegie Endowment for International Peace could do more for peace by helping the Foreign Service than by any other activity, since a strong Foreign Service preceded "treaties, arbitration and tribunals" (Gibson to Butler, August 24, 1924 [Box 1, Gibson Papers]).

Chapter II

1. National Business League of America, *Constitution and Official Directory* (6th ed., Chicago: National Business League of America, 1902), p. 4; and its *Endorsement of the Lodge Bill for the Reorganization of the Consular Service of the United States* (Chicago: National Business League, 1903), pp. 2-17; U.S. Congress, House, Committee on Foreign Affairs, *Reorganization of the Consular Service, Report No. 3305 to Accompany H.R. 16023* (58th Congress, 2nd Sess.), pp. 3-14; Henry L. Nelson, "The Need for Trained Diplomats and Consuls," *Harper's Weekly,* XLV (July 15, 1901), pp. 16-24.

2. A. L. Bishop, "Recent Reforms in the Consular Service," *Yale Review,* XVI, No. 2 (May 1907), pp. 39-55.

3. Copy of Executive Order for the Consular Service, November 10, 1905 (State Department File 120. 11/22, RG 59, N.A.).

4. U.S. *Statutes* 99 (April 6, 1906).

5. Copy of Executive Order for the Consular Service, June 27, 1906, Department of State *Biographical Register* (Washington: Government Printing Office,

1907), pp. 84-85. For a somewhat fuller account of the Orders of 1905 and 1906 and the Law of 1906, see Ilchman, *Professional Diplomacy in the United States,* pp. 88-94.

6. John Ball Osborne, *Education for the New Consular Service* (rev. ed., New York: North American Review Publishing Co., 1908), p. 12. From 1906 until 1915, 1,056 candidates were designated as eligible for the consular examination; 716, or 67.8%, appeared for the examination; of these, 313 or 43.7%, passed the examination and were certified eligible for appointment; 248 of those were actually appointed. (Statement of Wilbur J. Carr, Director of the Consular Service, December 31, 1915, in Swiggert, ed., "The Conference on Training for Foreign Service," p. 19.)

7. The National Business League of America was a nonpartisan group of businessmen and educators formed in 1897 to lobby for national legislation that would "enlarge the field of industrial and commercial activity." Besides consular reform, it endorsed the establishment of a Commerce Department, naval expansion, commercial reciprocity, improved roads, and national irrigation. See National Business League, *Constitution and Official Directory* (11th ed., Chicago: National Business League, 1907), pp. 1-3.

8. National Business League, *American Universities, American Foreign Service and an Adequate Consular Law* (2nd, amplified ed., Chicago: National Business League, 1909), pp. 3-4. The 18 institutions polled were: The Universities of California, Chicago, Illinois, Iowa, Kentucky, Michigan, Minnesota, Pennsylvania, Southern California, and Columbia, Cornell, George Washington, Harvard, Indiana, Northwestern, Stanford, and Yale.

9. *Ibid.,* pp. 5-51. Of the 18 universities, 3 (George Washington, Yale, and Columbia) jointly administered special schools or programs designed to prepare students for the consular service. Six others (Wisconsin, Illinois, Pennsylvania, Kentucky, Iowa and California) had recently established schools of commerce. One of their purposes was the training of men for overseas work for business or government. The other 9 schools did not have separate programs for consular preparation, but all had given serious thought to training men for overseas work. They had selected courses from their liberal arts curricula useful for men preparing for consular and overseas commercial work.

10. U. S. Congress, House, *National Consular School* (60th Cong., 2nd Sess., 1909, H. Res. 26991), pp. 1-4. The bill was introduced by Representative Frank O. Lowden and was rejected in the Foreign Affairs Committee. In the 50 years after 1909, proposals for a national school of Foreign Service, similar to the military academies, were revived several times in the twenties and the post-World-War-II period by Congressmen or members of the public. Each time the State Department opposed and defeated the suggestions as uneconomical, since the Department was certain it could recruit enough good diplomats from liberal arts courses at universities.

11. National Business League, *Resolution Disapproving of the Creation and Maintenance of a National Consular School by the United States Government*—adopted by the Board of Directors of the National Business League of America—(Chicago: National Business League, February 15, 1909), p. 1.

12. Lay, *Foreign Service of the United States,* p. 327.

13. National Business League, *American Universities,* p. 5.

14. *Ibid.,* p. 8.

15. *Ibid.,* pp. 8-9.

16. Osborne, *Education for the New Consular Service,* pp. 13-14.

17. To operate the special college for 5 years, George Washington University received over $125,000 from a variety of businessmen, educators, politicians, trade associations, and export firms. Among them were: J. Pierpont Morgan, J. Pierpont Morgan, Jr., Elbert H. Gary, Levi P. Morton, Seth Low, Otto Kahn, Paul Warburg, Frank Lowden, Mrs. John Hay, the South Carolina Cotton Manufacturers Association, the *American Exporter* magazine, and ten export firms. (National Business League, *American Universities,* p. 10.)

18. Richard D. Harlan, *The Two Prerequisites for the Permanent Improvement of the Consular Service: A New Law and a Special Training School*—an address delivered at Chicago, April 28, 1908—(Chicago: National Business League, 1908), p. 12. The two men who attended the College of Political Science and later went on to the most successful careers in the Foreign Service were Nelson Trusler Johnson and Dewitt Clinton Poole. See Nelson Trusler Johnson, "Reminiscences," *COHC* (1954), pp. 25-32; Poole, "Reminiscences," pp. 20-35.

19. See statement of Wilbur J. Carr, Director of Consular Service to the Conference on Foreign Service Training, December 31, 1915, in Swiggert, ed., "Conference on Training for Foreign Service," pp. 47-48.

20. National Business League, *American Universities,* pp. 15-49.

21. *Ibid.,* pp. 18-20.

22. Elihu Root to Richard Harlan, April 5, 1907, in Osborne, *Education for the New Consular Service,* p. iii.

23. Harlan, *Two Prerequisites,* p. 12.

24. Root to Harlan, March 17, 1908, in Osborne, *Education,* p. iv.

25. *Ibid.,* pp. 18-19.

26. *Ibid.,* p. 19. For an example of a consul who attended George Washington University and resented not being able to afford to go to Yale, thus joining the good fellowship there, see Johnson, "Reminiscences," pp. 30-32.

27. See below, Chap. 3.

28. See statement of Philander C. Claxton, United States Commissioner of Education, to the first National Conference on Foreign Service Training, December 31, 1915, in Swiggert, ed., "Conference on Training," p. 8.

29. John Barrett (Director General of the Pan American Union), Edward Ewing Pratt (Chief of the Bureau of Foreign and Domestic Commerce), and Glen Levin Swiggert (Assistant Secretary General of the Pan American Scientific Congress) joined Claxton and Carr in issuing invitations to representatives of the following institutions: the Universities of Alabama, California, Colorado, Ohio, Pennsylvania, Texas, Virginia, Washington, Illinois, Michigan, Minnesota, Missouri, North Carolina, and Wisconsin, as well as Yale University, Georgia School of Technology, University of Chicago, Tulane University, Johns Hopkins University, Harvard University, Dartmouth College, and the University of Cincinatti (*ibid.,* pp. 9-10).

30. *Ibid.,* p. 12.

31. *Ibid.,* pp. 58-59. The Committee consisted of 4 professors of history, government, or commerce; 7 deans of commercial colleges; 1 principal of a commercial high school; 2 representatives of business or business organizations; and a chairman, Glen Levin Swiggert, from the U.S. Bureau of Education.

32. Katherine Crane, *Mr. Carr of State: Forty-Seven Years of Service in the Department of State* (New York: St. Martin's Press, 1961), pp. 23-41.

33. See the dedication to Wilbur J. Carr as "The Devoted Pilot and Master Mariner in Foreign Service Reform," in Lay, *Foreign Service of the United States,* dedication page.

34. See below, Chap. 4.

35. Carr, "The Diplomatic and Consular Service," pp. 418-33. See also his "Diary," May 17, 1914 (Carr Papers), in which he revealed his state of mind while drafting this speech. Clearly, he felt closer to the businessmen he was addressing than to the diplomats within the Department or to Secretary of State Bryan.

36. Statement of Wilbur J. Carr to First Conference on Foreign Service Training, December 31, 1914, in Swiggert, ed., "Conference on Training," pp. 17-18.

37. *Ibid.,* pp. 20-25.

38. *Ibid.,* p. 25.

39. Lay, *The Foreign Service of the United States,* pp. 115, 122, 328; Carr, "Diary," July 4, 1918 (Carr Papers); Poole, "Reminiscences," pp. 57-8, 63-4; Johnson, "Reminiscences," pp. 32-5, 126-31; Joseph Ballantine, "Reminiscences," *COHC* (1961), pp. 5, 89-97, 121; Joseph C. White, "Reminiscences," *COHC* (1953), p. 133.

40. From 1900 to 1924, 74.8% of the diplomats attended one or more of the 8 "Ivy League" colleges as undergraduates. In the same period 24.2% of the consuls attended those same colleges. Only 9.2% of the diplomats had attended publicly supported colleges, while 32.2% of the consuls had. See figures compiled from State Department *Register,* in Ilchman, *Professional Diplomacy,* p. 171.

41. Statements of the representatives of the Universities of Illinois and Texas and Columbia University, in Swiggert, ed., "Conference on Training," pp. 41, 42, 49.

42. Statements of the representatives of the Universities of California, Illinois, and Pittsburgh, as well as Columbia and Stanford Universities, *ibid.,* pp. 46-49.

43. Statement of Ephraim D. Adams of Stanford, *ibid.,* pp. 37, 44.

44. Statement of Wilbur J. Carr, *ibid.,* pp. 45-50. Carr opposed a national graduate school for civil servants as too expensive. He not only thought a department course for prospective applicants too great a drain on the officials's time, but feared that a cram course in Washington would degenerate into a crass profit-making venture. The Department expressly forbade its members to tutor privately. See Wilson, *Education of a Diplomat,* p. 10; Department of State, *Consular Service of the United States: Information for Applicants, 1915* (Washington: Government Printing Office, 1915), p. 3.

45. Statement of Carr, in Swiggert, ed., "Conference on Training," p. 50.

46. Statement of Commissioner Claxton, *ibid.,* pp. 56-57.

47. Glen Levin Swiggert, ed., "Training for Foreign Service," U.S. Bureau of Education *Bulletin,* No. 27 (1921), p. iii; Bureau of Education, "Courses on International Relations," *Education Circular,* No. 7 (October 1921), pp. 1-4.

48. Georgetown University, School of Foreign Service *Bulletin of Information,* (Washington: Georgetown University, 1919), p. 1.

49. R. Gordon Hoxie, et. al., *A History of the Faculty of Political Science of Columbia University* (New York: Columbia University Press, 1955), p. 168.

50. James T. Shotwell, Introduction to Farrel Symons, ed., *Courses on International Affairs in American Colleges,* 1930-31 (Boston: World Peace Federation, 1931), pp. 1-3; Parker T. Moon, ed., *Syllabus on International Relations* (New York: Columbia University Press, 1925), *passim*; Bureau of Education, "Courses on International Relations," p. 3.

51. Glen Levin Swiggert, ed., "Practices and Objectives in Training for Foreign Service, Report of the National Conference on Foreign Service Training, Washington, December 26, 1923," Bureau of Education *Bulletin,* No. 21 (1924), pp. 3-4.

52. *Ibid.,* pp. 2-3.

53. See below, Chapter 3.

54. Swiggert, ed., "Practices and Objectives," p. 20.

55. *Ibid.,* pp. 20, 24.

56. Carr, "Diary," October 12, 13, 1922 (Carr Papers).

57. Swiggert, ed., "Practices and Objectives," p. 24.

58. See remarks of the educators, *ibid.,* pp. 15-20.

59. Ellery C. Stowell, "The Foreign Service School," *American Journal of International Law,* XIX, No. 4 (October 1925), pp. 763-64; "Report on Foreign Service Training," *American Consular Bulletin,* VI, No. 3 (March 1924), pp. 78-79.

60. See Carr's remarks to the entering consular class of 1921 regarding *esprit de corps,* in his "Diary," July 7, 1921 (Carr Papers).

61. See Bernadotte E. Schmitt's lecture to the Foreign Service School, "Diplomatic History and the Practice of Diplomacy," March 22, 1926 (State Department file 623, RG 59, N.A.).

Chapter III

1. Lewis Einstein, born New York, 1877; Columbia, A.B., 1898; A.M., 1899; appointed 3rd Secretary at Paris Embassy, 1903. (Lawrence Gelfand, Introduction to Einstein, *A Diplomat Looks Back,* pp. xv-xxix.)

Henry Fletcher, born Greencastle, Pa., 1873; practiced law, 1894-98; joined 1898 Rough Riders and served in Cuban campaign; served in Army in Philippines until 1901; appointed 2nd Secretary at Havana, May 1902. (U.S. Department of State, *Biographical Register* [1922], p. 119.)

Hugh Gibson, born Los Angeles, 1883; educated by tutors, attended Pomona College; certificate from L'Ecole des Sciences Politiques, 1906; appointed Secretary of the Legation at Tegucigalpa, 1908. (Galpin, ed., *Hugh Gibson,* and Gibson's "Reminiscences," *COHC* (1956), pp. 22-30.

Leland Harrison, born New York, 1883; attended Eton College, England; Harvard University, A.B., 1907; attended Harvard Law School, 1906-07; private secretary to Ambassador in Japan, 1907-08; 3rd Secretary at Tokyo, 1908. (U.S. Department of State, *Biographical Register* [1922], p. 129.)

Joseph Grew, born 1880; attended Groton School; Harvard, A.B., 1902; world travel, 1903-04; appointed Deputy Consul-General at Cairo, 1903; 3rd Secretary at the Embassy in Mexico City, 1906. (Heinrichs, *American Ambassador,* pp. 31-32.)

Franklin Mott Gunther, born New York, 1885; Harvard, A.B., 1907; attended L'Ecole des Sciences Politiques, 1907-08; private secretary to Ambassador in Japan, 1907-08; 3rd Secretary of Embassy at Paris, 1909. (U.S. Department of State, *Biographical Register* [1922], p. 126.)

Peter Augustus Jay, born Newport, R.I., 1877; attended Eton College, England, 1891-95; Harvard, A.B., 1900; private business in New York, 1901-02; appointed 3rd Secretary of Embassy at Paris, 1902. (*Ibid.,* p. 138.)

Basil Miles, born Philadelphia, 1877; University of Pennsylvania, A.B., 1897; Oxford, B. Litt., 1899; private business, 1899-1901; teacher in private academy, 1901-03; private secretary to Ambassador in Russia, 1903-05; appointed 3rd Secretary at Embassy in Berlin, 1905. (*Ibid.* [1918], p. 142.)

William Phillips, born Boston, 1878; attended private schools in Boston and Milton Academy; Harvard, A.B., 1900; attended Harvard Law School, 1900-02; private secretary to the Ambassador to Great Britain, 1903-05; appointed 2nd Secretary at the Legation in Peking, 1900. (Phillips, *Adventures in Diplomacy,* pp. 3-25.)

Hugh Wilson, born Evanston, Ill., 1885; attended Hill School, 4 years; Yale, A.B., 1906; attended L'Ecole des Sciences Politiques, 1906-07; world travel, 1907-08; private business in Chicago, 1908-11; private secretary to American Minister to Portugal, 1911; appointed Secretary of the Legation at Guatemala, 1912. (Wilson, *The Education of a Diplomat,* pp. 3-20.)

John Campbell White, born London, England, 1884, son of Henry White; privately tutored; Harvard, A.B. 1907; attended Harvard Law School, 1907-08; private secretary to Henry White at Rome and Paris, 1906-07; journalist in St. Paul and Baltimore, 1909-13; appointed Secretary of the Legation at Santa Domingo, 1913. (White, "Reminiscences," pp. 3-40.)

2. Wilbur J. Carr, born Hillsboro, Ohio, 1870; educated in Ohio public schools; attended University of Kentucky, 1888-91; Georgetown University, Ll.B., 1894; Columbian University (subsequently George Washington University), Ll.M., 1898; clerk in the Department of State, 1892-1902; appointed Chief of the Consular Bureau, 1902. (Crane, *Mr. Carr of State,* pp. 4-55; U.S. Department of State, *Biographical Register* [1922], p. 100.)

Joseph W. Ballantine, born in India of American missionary parents, 1888; Amherst, A.B., 1909; student interpreter in Japan, 1909-11; Deputy Consul in Kobe, 1911-12. (Ballantine, "Reminiscences," pp. 1-53.)

Nelson T. Johnson, born Washington, D.C., 1887; attended public elementary school in Oklahoma and private high school in Washington; attended George Washington University, 1905-07; Vice and Deputy Consul-General at Mukden, 1909-10. (Johnson, "Reminiscences," pp. 1-35.)

Tracy H. Lay, born Gadsden, Ala., 1882; studied civil engineering at the Alabama Polytechnical Institute, 1900-04; businessman in Alabama, 1904-08; secretary to member of Congress, 1911-12; appointed Deputy Consul-General at London, 1912. (U.S. Department of State, *Biographical Register* [1922], p. 145.)

George S. Messersmith, born Fleetwood, Pa., 1883; graduate of Keystone State Normal School, Kutztown, Pa., 1900; attended Delaware College, 1902-11; secretary of the State Board of Examiners of Delaware, 1912-14; Vice-President, State Board of Education of Delaware, 1912-14; appointed Consul at Fort Erie, 1914-16; Consul at Curacao, 1916-19; Consul at Antwerp, 1919-22. (U.S. Department of State, *Biographical Register* [1925], p. 161.)

DeWitt Clinton Poole, born Vancouver Barracks, Washington, 1885; public school in Wisconsin; University of Wisconsin, A.B., 1906, studying with Paul Reinsch; newspaper work, Moline, Ill., 1906-19; George Washington University, Master of Diplomacy, 1910; Deputy Consul-General at Berlin, 1911-12. (Poole, "Reminiscences," pp. 1-41.)

3. For a description of the intellectual milieu of progressive reform, see Robert Wiebe, *The Search for Order: 1877-1920* (New York: Hill and Wang, 1967), pp. 1-195; Haber, *Efficiency and Uplift*, pp. ix, 1-12.

4. Max Weber, *From Max Weber: Essays in Sociology*, translated and edited by H. H. Gerth and C. Wright Mills (New York: Oxford University Press, 1946), pp. 77-128.

5. Besides Fletcher, Joseph Grew, William Phillips, Lewis Einstein, George Summerlin, Hugh Wilson, and Craig Wadsworth all had close personal connections with T. R. For Grew and Phillips, see below, pp.   . Einstein later wrote an appreciation of T. R., see *Roosevelt: His Mind in Action,* see *passim.* Summerlin, a graduate of West Point, met Roosevelt and Fletcher during the Cuban campaign. (U.S. Department of State, *Biographical Register* [1922], p. 185.) Wilson responded to the general appeal of Roosevelt while an undergraduate at Yale (See Wilson, *Education of a Diplomat,* p. 6.) Wadsworth joined the Rough Riders in Cuba and was on the Roosevelt staff when T. R. was governor of New York from 1899 to 1900. He was appointed 3rd Secretary at London in 1902. (U.S. Department of State, *Biographical Register* [1926], p. 197.)

6. "Rough Riders," 1909 (Box 2, Fletcher Papers). While serving in Cuba, Fletcher met George Summerline and Craig Wadsworth. The former became Fletcher's chief assistant in Chile and Mexico from 1914 to 1919. Wadsworth became Fletcher's second in command in Brussels from 1922 to 1925. (U.S. Department of State, *Biographical Register* [1926], pp. 192, 197.)

7. Fletcher to Roosevelt, January 17, 1902 (Box 2, Fletcher Papers).

8. Sydney Smith, Chief of the Diplomatic Bureau, to Fletcher, May 22, 1902.

9. Smith to Fletcher, March 10, 1905 (Box 2, Fletcher Papers.)

10. For Grew's early response to Theodore Roosevelt, see Heinrichs, *American Ambassador,* p. 11. For his response to the teaching of Archibald Carey

Coolidge, see Coolidge, and Lord, *Life and Letters*, pp. 43-49; Grew to Coolidge, April 20, 1920 (Grew Papers).

11. Cf. Wilson, *Education of a Diplomat*, p. 8.

12. Phillips, *Ventures in Diplomacy*, pp. 5-6. In 1919 Phillips wrote a eulogy of T. R. in which he praised the dead President's encouragement of public service by young men. "He lived to see his ideal triumph and young Americans respond as an unit to the call of the nation. His influence will live forever and will be realized in the words 'Service to the State!'" (p. 45). Cf. Einstein, *Roosevelt*, pp. 3-5.

13. Philips, *Ventures in Diplomacy*, p. 8.

14. Hay's recommendation that Phillips get a law degree was not a capricious suggestion designed to put off a job-seeker. One of the reformers of Foreign Service education, Andrew D. White, recommended that all aspirants for diplomatic work have Ll.B.'s to help them in their work, give the service extra prestige, and give unsuccessful job applicants a career to return to when the State Department rejected them. See Andrew D. White, "The Diplomatic Service of the United States: With Some Hints toward Its Reform," *Smithsonian Miscellaneous Collections*, XLVIII (June 13, 1905), p. 130.

15. Phillips, "Reminiscences," pp. 9-10.

16. *Ibid.*, p. 17.

17. *Ibid.*, pp. 16-17.

18. Phillips, *Ventures in Diplomacy*, p. 14.

19. Sydney Smith to Henry Fletcher, March 10, 1905 (Box 2, Fletcher Papers).

20. Phillips, "Reminiscences," pp. 18-27; and his *Ventures in Diplomacy*, pp. 16-32.

21. Phillips, "Reminiscences," p. 28.

22. *Ibid.*, pp. 28-37.

23. Roosevelt to George L. von Meyer, December 26, 1904; same to Richard Harding Dana, January 3, 1905. (In Morison, ed., *Letters of Theodore Roosevelt*, Vol. IV, pp. 1079, 1089-90.

24. Phillips, *Ventures in Diplomacy*, pp. 33-46.

25. Phillips, "Reminiscences," p. 39.

26. *Ibid.*, pp. 37-44.

27. *Ibid.*, p. 36; *Ventures in Diplomacy*, p. 21.

28. An influential senator threatened to block a State Department appropriation unless the 3rd Assistantship was given to his son. (Phillips, *Ventures in Diplomacy*, pp. 45-46.)

29. Phillips, "Reminiscences," p. 50.

30. *Ibid.*, pp. 50-58.

31. *Ibid.*, pp. 58-59.

32. Edward M. House, "Diary," January 7, 1914 (House Papers, Sterling Library, Yale University).

33. Phillips, *Ventures in Diplomacy*, pp. 59-63. Bryan to Phillips, March 13, 1914 (Phillips Papers).

34. For Einstein, see Einstein, *A Diplomat Looks Back*, pp. xv-xxix, 3-15. For Grew, see Heinrichs, *American Ambassador*, pp. 3-19. For Harrison, see his "Eton College" (Box 18, Harrison Papers); and U.S. Department of State, *Biographical*

Register (1922), p. 129. For Wilson, see his *Education of a Diplomat,* pp. 3-19, and *Diplomacy as a Career,* pp. 1-52. For Gibson, see Galpin, *Hugh Gibson,* pp. 121-61.

35. National Civil Service Reform League, *Report on the Foreign Service* (hereafter cited as NCSRL *Report*) (New York: National Civil Service Reform League, 1919), p. 103.

36. House, "Diary," April 3, 4, 18, 1913 (House Papers).

37. Archibald Carey Coolidge to Edwin Morgan, August 3, 1913, in Coolidge and Lord, *Life and Letters,* p. 151.

38. Carr, "Diary," February 17, 1914 (Carr Papers).

39. *Ibid.*

40. *Ibid.,* April 17, 1914.

41. *Ibid.,* April 17, 28, May 17, November 17, December 1, 1914 (Phillips, "Reminiscences," p. 41).

42. NCSRL *Report,* p. 42.

43. Galpin, ed., *Hugh Gibson,* pp. 121-126.

44. Carr, "Diary," August 7, 1914 (Carr Papers).

45. Galpin, *Hugh Gibson,* pp. 115-33; Joseph Grew to his mother, January 8 and 29, 1915, in Joseph Grew, *Turbulent Era: A Diplomatic Record of Forty Years, 1904-1945,* ed. Walter Johnson (Boston: Houghton-Mifflin, 1952), Vol. 1, pp. 157-160, 164-165; Wilson, *Education of a Diplomat,* pp. 180-83. See editorial in the *Milwaukee Journal,* February 7, 1918, which reports approvingly of the speeches in favor of the war effort that two touring diplomats, Gibson and Grew, were making (copy in Box 2, Gibson Papers).

46. Carr, "Diary," December 2 and 23, 1914; June 12, 1915 (Carr Papers); Phillips, "Reminiscences," pp. 46-47; Phillips, "Diary," June 14, 1915 (Phillips Papers).

47. Phillips, "Reminiscences," pp. 50-53; his "Diary," December 1, 15, February 17, March 1, 2, 3, 4, April 3 (Phillips Papers).

48. David F. Trask, *The United States in the Supreme War Council: American War Aims and Inter-Allied Strategy, 1917-1918* (Middletown, Conn.: Wesleyan University Press, 1961), pp. 15-52, 151-78; W. B. Fowler, *British-American Relations, 1917-1918: The Role of Sir William Wiseman* (Princeton: Princeton University Press, 1969), pp. 36-60; Gelfand, *The Inquiry,* pp. 32-78; Daniel R. Beaver, "Newton Baker and the Genesis of the War Industires Board, 1917-1918," *The Journal of American History,* LII, No. 1, (January 1965), pp. 43-58.

49. Phillips, "Diary," July 12, 14, 1917 (Phillips Papers), Carr, "Diary," July 10, 1918 (Carr Papers); Hugh Wilson, *Education of a Diplomat,* pp. 201-05; Joseph C. Grew to Ellis Dresel, May 23, 1917, in Grew, *Turbulent Era,* Vol. 1, pp. 327-30; Einstein, *A Diplomat Looks Back,* pp. 164-72.

50. Carr, "Diary," July 10, August 31, 1918, (Carr Papers); House, "Diary," August 27, 1918 (House Papers); Gelfand, *The Inquiry,* p. 134.

51. Heinrichs, *American Ambassador,* pp. 38-39; Gelfand, *The Inquiry,* pp. 160-61; James T. Shotwell, *At the Paris Peace Conference* (New York: Macmillan, 1937), pp. 16-17.

52. Heinrichs, *American Ambassador,* p. 41.

53. House, "Diary," December 3, 14, 1918 (House Papers).

54. Joseph C. Grew to Hugh Gibson, January 18, 1920 (Grew Papers).

55. Carr, "Reasons Why the State Department Should Be Reorganized," December 4, 1919; letter to transmittal, Carr to Lansing, December 4, 1919 (Carr Papers).

56. Henry Morgenthau to Herbert Hoover, August 12, 1919 (Frank L. Polk Papers, Sterling Library, Yale University).

57. Hugh Gibson to Arthur Bliss Lane, July 18, 1919 (Lane Papers, Sterling Library, Yale University). Cyrus Adler to Gibson, July 20, 1920; Gibson to Fred Morris Dearing, April 13, 1921; same to same, July 28, 1921; William R. Castle to Gibson, September 22, 1921; same to same, December 9, 1921 (Box 7, Gibson Papers).

58. Telegram, Frank Polk to Robert Lansing, September 12, 1919 (Box 1, Lane Papers).

59. Hugh Gibson to Joseph C. Grew, May 10, 1919; same to William Phillips, May 22, 1919; same to Arthur Bliss Lane, July 18, 1919; same to same, July 26, 1919. (Lane Papers).

60. Hugh Gibson to Arthur Bliss Lane, July 26, 1919 (Lane Papers).

61. *American Consular Bulletin,* IV, No. 11 (November 1922), p. 320.

62. Testimony of Robert F. Skinner, Consul General at London, U.S. Congress, House Committee on Foreign Affairs, *Hearings on H.R. 12543: The Reorganization and Improvement of the Foreign Service of the United States* (67th Congress, 4th Sess., December 12, 1922), p. 77.

63. William Phillips to Richard Cameron Beer, January 29, 1917 (Box 122, Beer Family Papers, Sterling Library, Yale University).

64. Richard C. Beer to Mrs. William C. Beer, June 22, 1922; same to Thomas Beer, October 5, 1922; same to Mrs. William C. Beer, October 30, 1922; same to same, November 9, 1922; same to Alice Beer, November 23, 1922 Box 122, Beer Family Papers).

65. Carr, "What Your Consuls Do," n.d. (1922), Draft Ms. (Box 17, Carr Papers).

66. Testimony of Wilbur J. Carr, U.S. Congress, House Committee on Foreign Affairs, Hearings on H.R. 15857 and H.R. 15953, *Further Regulating the Granting of Visas by Diplomatic and Consular Officers of the United States and for Other Purposes* (66th Congress, 3rd Sess., January 22, 1921), p. 16.

67. Lansing to Porter, December 6, 1919 (Vol. XLVII, Lansing Papers, Manuscript Division, Library of Congress); same to same, January 21, 1920 (State Department File 111/52a, N.A.); Carr memo, "Reasons Why State Department Should Be Reorganized," December 4, 1919 (Carr Papers).

68. Charles Evans Hughes, "Some Observations on the Conduct of Our Foreign Relations," *American Journal of International Law,* XVII, No. 3 (July 1922), pp. 359-60; his "Some Aspects of the Work of the State Department," *ibid.,* p. 371; and his Testimony on H.R. 12543, December 11, 1922, *ibid.,* pp. 6-7.

69. Charles Evans Hughes, quoted in *American Consular Bulletin,* V, No. 2

(February 1923), p. 37.

70. Carr, "Reorganization in Prospect," *American Consular Bulletin,* III, No. 2 (April 1921), p. 5.

71. Lansing to Porter, January 21, 1920 (State Department File 111/52a RG 59, N.A.).

72. *Ibid.*

73. Carr to Joseph W. Mauch, May 15, 1920 (Carr Papers).

74. Carr to Nicholas Murray Butler, President of Columbia University, December 4, 1922 (Butler Papers, Butler Library, Columbia University). Carr to Julius Barnes, U.S. Chamber of Commerce, December 17, 1922; Carr to President Warren G. Harding, January 19, 1923 (Carr Papers).

75. NCSRL *Report.*

76. Stewart, *History of the National Civil Service Reform League,* pp. 200-01.

77. The most interesting of the books and articles were: Arthur Sweetser, "Why the State Department Should Be Reorganized," *World's Work,* XXXIX (March 1920), pp. 511-15; William H. Crawford, "An Interview with Charles Evans Hughes," *World's Work,* XL (June 1921), pp. 127-31; Wilbur J. Carr, "To Bring Our Foreign Service Up to Date", *Independent,* CV (February 26, 1921), pp. 207-30; Maurice Francis Egan, "More Business in Diplomacy," *Colliers,* LXX (February 4, 1922), pp. 22-24; NCSRL, *The Foreign Service: Report of the Committee on Foreign Service in the First Year of the Administration of President Harding* (New York: NCSRL, 1922); Samuel McClintock, "A Unified Foreign Service," *American Journal of International Law,* XVII, No. 2 (April 1923), pp. 110-114; A. L. Dennis, "The Foreign Service of the United States," *North American Review,* CCXIX (February 1924), pp. 3-40. Other articles on Foreign Service Reform are listed in Ilchman, *Professional Diplomacy,* pp. 153, 165.

78. NCSRL *Report,* p. 49.

79. *Ibid.,* p. 57.

80. *Ibid.,* p. 103.

81. *Ibid.,* pp. 114-15. See letter of E. J. Hale to Frank L. Polk, June 9, 1920 (Drawer 85, File 211, Polk Papers), for Hale's charge that he had been unjustly accused of peculation by the *Report* and by Rep. Rogers who had broken the story on the floor of the House. Hale claimed that the League and Rogers had accused him out of political motives; after all, several *Republican* diplomats had received pay while away from their posts, and no issue had been raised. Hale also suggested that Republicans in the State Department, like Phillips and Carr, had told Rogers about his drawing pay in order to embarrass President Wilson. See Frank L. Polk to E. J. Hale, June 12, 1920 (Polk Papers), for Polk's refutation of all Hale's charges.

82. NCSRL *Report,* pp. 19, 83.

83. Francis King Carey to Frank L. Polk, January 1, 1920; same to Robert Lansing, January 15, 1920; same to Senator John W. Smith, February 13, 1920 (Drawer 85, File 212, Polk Papers).

84. Francis Carey King to Robert Lansing, January 15, 1920 (Polk Papers).

85. Carr, "Diary," February 27, 1920 (Carr Papers).

86. NCSRL *Report,* p. 72.

87. *Ibid.,* pp. 32-33.

88. *Ibid.*, p. 77, chart.
89. *Ibid.*
90. *Ibid.*, p. 34.
91. *Ibid.*, pp. 31-32. See testimony of J. Butler Wright, U.S. Congress, House Committee on Foreign Affairs, *Hearings on H.R. 17 and H.R. 6357, Foreign Service of the United States* (68th Congress, 1st Session, January 22, 1924), p. 57.
92. NCSRL *Report,* p. 18.
93. The Joint Committee on Reorganization of the United States Foreign Service was made up of the American Manufacurers Export Association, the National Foreign Trade Council, as well as the National Civil Service Reform League. The business members of the Committee were: H. G. Cole (Standard Oil of New York), W. W. Nichols (Allis-Chalmers), W. L. Saunders (Ingersoll-Rand Corp.), Edward N. Hurley (Hurley Machine Co.), Alba B. Johnson (Baldwin Locomotive Works), and M. R. Audin (International General Electric). This Committee was in the closest contact with the Consular Bureau. See W. W. Nichols to Wilbur J. Carr, September 9, 1924 (State Department, 120, Rogers Act, File 2, RG 59, N.A.).
94. See speech of Rep. John Jacob Rogers in House, *U.S. Congressional Record* (68th Congress, 1st Session, April 24, 1924, LXV, Pt. 8), p. 7562.
95. Carr, "Reasons Why State Department Should Be Reorganized," December 4, 1919 (Carr Papers); and his "Reorganization in Prospect," p. 14; Charles Evans Hughes's speech to the United States Chamber of Commerce, June, 1922, in *American Journal of International Law,* XVI, No. 3 (July 1922), pp. 358-59.
96. Stewart, *History of the National Civil Service Reform League,* p. 206.
97. Robert P. Skinner (American Consul General in London) to Secretary of State Colby, November 10, 1920 (State Department File 111/53, RG 59, N.A.); Robert Frolingham (Secretary, American Chamber of Commerce in London) to Colby, December 23, 1920 (State Department File 111/54, RG 59, N.A.).
98. Claude G. Dawson (American Consul-General in Mexico City) to Secretary of State Hughes, December 29, 1922 (State Department File 111/118, RG 59, N.A.); G. Bie Ravndal (American Consul in Constantinople) to Secretary of State Hughes, February 7, 1923 (State Department File 111/127, RG 59, N.A.).
99. Julius H. Barnes (President of the U.S. Chamber of Commerce) to Rep. John Jacob Rogers, December 23, 1922, quoted in *Hearings on H.R. 17 and H.R. 6357* (January 24, 1923), pp. 140-41.
100. Carr, "Diary," March 3, 1923 (Carr Papers).
101. Carr, "Reasons Why State Department Should Be Reorganized," December 4, 1919 (Carr Papers).
102. Wilson, *Diplomacy as a Career,* p. 23.
103. Carr to Julius Barnes, December 17, 1922 (Carr Papers).
104. Joseph C. Grew to J. Butler Wright, January 18, 1920, in Grew, *Turbulent Era,* Vol. 1, pp. 409-10.
105. *Ibid.*
106. William Phillips, "Cleaning Our Diplomatic House," *Forum,* LXIII (February 1920), pp. 167-68. Hugh Gibson, "Eighty-eight Points on the Diplomatic Service Versus the Consular Service" (unpublished ms., n.d. [1923?]); Gibson to J. Butler Wright, December 2, 1919 (Boxes 9 and 14, Gibson Papers).

107. Joseph C. Grew to J. Butler Wright, January 18, 1920, in Grew, *Turbulent Era,* Vol. I, pp. 409-410.

108. Joseph C. Grew to Hugh Gibson, January 18, 1920 (Box 9, Gibson Papers).

109. Testimony of J. Butler Wright, in *Hearings on H.R. 17 and H.R. 6357* (January 23, 1924), p. 57.

110. Testimony of Frank L. Polk, *ibid.,* pp. 95-96; testimony of John W. Davis, *ibid.,* pp. 89-90.

111. *Ibid.,* p. 90.

112. *Ibid.*

113. Testimony of J. Butler Wright, in *Hearings on H.R. 17 and H.R. 6357* (January 23, 1924), p. 57.

114. *Ibid.,* p. 58.

115. See Joseph C. Grew to J. Butler Wright, January 18, 1920, in Grew, *Turbulent Era,* Vol. I, pp. 409-10, where Grew criticizes Gibson's strategy of arguing before Congress that political rather than business or economic considerations demanded the reform of the Foreign Service. See Gibson, "Eighty-eight Points"; Gibson to F. W. Huntington Wilson, January 19, 1921; and Gibson to Fred Morris Dearing, March 31, 1921 (Boxes 14 and 9, Gibson Papers).

117. See letters from the following diplomats opposed to amalgamation: T. L. Daniels, Lawrence Dennis, H. Percival Dodge, Frank Mott Gunther, Barton Hall, Peter Augustus Jay, Stewart Johnson, H. Dorsey Newson, John C. White, Charles Wilson and Orme Wilson. (All in Box 14, Gibson Papers.)

118. Gibson to William R. Castle, January 3, 1923 (Box 14, Gibson Papers).

119. Testimony of Hugh Gibson, in *Hearings on H.R. 17 and H.R. 6357* (January 22, 1924), pp. 41-42, 47.

120. *Ibid.,* pp. 44-45.

121. *Ibid.,* pp. 89-93.

122. Joseph C. Grew, "Danish Foreign Service Reorganization," *American Consular Bulletin* III, No. 18 (October 1921)..p. 2.

123. "World Wide Reorganization," *American Consular Bulletin,* III, No. 3 (May 1921) pp. 2-4.

124. Henry P. Fletcher (Ambassador to Belgium) to Warren G. Harding, August 21, 1922; same to same, September 4, 1922; same to Charles Evans Hughes, personal, September 20, 1922 (Box 10, Fletcher Papers).

125. Norton, "Foreign Office Organization: A Comparison of the Organization of the British, French, German and Italian Offices with That of the Department of State of the United States of America," pp. ii-xi.

126. *Ibid.,* pp. 2-4.

127. Carr, "Diary," March 8, 1923 (Carr Papers).

128. Crane, *Mr. Carr of State,* p. 279.

129. Two consuls-general, at London and Paris, received $12,000 per year, but Carr intended to have those salaries reduced to $8,000 when the incumbents in those posts left.

130. See letter of William Phillips to Richard Cameron Beer, January 29, 1917 (Box 121, Beer Family Papers). The letter appointed Beer a consular clerk in the

Bahamas, and informed him that the Department could not pay his passage to his post.

131. It is interesting to note that while the charge of snobbery was most often leveled at the junior secretaries in the diplomatic service, the same criticism could have applied to those consular clerks who were wealthy enough to pay their way to their posts. William Phillips once remarked to Carr that he believed there was as much snobbery among consuls as among diplomats. (See Carr's "Diary," February 5, 1923 [Carr Papers]). Richard C. Beer was an example of the consular clerks who detested their superiors in the consular branch as social inferiors. Indeed, he once described them as "hicks." (See Richard C. Beer to Alice Beer, November 23, 1922 [Box 122, Beer Family Papers]).

132. Testimony of Robert P. Skinner, in *Hearings on H.R. 12543* (December 11, 1922), p. 15.

133. Testimony of Carr, *ibid.* (December 13, 1922), p. 33.

134. Carr, "Diary," March 8, 1923 (Carr Papers). In having Julius Lay testify to the hardships which had forced him to leave the consular service, Carr was being a bit disingenuous. When Lay first announced his intention of resigning, Carr wrote in his diary that he suspected that the real reason for Lay' departure was his wife's extravagance. (See Carr, "Diary," February 12, 1920 [Carr Papers]). "Julius Lay now talks about returning to the service at the end of a year. [Actually, he did not return until 1924.] I begin to suspect financial embarrassment. Possibly Ann has been spending too freely."

134a. Testimony of Lay, in *Hearings on H.R. 17 and H.R. 6357* (January 24, 1924), p. 110.

135. Memo, Carr to Henry Fletcher and Robert Lansing, n.d. (1919, 1920?), Box 16, Carr Papers.

136. Carr, draft of Report to Accompany H.R. 13880, p. 2, January 1923 (Box 17, Carr Papers).

137. That at least some consular officers had vague feelings of carrer insecurity is shown by the advertisements for a Dale Carnegie-type self-improvement course which ran in nearly every issue of the 1923 volume of the *American Consular Bulletin*. One of the several testimonials to the effectiveness of the course in raising one's prestige came from the president of the A & W Root Beer Company.

138. Rogers Act, Section 5, Executive Order 4022, Departmental Order 295, in Lay, *Foreign Service of the United States,* p. 423-24.

139. Testimony of Robert P. Skinner, in *Hearings on H.R. 12543* (December, 1922), p. 77.

140. Testimony of Gibson, *ibid.,* pp. 21-22.

141. Memo, E. C. Wilson to J. Butler Wright, November 7, 1923 (State Department File 111/155, RG 59, N.A.).

142. Fred Morris Dearing (American Minister to Portugal) to William Phillips, July 7, 1923 (State Department 111/248, RG 59, N.A.). Enclosed is a copy of Einstein's circular. See also Einstein to Henry P. Fletcher (Ambassador to Holland), June 20; Dearing to Einstein, July 2; Gibson to Fletcher, October 23; Fletcher to Gibson, October 26; Dearing to Fletcher, November 10, 1923 (Box 10, Fletcher Papers). Einstein to Assistant Secretary of State Leland Harrison, September 3, 1923

(Box 4, Harrison Papers).

143. See Gibson's circular of October 22, 1923, and replies to it in (Box 14, Gibson Papers).

144. Joseph G. Grew to Hugh Gibson, November 12, 1923 (Box 14, Gibson Papers).

145. Carr, "Diary," February 5, 1923 (Carr Papers).

146. *Ibid.*, March 5, 1923.

147. *Ibid.*, March 8, 1923.

148. The text of the Act is in U.S. Department of State, *The American Foreign Service* (Washington: Government Printing Office, 1929), pp. 13-20. Executive Order 4022, June 7, 1924, is in *ibid.*, pp. 925-26.

149. "The Rogers Act is Law!" *American Consular Bulletin,* VI, No. 7 (July 1924), pp. 244, 246, 247-48, 250, 258-59.

150. Crane, *Mr. Carr of State,* p. 279. Over 100 letters of congratulations to Carr are among the Carr Papers for July-September 1924.

151. John Jacob Rogers to Secretary of State Hughes, August 31, 1922 (State Department 111/104. RG 59, N.A.); Wilbur J. Carr to Secretary of State, August 17, 1922 (State Department File 120, Rogers Act Folder 1, RG 59, N.A.).

152. Memo, Carr to Phillips, September 1, 1922 (State Department 111/223, RG 59, N.A.); Carr, "Diary," October 12, 1922 (Carr Papers).

153. Carr to Hughes, January 20, 1923 (Carr Papers); Hughes (initialed by Carr) to President, January 20, 1923 (State Department 111/253a, RG 59, N.A.).

154. Carr, "Diary," February 12, 13; March 1, 2, 1923 (Carr Papers).

155. U.S. *Congressional Record* (67th Congress, 4th Sess., February 6, 1923), XLIV, Part II, pp. 3143-67; *ibid.*, (68th Congress, 1st Sess., April 24), XLV, Part 8, pp. 7562-73.

156. On February 8, 1923, the motion to recommit to reduce the pension was defeated 73 for, 180 against. The bill passed 203 to 27 (*ibid.*, XLIV, Part ii, p. 3285). On May 1, 1924, the motion to recommit was defeated 110 for, 201 against; the bill passed 134 to 27 (*ibid.*, XLV, Part 8, p. 7635).

157. Connally of Texas, *ibid.* (February 6, 1923), XLIV, Part ii, p. 3147; (April 24), XLV, Part 8, p. 7573. Collins of Mississippi, p. 7565. By 1946 Connally had changed his position on foreign affairs, and as Chairman of the Senate Committee on Foreign Relations, he sponsored the Foreign Service Act of 1946.

158. Rogers of Massachusetts, *ibid.* (February 6, 1923), XLIV, Part 11, pp. 3143-47, 3165; (April 24, 1924), XLV, Part 8, p. 7562.

159. U.S. Congress, Senate, Committee on Foreign Relations, *Reorganization of the Foreign Service,* Senate Report 1142 (67th Congress, 4th Sess., February 1923), p. 15.

160. U.S. *Congressional Record* (67th Congress, 4th Sess., February 28, 1923), XLIV, Part 12, p. 4842.

161. Carr, "Diary," March 5, 1923 (Carr Papers).

162. Lodge of Massachusetts, U.S. *Congressional Record,* May 15, 1924 (68th Congress, 1st Sess.), XLV, Part 9, p. 8622.

163. See below, chap. 5.

Chapter IV

1. See above, Chap. 2 and 3.

2. See esp. the lectures of Ellery C. Stowell, Tracy Lay, Bernadotte Schmitt, William Castle, Dana Munro, Stokely Morgan, Leland Harrison, Paul Culbertson, and Alanson Houghton, in "Lectures to the Foreign Service School" (hereafter cited as FSS), 7 vols., State Department File #623, RG 59, N.A.

3. Stowell, "The Foreign Service School," *American Journal of International Law,* XIX, No. 4 (October 1925), pp. 763-65; and his "Reforms in the State Department and Foreign Service," *ibid.,* XXII, No. 3 (July 1928), p. 608.

4. "The Foreign Service School Opens," *Foreign Service Journal,* 11, No. 5 (May 1925), p. 176.

5. Ellery C. Stowell, "Examinations for the American Foreign Service," *American Journal of International Law,* XXIV, No. 3 (July 1930), p. 579; Executive Order 4011, June 7; Departmental Order 296, June 9, 1924.

6. This "realistic" criticism of American studies of international relations was quite widespread for the 15 years after World War II. See, for example, Kirk, *The Study of International Relations,* pp. 10-12. Also the review column in the journal *World Politics,* from 1948-60.

7. See above, Chap. 1.

8. Carr, "Diary," April 21, 1925 (Carr Papers).

9. Lectures to the FSS: J. Butler Wright, April 21 and November 2, 1925; Joseph Grew, April 20 and November 2, 1925; Tracy Lay, November 5, 1925; Wilbur Carr, April 21, 1925, and October 5, 1926.

10. Wright to FSS, April 21 and November 2, 1925; Grew to FSS, April 20, 1925.

11. Heinrichs, *American Ambassador,* p. 50. Cf. Phillips, *Ventures in Diplomacy,* p. 32.

12. Wilbur J. Carr to FSS, April 21, 1925.

13. Henry White, *Diplomacy and Politics,* p. 3.

14. See "Family" file (Box 5, Harrison Papers).

15. *Ibid.*

16. All of these diplomats were wealthy and many attended Harvard from 1895 to 1905. See above, Chap. 3, and below, Chap. 5.

17. Fred Morris Dearing to Lewis Einstein, July 2, 1923 (Box 10, Fletcher Papers).

18. Not all of the first generation were happy with the results of the enlarged Foreign Service. William Phillips, one of the drafters of the Rogers Act, reminisced at the end of his career that after 1924, the Service got too big to allow for the close kinship he found in the "Family." (Phillips, *Ventures in Diplomacy,* pp. 36-38.) The importance of the FSS and the F.S. Association was that the first generation realized that their old method of encouraging group spirit was insufficient for the post-Rogers-Act period.

19. Grew to FSS, April 29, 1925.

20. See recommendation to do this in Lewis Einstein to Undersecretary of State Henry P. Fletcher, April 23, 1923 (Box 11, Fletcher Papers).

21. See, for example, "World Wide Reorganization," *American Consular Bulletin,* III, No. 3 (May 1921), pp. 2-4; Grew, "Danish Foreign Service Reorganization," *ibid.,* III, No. 10 (October 1921), p. 2.

22. Tracy Lay to FSS, April 25, 1925.

23. Grew to FSS, April 29, 1925.

24. J. Butler Wright to FSS, October 4, 1926.

25. William R. Castle, "Germany Since the War," to FSS, March 20, 1926.

26. Grew to FSS, April 29, 1925.

27. Representative Sisson of Mississippi, U.S. *Congressional Record,* February 6, 1923 (67th Congress, 4th Sess.), XLIV, Part II, p. 3167; Rep. Collins of Mississippi, *ibid.,* April 24, 1924 (68th Congress, 1st Sess.), XLV, Part 8, p. 7565.

28. Grew to FSS, April 29, 1925.

29. Allen Dulles to FSS, August 10, 11, 12, 13, 1925.

30. For the opposite view—that modern communications had rendered diplomats superfluous—see William E. Borah, "The Perils of Secret Treaty Making: How Conspiring Diplomacy and Public Ignorance Create War," *Forum,* LX (December 1918), pp. 657-72.

31. Dulles to FSS, August 10, 1925.

32. *Ibid.*

33. Dulles to FSS, August 11, 1925. Cf. Fred Morris Dearing to Leland Harrison, October 10, 1923 (Box 4, Harrison Papers), for difficulties caused by the American press.

34. Dulles to FSS, August 11, 12, 13, 1925. Dulles' later career in the O.S.S. and the C.I.A. would imply that his advice was either ironic or disingenuous.

35. Dulles to FSS, August 11, 12, 1925.

36. Dulles to FSS, August 11, 1925.

37. Dulles to FSS, August 12, 1925.

38. Bernadotte E. Schmitt, "Diplomatic History and the Practice of Diplomacy," to FSS, March 22, 1926.

39. See above, Chaps. 2 and 3.

40. Lay, "The Relation of Economic to Political Matters," to FSS, April 29, 1925.

41. *Ibid.*

42. *Ibid.*

43. *Ibid.*

44. William R. Castle, "New States of Europe," to FSS, August 10, 1925.

45. *Ibid.*

46. Levin, *Woodrow Wilson and World Politics,* pp. 1-49.

47. For the opposite liberal viewpoint—that an enlightened public opinion, rather than a diplomatic guild, should control foreign policy—see William T. Ellis, "Frank Words on the 'Trained' Diplomats," *Outlook,* CXXVII (March 1921), p. 383; Bruce Bliven, "The Diplomat as High Priest," *New Republic,* XXIX (January 4, 1922), p. 145; Manley O. Hudson, "The Liberals and the League," *Nation,* CXVI (April 4, 1923), pp. 383-84.

48. Ellery C. Stowell, "Sources and Principles of International Law," to FSS, April 20, 1926.

49. See Grew to Charles Evans Hughes, March 2, 1925; and Grew to Hugh Wilson, January 19, 1925; in the Minutes of Foreign Service Personnel Board, July 10, 1926 (Grew Papers).

50. Department of State, *The American Foreign Service: General Information for Applicants* (Washington, 1925), p. 3.

51. Francis White to FSS, May 18, 1925.

52. *Ibid.*

53. White to FSS, May 18, 1925; Dana Munro, "Basis of American Intervention in the Caribbean," to FSS (n.d.); Stokely Morgan, "American Problems and Policy in Central America," to FSS, January 18, 1926.

54. Morgan, "American Problems."

55. *Ibid.*

56. Munro, "Basis of American Intervention."

57. Morgan, "American Problems."

58. *Ibid.*

59. *Ibid.*

60. See the following lectures to FSS: Alanson B. Houghton, "Disarmament," March 18, 1926; John V. MacMurray, "The Far East and the Pacific," April 29, 1925; A. N. Young, "Department of State and Foreign Loans," August 27, 1925; Dr. Wallace McClure, "American Commercial Policy," June 10, 1925; Leland Harrison, "Policy of U.S. Government Regarding Granting of Licenses to Cables," June 17, 1925; Paul B. Culbertson, "The Petroleum Situation," June 12, 1925; Alanson B. Houghton, "The Rubber Situation," March 18, 1926; Charles C. Hyde, "Relations of International Law to the United States and the Work of the Foreign Service Officer," June 5, 1925; Preston Kemler, "Activities of the Soviet Regime in the United States," January 6, 1926.

61. Houghton, "Disarmament," March 18, 1926.

62. See Robert Ferrell, *Peace in Their Time* (New Haven: Yale University Press, 1952), pp. 81-84, for an extremely favorable view of Castle.

63. Castle to FSS, March 20, 1926.

Chapter V

1. U.S. Department of State, *American Foreign Service: Information for Applicants and Sample Examination Questions* (Washington: Government Printing Office, 1926), pp. 2-4, 11-13; and its *Biographical Register* (1930), p. 289.

2. *American Foreign Service* (1925), p. 3; John Bassett Moore, "A Decalogue for Diplomats," reprinted from *The Review of Reviews* (July 1930), in Edward M. Borchard, ed., *The Collected Papers of John Bassett Moore*, (New Haven: Yale University Press, 1945), Vol. VI, pp. 339-41.

3. "The Rogers Act is Law!" *American Consular Bulletin,* VI, No. 7 (July 1924), p. 224.

4. Examples of case studies with theoretical conclusions are: Reinhard Bendix, "Bureaucracy: The Problem and Its Setting," *American Sociological Review,* XII (1947), pp. 493-507; Peter M. Blau, "Cooperation and Competition in a Bureaucracy," *American Journal of Sociology,* LIX (1954), pp. 530-35; and his *The Dynamics of Bureaucracy* (rev. ed., Chicago: University of Chicago Press, 1963), pp. 231-65; Melville Dalton, *Men Who Manage: Fusion of Feeling and Theory in Administration* (New York: John Wiley and Sons, 1959), pp. 1-109; Philip Selznick, "Foundations of the Theory of Organization," *American Sociological Review,* XIII (1948), pp. 24-35; Charles Hunt Page, "Bureaucracy's Other Face," *Social Forces,* XXV (1946), pp. 88-94.

5. Charles Evans Hughes, Foreword to Lay, *The Foreign Service of the United States,* p. vii.

6. Wilson, *Diplomacy as a Career,* pp. 20, 38-40. Hugh Gibson "Diplomacy" (unpublished MS, Box 3, Gibson Papers).

7. Lay, *The Foreign Service,* pp. 190-228; NCSRL *Report,* p.91; Brookings Institution, "The Bureau of Foreign and Domestic Commerce," *Service Mongraphs of the United States Government,* No. 29 (Baltimore: Johns Hopkins University Press, 1925); pp. 17-24; U.S. Congress, Senate, *Foreign Commerce of the United States, Letters from Heads of Departments,* Doc. No. 190 (66th Congress, 2nd Sess., 1919), pp. 2-10; U.S. Congress, House, Committee on Foreign Affairs, *Hearing on H.R. 9937 and H.R. 10213, Relative to the Foreign Intercourse of the United States* (67th Congress, 3rd Sess., 1922), pp. 3-19; Calvin Coolidge, *Establishing a System of Cooperation Abroad,* Executive Order No. 3987 (April 4, 1924), p. 1.

8. Amatai Etzioni, *Modern Organizations* (Englewood Cliffs, N.J.: Prentice-Hall, 1964), chap. 8, pp. 75-93; William E. Mosher and J. Donald Kingsley, *Public Personnel Administration* (New York: Harper and Brothers, 1936), pp. 3-37; William E. Mosher, "Public Service as a Career," *Annals of the American Academy of Political And Social Science,* CLXIX, No. 2 (April 1933), pp. 130-43; Morris Janowitz and Dell Wright, "The Prestige of Public Employment: 1929 and 1954," *Public Administration Review,* XIV, No. 1 (Winter 1956), pp. 36-40; Carr-Saunders, *Professions,* pp. 3-10; William H. Form, "Occupations and Careers," *International Encyclopedia of the Social Sciences* (New York: Macmillan and the Free Press, 1968), Vol. XI, pp. 252-53; Talcott Parsons, "Professions," *ibid.,* Vol. XII, pp. 536-46; Bendix, "Bureaucracy," *ibid.,* Vol. II, pp. 206-09.

9. Israel Gerver and Joseph Bensman, "Toward a Sociology of Expertness," *Social Forces,* XLII (1954), pp. 226-35.

10. Leonard D. White, *Government Careers for College Graduates* (Chicago: Civil Service Assembly of the United States and Canada, 1937), p. 7; Lucius Wilmerding, Jr., *Government by Merit: An Analysis of the Problem of Governmental Personnel* (New York: McGraw-Hill, 1935), pp. 1-2, 84-86; Commission of Inquiry on Public Service Personnel, *Better Government Personnel,* Report of the Commission (New York: McGraw-Hill, 1935), pp. 27-29.

11. Carr-Saunders and Wilson, *Professions,* p. 498. Alfred North Whitehead,

Science and the Modern World, (New York: Macmillan, 1925), p. 294. Form, "Occupations and Careers," pp. 252-53.

12. Representative R. Walton Moore of Virginia, U.S. *Congressional Record,* February 6, 1923 (6th Congress, 4th Session), LXIV, Part II, p. 3163. Representative C. Charles Linthicum of Maryland, *ibid.,* April 24, 1924 (68th Congress, 1st Session), LXV, Part 8, p. 7569.

13. For a somewhat different account of the diplomats' success in defining their career as a profession, see Waldo Heinrichs' "Bureaucracy and Professionalism in the Development of American Career Diplomacy," in *Twentieth Century American Foreign Policy,* edited by John Braemer et al. (Columbus: Ohio State University Press, 1971), pp. 119-206. Heinrichs observed many of the bureaucratic restraints which impelled diplomats to define their career the way they did. Yet perhaps he credited them with more capacity than they possessed to develop an autonomous profession. The diplomats were not necessarily at fault for this failure. The practice of diplomacy was totally dependent upon Foreign Service officers being employed by a large, complex organization—the State Department. Hence it was not surprising that intraservice and interdepartmental politics determined so large a part of the diplomats' conception of their career and world politics.

14. U.S. Department of State, *American Foreign Service* (1927), p. 3.

15. Carr, "Diary," April 17, 28, and August 1, 1914 (Carr Papers); Phillips, "Reminiscences," *COHC* (1951), pp. 67-70; Phillips, "Diary," February 17, March 1, 2, 3, and April 1, 4, 1917 (Phillips Papers).

16. Carr, "Diary," July 10 and August 31, 1918 (Carr Papers); Phillips, "Reminiscences," p. 69; Grew to Hugh Gibson, January 19, 1920 (Grew Papers).

17. Carr, "Diary," June 10, 1915 (Carr Papers); Phillips, "Reminiscences," p. 65.

18. Carr, "Diary," April 28, 1914 (Carr Papers); Phillips, *Ventures in Diplomacy,* p. 72.

19. Fletcher to Colby, January 20; Gibson to Fletcher, February 11, 1920; Fletcher to Colby, "open letter," July 12, 1920 (Box 8, Fletcher Papers). Carr, "Diary," April 7, 1920 (Carr Papers).

20. Elliot Wadsworth to Fletcher, June 19, 1920 (Box 8, Fletcher Papers); Lewis Einstein's section on Wilson's attack on the Foreign Service, in the *Republican Campaign Textbook for 1920* (Washington: Republican National Committee, 1920), pp. 115-17, 231-32.

21. Henry White to Nicholas Murray Butler, January 27, 1921 (Butler Papers).

22. Harding to Fletcher, 34 personal letters, 1921 to 1923; Phillips to Fletcher, September 12, 1922 (Boxes 1 and 9, Fletcher Papers). Fletcher was Harding's closest friend among diplomats, and the President often attended parties at the farm where Phillips and Harrison spent their summers. Thirty years after these *fêtes,* Phillips observed that he did not like their low tone ("Reminiscences," p. 83). At the time, however, he seemed to enjoy himself (Phillips to Fletcher, September 12, 1922 [Box 9, Fletcher Papers]).

23. NCSRL *Report,* pp. 11-12.

24. Grew, "Diary," September 16, 1924 (Grew Papers).

25. Phillips to Fletcher, March 3, 1922 (Box 9, Fletcher Papers); Grew's

farewell speech to Hughes, March 5, 1925, (Grew Papers).

26. Fletcher to Harding, August 8; Phillips to Fletcher, August 22, 1922 (Box 9, Fletcher Papers).

27. Betty Glad, *Charles Evans Hughes and the Illusion of Innocence: A Study in American Diplomacy* (Urbana: University of Illinois Press, 1966), p. 136.

28. Hughes, testimony, *Hearings on H.R. 12543* (December 11, 1922), p. 7.

29. For the diplomats' ideal, see Moore, "A Decalogue For Diplomats," pp. 339-41, or Wilson, *Diplomacy as a Career,* pp. 37-41. For the consuls' ideal, see U.S. Department of State, *American Consular Service* (1923), p. 2; Wilbur J. Carr, "What Your Consuls Do," n.d. [1922] (Box 17, Carr Papers).

30. Norton, "Foreign Office Organization," p. 45; Stowell, "Reforms within the Department of State," pp. 607-09. On December 17, 1927, Senator Pat Harrison of Mississippi introduced Senate Resolution 76, "To Investigate the Administration of the Act for the Reorganization of the Foreign Service," 70th Congress, 1st Sess. Senator George H. Moses of New Hampshire chaired a subcommittee of the Committee on Foreign Relations to investigate the grievances of consuls. They concluded Consuls were discriminated against under the Rogers Act. See U.S. Congress, Senate, *Report No. 1069* (70th Congress, 1st Sess.), pp. 2-7.

31. Johnson, "Reminiscences," pp. 170-88; Stanley K. Hornbeck to Nelson T. Johnson, October 31, 1920 (Box 137, Hornbeck Papers); Ballantine, "Reminiscences," pp. 110, 125-30; J. C. White, "Reminiscences," p. 133.

32. Carr to Foreign Service School, April 24, 1925 (State Department File 623, RG 59, N.A.). See Carr's remarks to the Conference on Training for National Service held at the University of Minnesota in 1932, in *University Training for National Service* (Minneapolis: University of Minneapolis Press, 1932), pp. 146-59.

33. Carr, "Diary," December 23, 1914 (Carr Papers). J. M. Blackford, *The Job, the Man and the Boss* (New York: Macmillan, 1910), *passim,* was Carr's source.

34. Carr, "Diary," August 16, 1921 (Carr Papers); Department of State, Legal Advisor's Office *Consular Reorganization,* 1922-23 (Washington: Government Printing Office 1922), pp. 2-4; Grew, "Diary," May 28-June 6, 1924 (Grew Papers); J. H. Dunderdale, "Effective Methods of Interview," United States Bureau of Labor Statistics *Bulletin,* No. 311 (1922), pp. 30-38; H. C. Link, *Employment Psychology* (New York: Macmillan, 1920, pp. 49-53, 64-65 Carr's favorite source for a "scientific" method of selection); Hugh Gibson to Frederick R. Dolbeare, May 11, 1920, cc. J. Pierpont Moffat; Gibson to Moffat, July 23, 1920 (Moffat Papers , Houghton Library, Harvard University).

35. See "Guide for Evaluating Oral Examinations, 1924" (Box 15, Harrison Papers).

36. Mosher and Kingsley, *Public Personnel Administration,* pp. 129-42; Walter V. Bingham and Bruce V. Moore, *How to Interview* (New York: Harper 1931), pp. 40, 56-57.

37. Muriel Morse and Joseph W. Hawthorne, "Some Notes on Oral Exams," *Public Personnel Review,* VII, No. 1 (January 1946), pp. 15-18; Raymond B. Cattell, *The Description and Measurement of Personality* (New York: World Book Co., 1957), p. 761.

38. Walter V. Bingham, *Oral Examinations in Civil Service Recruitment: With Special Reference to Experience in Pennsylvania* (Chicago: Civil Service Assembly of the United States and Canada, 1943) p. 10.

39. Donald R. Morrison, "The Interview in Personnel Selection," in J. J. Donovan, ed., *Recruitment and Selection in the Public Service* (Chicago: Public Personnel Association, 1968), pp. 212-38; Albert P. Maslow, *Oral Tests: A Survey of Current Practices* (Chicago: Civil Service Assembly of the United States and Canada, 1952), p. 4.

40. The qualities sought by Carr's guide ironically resembled the same qualities diplomats admired in a good clubman. See Leland Harrison to Judge John Vayne, May 29, 1925, recommending Joseph Grew for membership in the Burning Tree Club (Box 17, Harrison Papers).

41. For sample oral examinations of 1924-25, see "Oral Exams" (Box 15, Harrison Papers).

42. Ellery C. Stowell, "Examinations for the Foreign Service," *American Foreign Service Journal,* XVII, No. 8 (August 1940), p. 579; Grew "Diary," October 15, 1924, and January 14, 1925 (Grew Papers).

43. Robert D. Murphy, *Diplomat Among Warriors* (New York: Doubleday, 1964), pp. 121-23; Ballantine, "Reminiscences," p. 170; Robert P. Skinner, testimony, *Hearings on H.R. 12543,* December 12, 1922), p. 78; U.S. Congress, House, Committee on Foreign Affairs, *Report to Accompany H.R. 13880,* Foreign Service of the United States (67th Congress, 4th Sess., January 1923), p. 2.

44. Carr, "Diary," March 3, 1923 (Carr Papers).

45. Crane, *Mr. Carr of State,* p. 269; Stowell, "Examinations for Foreign Service," p. 576; G. Howland Shaw, "The American Foreign Service," *Foreign Affairs,* XIV, No. 2 (January 1936), p. 327, Norton, "Foreign Office Organization," p. 57.

46. Copy in U.S. Department of State, *The American Foreign Service* (1929), pp. 35-47.

47. Copy in Box 15, Harrison Papers.

48. Sections 3, 14, 15, Rogers Act.

49. Minutes of the Foreign Service Personnel Board (hereafter cited as FSPB), June 20, 1924 (copy in Grew Papers).

50. See statistics compiled by Ilchman, in *Professionaal Diplomacy,* p. 226.

51. Minutes of the Board of Examiners of the Foreign Service, May 1936 (Record Center of the Department of State); Robert P. Skinner, "Ten Years under the Rogers Act," *American Foreign Service Journal,* XI, No. 7 (July 1934), p. 342.

52. See statistics compiled by Ilchman, in *Professional Diplomacy,* pp. 170, 226.

53. William Castle, "The Harvard Clique," *American Foreign Service Journal,* VII, No. 11 (November 1930), p. 12. Editorial, *ibid.,* XXVII, No. 6 (June 1940), p. 318. Minutes of the Board of Examiners of the Foreign Service, September 1938.

54. Grew to American Foreign Service Association, Grew "Diary," September 14, 1924 (Grew Papers).

55. Frederick Van Dyne, *Our Foreign Service: The ABC of American Diplo-*

macy (Rochester: The Lawyers' Cooperative Publishing Co., 1909), p. 77.

56. "Questions for Oral Examinations for the Foreign Service" (Box 15, Harrison Papers).

57. Grew to Gibson, July 15, 1924 (Grew Papers).

58. Grew, "Diary," October 31, 1924 (Grew Papers).

59. *Ibid.*

60. *Ibid.*

61. *Ibid.*

62. Grew to Hugh Wilson, January 19, 1925 (Grew Papers).

63. *Ibid.*

64. *Opportunities for Women in the Foreign Service* (New York: National Federation of Women's Clubs, 1928), pp. 1-4; Herbert Wright, "Can a Woman Be a Diplomat?" *American Foreign Service Journal*, XVII, No. 8 (August 1940), p. 454; Stowell, "Examinations for the American Foreign Service," pp. 577-78.

65. Hugh Gibson to Joseph C. Grew, April 6, 1925; Michael J. O'Prune [Gibson] to Grew, April 20, 1925; Wee Willie Winkie [Grew] to O'Prune, May 15, 1925 (Box 1, Gibson Papers).

66. Office of Equal Opportunity, Department of State, "A Chronology of Key Negro Appointments in the Department of State and the Foreign Service," May 1969 (mimeographed), pp. 3-4.

67. Ludlow Werner, "Negroes In the Foreign Service," *New York Age*, October 10, 1942; Phillips, "Diary," January 31, 1919 (Phillips Papers).

68. Office of Equal Opportunity, "A Chronology of Key Negro Appointments," pp. 3-4.

69. Phillips, "Diary," January 31, 1919, (Phillips Papers).

70. Stowell, "The Foreign Service School," pp. 765-66.

71. See Phillips's comments on David K. E. Bruce, in his "Diary," March 15, 1924 (Phillips Papers). See also, Grew, "Diary," September 14, 1924 (Grew Papers); Nancy H. Hooker, ed., *The Moffat Papers* (2 vols. Cambridge: Harvard University Press, 1956), pp. 11-23; Murphy, *Diplomat among Warriors*, pp. 17-21; J. Rives Childs, *Foreign Service Farewell* (Charlottesville: University of Virginia Press, 1969), pp. 11-23; Willard L. Beaulac, *Career Ambassador* (New York: Macmillan, 1951), p. 6.

72. Gibson to Moffat, July 23, 1920 (Moffat Papers). Wilson to Fletcher, January 23, 1923; Wright to Fletcher, July 21, 1924 (Boxes 10 and 11, Fletcher Papers). See below, Chap. 6.

73. William Phillips, Leland Harrison, Benjamin Strong, James F. Curtis, and Elliot Wadsworth to National Savings and Trust Co., November 29, 1922 (Box 7, Harrison Papers). Henry P. Fletcher to A. W. Fiedler (executive of the estate of Willard Straight), January 30, 1920; Fletcher to Reginald Hudekoper (lawyer to the Family), January 30, 1920 (Box 8, Fletcher Papers).

74. H. F. Taft (Western Union official) to Leland Harrison, October 7, 1923 (Box 5, Harrison Papers). Taft asked Harrison for $2.50 to renew the cable address "FAMILY" for 1718 H Street.

75. Leland Harrison to James A. Logan, June 10, 1921, listing occupants of 1718 H Street (Box 7, Harrison Papers); Henry P. Fletcher to the Secretary of the

Chevy Chase Club, January 12, 1920, paying Leland Harrison's dues, while the latter was at the Paris Peace Conference (Box 8, Fletcher Papers). Harrison to James Logan, August 5, 1921, listing occupants of 1718 H Street; Grew to Harrison, January 10, 1922; same to same, July 3, 1922, inquiring about the health of residents of 1718 H Street and saying that Grew would stop there in Washington; Harrison to Logan, February 10, 1922, telling of fire at 1718 H; Elliot Wadsworth to Leland Harrison, December 19, 1922, assessing dues for wedding presents to Family members; memorandum, n.d. (1924), listing inscriptions of marriages on "Family Cup," all headed "In Memorian" (Boxes 5 and 7, Harrison Papers). Elliot Wadsworth to Henry P. Fletcher, May 26, 1920, inquiring who Fletcher and "the European members of the Family" support for the Republican presidential nomination in 1920; William Phillips to Fletcher, July 26, 1922, telling of summer at the Family farm in Bethesda, Md.; same to same, September 12, 1922, telling of Harrison and Phillips' summer; telegram, James A. Sterling to Henry P. Fletcher, April 9, 1923, informing him of the marriage of a Family member (Boxes 8, 9, and 10, Fletcher Papers).

76. Leland Harrison to Henry P. Fletcher, June 19, 1923, giving news of the Harvard Commencement (Box 10, Fletcher Papers).

77. Edward Bell (First Secretary to Peking) to Henry P. Fletcher, March 22, 1924, reminiscing about China; J. Butler Wright to Henry P. Fletcher, April 23, 1924, reminiscing (Box 11, Fletcher Papers).

78. Hugh Gibson to Henry P. Fletcher, February 21, 1920 (Box 8, Fletcher Papers). Fletcher to Grew, November 7, 1921 cc. to Harrison; Fred Morris Dearing to Harrison and and Fletcher, January 13, 1922 (Box 7, Harrison Papers). James Logan to Fletcher (confidential), April 28, 1922; William Phillips to Fletcher, May 9, 1922 (Box 8, Fletcher Papers). Dearing to Harrison, May 27, June 3, and June 13, 1922 (Box 4, Harrison Papers); Phillips to Fletcher, August 22, 1922 (Box 9, Fletcher Papers); Lewis Einstein to Harrison, March 6, 1923 (Box 7, Harrison Papers); Einstein to Fletcher, June 20, 1923 (Box 10, Fletcher Papers); Einstein to Harrison, June 27 and September 3, 1923 (Box 4, Harrison Papers); Fletcher to Phillips, October 2, 1923 (Box 10, Fletcher Papers); Dearing to Harrison, October 22 and November 26, 1923 (Box 4, Harrison Papers). Dearing to Fletcher, November 10, 1923; Phillips to Fletcher, January 25; Hugh Gibson to Fletcher, March 7; Grew to Fletcher, March 12; William R. Castle to Fletcher, July 21; J. Butler Wright to Fletcher, July 31, 1924 (Boxes 10 and 11, Fletcher Papers).

79. For a discussion of the theoretical implications of horizontal lines of communications in bureaucracies, see Richard L. Simpson, "Vertical and Horizontal Communications in Formal Organizations," *Administrative Science Quarterly,* IV (1959), pp. 188-96; Blau, *Dynamics of Bureaucracy,* pp. 121-64, 231-65.

80. See esp. Fred Morris Dearing to Harrison and Fletcher, January 13, 1922; Dearing to Harrison, August 23, September 1, and December 4, 1922, February 23, 1923 (Boxes 4 and 7, Harrison Papers). Phillips to Fletcher, August 22, 1922; Castle to Fletcher, July 21, 1924 (Boxes 9 and 11, Fletcher Papers).

81. J. Pierpont Moffat, "Diary," May 10 and August 26, 1918; Phillips to Hugh Gibson, cc. Moffat, October 2, 1919; Hugh Gibson to Frederick Dolbeare, cc. Moffat, May 11, 1920; Gibson to Moffat, July 23, 1920 (Moffat Papers). Hugh

Gibson to Fletcher, February 21, 1920; M. E. Hanna to Fletcher, December 10, 1929; James A. Sterling to Fletcher, January 16, 1922; Charles Evans Hughes to Summerlin, cc. Fletcher, April 15, 1922; Gibson to Fletcher, February 17, 1924; Basil Miles to Fletcher, February 19, 1924; Summerlin to Fletcher, February 18; Franklin Mott Gunther to Fletcher, February 21; Edward Bell to Fletcher, March 22; J. Butler Wright to Fletcher, April 23, 1924; and Grew to Fletcher, June 29, 1925 (Boxes 8, 9, 11, Fletcher Papers). Phillips, "Diary," September 10, 1923 (Phillips Papers); Phillips, "Reminiscences," p. 78; Grew "Diary," April 22, 1924 (Grew Papers).

82. Minutes of the FSPB, June 20, 1924; March 14, December 7, 1925 (copy in Grew Papers). Grew to Secretary of State Frank B. Kellog, March 12; Grew to Carr, March 18, 1925 (Grew Papers). Grew to Fletcher, July 21; Castle to Fletcher, July 21; Wright to Fletcher, July 31; Wright to Fletcher, July 31, 1925 (Fletcher Papers).

83. Department of State, *American Foreign Service* (1926), pp. 10-11.

84. See Grew's speech of farewell to Charles Evans Hughes, March 5, 1925; Grew, "Diary," March 5, 1925 (Grew Papers).

85. Minutes of FSPB, December 7, 1925 (Grew Papers).

86. Grew to Secretary of State Charles Evans Hughes, January 19, 1925; Grew to Secretary of State Kellogg, March 12, 1925; Grew "Diary," March 15 and October 15, 1925 (Grew Papers).

87. Minutes of FSPB, July 11, 1925; March 25, 1927 (Grew Papers). Grew to Lawrence Dennis, March 30, 1927 (State Department File 123C421/71, RG 59, N.A.).

88. Lawrence Dennis, "Reminiscences," *COHC* (1965), pp. 17-20; Norton, "Foreign Office Organization," pp. 39-41.

89. Department of State, *American Foreign Service* (1926), p. 13.

90. "Republican National Committee" (Box 21, Fletcher Papers).

91. Fletcher to Joseph B. Grundy, August 12, 1920; same to same, October 14, 1924 (Boxes 7 and 11, Fletcher Papers).

92. See 34 letters from Harding to Fletcher, 1920-23; Fletcher to Senator George Pepper, November 13; same to Senator David Reed, November 14; same to Speaker Frederick Gillette, December 14, 1922 (Boxes 1 and 9, Fletcher Papers).

93. Telegram, Fletcher to Senator Frank B. Brandage, November 3; Brandage to Fletcher, November 4, 1920; Fletcher to Sen. Pepper, November 13; same to Sen. Reed, November 14; same to Sen. Frank B. Kellogg, November 14; same to Speaker Gillette, December 13; same to Sen. Medill McCormack, December 14, 1922; same to Sen. Pepper, November 5, 1924 (Boxes 7, 9, 11, Fletcher Papers).

94. Fletcher to Gibson, July 28, 1922 (Box 9, Fletcher Papers).

95. Fletcher to Sen. Pepper, November 13; same to Sen. Reed, November 14, 1922; same to Charles Evans Hughes, "entirely personal," January 19, 1923 (Boxes 9 and 10, Fletcher Papers).

96. Fletcher to Sen. Reed, "entirely personal," August 27; Reed to Fletcher, September 21; E. A. VanValkenberg (editor *Philadelphia North American)* to Fletcher, September 28; Janet H. Stewart (editor *PNA*) to Fletcher, October 24; Hughes to Fletcher, "confidential," October 31, 1923 (Box 10, Fletcher Papers).

97. Reed to Fletcher, November 2, 1923 (Box 10, Fletcher Papers).

98. Fletcher to Reed, November 13, 1923 (Box 10, Fletcher Papers).

99. Pepper to Fletcher, November 19; Fletcher to Gillette, December 14; Gillette to Fletcher, December 19, 1923 (Box 10, Fletcher Papers).

100. Reed to Fletcher, January 5, 1924 (Box 11, Fletcher Papers).

101. Phillips to Fletcher, January 7, 25, 1924 (Box 11, Fletcher Papers).

102. Secretary of State Hughes to Fletcher, February 17, 1924 (Box 11, Fletcher Papers).

103. Telegram, Gibson to Fletcher, February 17; Miles to same, February 19; Gunther to same, February 21; Einstein to same, February 23; Gibson to same, March 7; Grew to same, March 12; Bell to same, March 22, 1924 (Box 11, Fletcher Papers).

104. Carr, "Diary," March 6, 1924 (Carr Papers).

105. Memorandum, Edward J. Norton to FSPB, February 8, 1927 (State Department File E617, RG 59, N.A.); Ballantine, "Reminiscences," p. 110.

106. Carr, "Diary," July 6, 1921 (Carr Papers).

107. Carr to FSS, October 15, 1925 (State Department File 623, RG 59, N.A.); "Foreign Office Organization," p. 32.

108. Carr, "Diary," February 6, 1924 (Carr Papers).

109. Hugh Gibson, testimony, *Hearings on H.R. 12543* (December 12, 1922), p. 21; testimony of Charles Evans Hughes, *ibid.,* p. 6. Lewis Einstein to members of Diplomatic Branch, June 20; Dearing to Einstein, July 2, 1923 (copies in Box 10, Fletcher Papers). Einstein to Harrison, September 3, 1923 (Box 4, Harrison Papers). Gibson to members of the Diplomatic Branch, October 23; Dearing to Fletcher, November 10, 1923 (Box 10, Fletcher Papers). Phillip Phillips, "Diary," November 14, 1914 (Phillips Papers); Dearing to Harrison, November 26, 1923 (Box 4, Harrison Papers). Compare Fletcher's view as expressed in Fletcher to Gibson, November 2, 1923. Fletcher suggest that consuls already in the service at the time of the Rogers Act be excluded from diplomatic work in the future, but that the recruits of the new Foreign Service have both consular and diplomatic assignments. This procedure was followed in practice (see Box 10, Fletcher Papers).

110. T. L. Daniels to Hugh Gibson, November 5, 1923; Lawrence Dennis to same, November 1, 1923; Franklin Mott Gunther to same, November 17, 1923; Butron Hall to same, November 9, 1923; Peter Augustus Jay to same, October 22, 1923; Stewart Johnson to same, November 13, 1923; H. Dorsey Newson to same, November 8, 1923; John C. White to same, October 29, 1923; Charles Wilson to same, November 3, 1923; Orme Wilson to same, November 6, 1923 (Box 14, Gibson Papers).

111. Section 6, Rogers Act.

112. Grew, "Diary," May 28-June 6, 1924 (Grew Papers); Carr, "Diary," September 1, 1921, and June 7, 1924 (Carr Papers).

113. Wilson, *Diplomat between Two Wars,* pp. 169-70; Grew, "Diary," May 28-June 6, 1924 (Grew Papers).

114. Grew, "Diary," May 28-June 6, 1924 (Grew Papers).

115. Grew's informal method of administration and his suspicion that precise rules of procedure could wreck the morale of subordinate officers preceded by

a decade similar advice given to aspiring young executives at the Harvard Business School by Chester I. Barnard, President of the New Jersey Bell Telephone Company. Barnard's admonitions to executives to supervise offices by friendship rather than formal rulings became standard administrative theory for decades after the thirties. See below, Epilogue. See also, Chester I. Barnard, *The Function of the Executive* (Cambridge: Harvard University Press, 1938), *passim*.

116. Crane, *Mr. Carr of State,* p. 241; Carr, "Diary," June 6, 1924 (Carr Papers).

117. Grew, "Diary," May 21-27, 1924 (Grew Papers); NCSRL *Report,* p. 7.

118. Grew, "Diary," May 21-27 (Grew Papers). As a further balm to Carr's feelings, Grew decided that the outsider to be selected for the job of personnel director should be former Consul-General Julius Lay. Lay had resigned from the Service in 1920 to take a job with the investment house of Speyer Brothers; later he testified for the Rogers bill at Carr's behest. Lay was far more acceptable to Carr than the men presented by Hugh Gibson and Hugh Wilson, who preferred either Basil Miles or William Castle, since Miles was a Family member and Castle very close to the Family.

119. Grew, "Diary," May 28-June 6, 1924 (Grew Papers).

120. Executive Order 4022, June 7; Departmental Order No. 295, June 9, 1924.

121. Grew, "Diary," May 28-June 6, 1924 (Grew Papers); Carr, "Diary," June 10, 1924 (Carr Papers). Although he was exasperated with Carr, Grew truly liked him, in a rather condescending manner (e.g., Grew, "Diary," May 11 and July 1, 1921 [Grew Papers]).

122. The Executive Board consisted of Wright, Norton, and Eberhardt. For its powers, see Departmental Order, No. 295.

123. Circular instruction, Grew to Foreign Service officers, July 28, 1924 (Grew Papers).

124. *Ibid.*

125. Gibson to Grew, September 2, 1924; Grew, "Diary," September 14, 1924; Castle to Moffat, January 25, 1925; Moffat, "Diary," February 10, 1925 (Moffat Papers); Norton, "Foreign Office Organization," p. 42.

126. Norton, "Foreign Office Organization," pp. 31-43; Memorandum, Norton to FSPB, February 8, 1927 (State Department File E617, RG 59, N.A.).

127. Castle to Moffat, January 20, 1925 (Moffat Papers).

128. Grew, "Diary," September 30, 1924 (Grew Papers). For another view of Skinner, see Poole's "Reminiscences," pp. 63-64. Skinner "was a man of great energy, very sharp intellect, and wide culture. He not only performed his normal consular functions well, but participated in the cultural life of Southern France and was one of those who helped in the revival of Provençal." Poole was Skinner's assistant at Berlin in 1913; Skinner was American consul at Marseilles from 1879 to 1908. (Department of State, *Biographical Register* [1922], p. 180.)

129. Skinner to FSPB, October 2, 1925 (Copy in Grew Papers).

130. Grew to Wright and Carr, October 17, 1925 (Grew Papers).

131. Minutes of FSPB, November 24, December 7, 1925 (copy in Grew Papers).

132. Norton, "Foreign Office Organization," p. 47.

133. Castle to Moffat, January 20, 1925 (Moffat Papers).

134. Louis Goethe Dreyfus, Jr. (Consular Inspector) to Edward Norton, January 14, 1927, in memorandum, Norton to FSPB, February 8, 1927 (State Department File E617, RG 59, N.A.).

135. Letter from unnamed consul of class VII received by Norton in July 1926. Quoted in Norton memo to FSPB, February 8, 1927.

136. *Ibid.*

137. *Ibid.*

138. *Ibid.*

139. Heinrichs, *American Ambassador,* p. 124, and his "Professionalism and Bureaucracy," pp. 176-79.

140. U.S. Congress, Senate, *Report 1069* (70th Congress, 1st Sess., May 3, 1928), pp. 1-5; George Moses, S4382, *Foreign Service Personnel Administration,* 70th Congress, 1st Sess., May 3, 1928.

141. U.S., *Statutes* 1207, February 23, 1931; Stowell, "The Moses-Linthicum Act and the Foreign Service," p. 516.

142. Ilchman, *Professional Diplomacy,* p. 200.

143. Skinner, "Ten Years under the Rogers Act," p. 342.

144. *Ibid.*

Chapter VI

1. Gibson, "Diplomacy" (Box 3, Gibson Papers).

2. *Ibid.*

3. See Harold Nicolson, *Diplomacy,* (3rd rev. ed., New York: Oxford University Press, 1963), *passim,* for a statement by a British diplomat, greatly admired by American Foreign Service officers, of the mutual obligations of professional diplomats, politicians, and the public.

4. Karl Mannheim, "Orientations of Bureaucratic Thought," in Robert K. Merton, et. al., *A Reader in Bureaucracy* (Glencoe, Ill.: The Free Press, 1952), pp. 360-61; Merton, "Bureaucratic Structure and Personality," *ibid.,* pp. 361-71.

5. Dexter Perkins, "The Department of State and American Public Opinion," in Gordon Craig and Felix Gilbert, eds., *The Diplomats* (Princeton: Princeton University Press, 1953), pp. 282-308.

6. *Ibid.*

7. For harsh criticism of State Department action regarding the refugees from Nazism in the late '30s, see Arthur D. Morse, *While Six Million Died: A Chronicle of American Apathy* (New York: Random House, n.d.), pp. 32-36, 38-42, 93-97; David Wyman, *Paper Walls: America and the Immigration Crisis, 1938-1941* (Amherst: University of Massachusetts Press, 1969), pp. 114, 138-40, 178; Henry Feingold, *The Politics of Rescue: The Roosevelt Administration and the Holocaust,*

1938-1941 (New Brunswick: Rutgers University Press, 1970), pp. 17, 131-207.

8. See testimony of Wilbur J. Carr and John Jacob Rogers to House Committee on Foreign Affairs, in *Hearings on H.R. 15857 and H.R. 15953, Further Regulating the Granting of Visas by Diplomatic and Consular Officers of the United States and For Other Purposes* (66th Cong., 3rd Sess., January 22, 24, 28, 31, 1921), pp. 10, 15.

9. See John Higham, *Strangers in the Land* (New York: Atheneum, 1963), *passim,* for the intellectual history of American nativism.

10. Poole, "Reminiscences," pp. 27-29.

11. Henry Morgenthau to Herbert Hoover, August 12, 1919 (Polk Papers). Hugh Gibson to Arthur Bliss Lane, July 18, 1919; same to same, July 26, 1919; Gibson to Joseph C. Grew, May 10, 1919; same to William Phillips, May 22, 1919 (Lane Papers). Vladimir Petrov, *A Study in Diplomacy: The Story of Arthur Bliss Lane* (Chicago: Henry Regnery, 1971), pp. 83-98.

12. Testimony of Wilbur J. Carr to House Committee on Foreign Affairs, *Hearings on H.R. 15857 and H.R. 15953,* pp. 15-16.

13. *Ibid.*

14. W. W. Husband (U.S. Commissioner General of Immigration), lecture to FSS, April 25, 1925.

15. Department of State, *Biographical Register* (1925-32, 1946), *passim.*

16. Besides the lectures of Nelson T. Johnson discussed below, see Preston Kumler (Div. of Eastern European Affairs), "Activities of the Soviet Regime in the United States," January 6, 1926; Franklin DuBois (Chief of the Visa Office, DOS), "Foreign Relations as Affected by Visa Requirements," April 23, 1925; Husband to F.S.S., April 25, 1925.

17. Johnson to FSS, November 19, 1925.

18. Russell D. Buhite, *Nelson T. Johnson and American Policy Toward China: 1925-1941* (East Lansing: Michigan State University Press, 1968), pp. 19-38, 150-53.

19. Johnson to FSS, November 19, 1925. Cf. Raymond Leslie Buell, "The Development of Anti-Japanese Agitation in the United States," I and II, *Political Science Quarterly,* XXXVII-XXXVIII, No. 4 and No. 1 (December 1922, March 1923), pp. 605-38, 57-81.

20. Johnson to FSS, November 19, 1925.

21. *Ibid.*

22. Madison Grant, *The Passing of the Great Race: The Racial Basis of European History* (New York: Charles Scribner's Sons, 1919).

23. Johnson to FSS, November 19, 1925.

24. Earl Packer (Division of Eastern European Affairs), "The Revolution of 1917," December 22, 1925; Preston Kumler (Div. E.E.A.), "Activities of the Soviet Regime in the United States," January 6, 1926; Robert F. Kelley (Chief, Div. E.E.A.), "The Foreign Policy of the Bolshevik Regime," December 30, 1925; and his "Essential Factors Involved in the Establishment of Normal Diplomatic Relations with the Soviet Regime," January 7, 1926.

25. Kelley to FSS, January 7 1926.

26. DuBois to FSS, April 23, 1925.

27. Phillips, "Diary," May 18, 1923 (Phillips Papers).

28. Cyrus Adler to Hugh Gibson, July 20, 1920; Gibson to Fred Morris Dearing, April 13, 1921; same to same, July 28, 1921; William R. Castle to Gibson, September 22, 1921; same to same, December 9, 1921 (Box 9, Gibson Papers).

29. Gibson to J. Pierpont Moffat, June 11, 1920 (Moffat Papers).

30. Richard Cameron Beer to Mrs. William C. Beer, November 19, 1922 (Box 122, Beer Family Papers).

31. Richard C. Beer to Ann Beer, November 23, 1922 (Box 122, Beer Family Papers).

32. DuBois to FSS, April 23, 1925.

33. Rodman W. Paul, *The Abrogation of the Gentleman's Agreement* (Cambridge: Alpha Chapter of Phi Beta Kappa, 1936)), pp. 58-68.

34. *Ibid.*

35. DuBois to FSS, April 23, 1925.

36. Husband to FSS, April 25, 1925.

37. *Ibid.*

38. Wyman, *Paper Walls, passim.*

39. Lewis Einstein to James McDonald, October 19, 1933 (Einstein Papers).

40. *Ibid.*

41. George F. Kennan, *Memoirs: 1925-1950* (Boston: Atlantic, Little, Brown, 1967), pp. 109, 139. Cf. Hugh Gibson's admonition to diplomats to resist the soft-headed tendency of American politicians to meddle in the internal affairs of Germany by demanding that maltreatment of Jews cease (Gibson, "Diplomacy," Box 3, Gibson Papers).

42. Herbert Feis, *The Diplomacy of the Dollar: The First Phase, 1919-1932* (Baltimore: Johns Hopkins University Press, 1950), pp. 1-7; A. N. Young, "The Department of State and Foreign Loans," lecture to FSS, August 27, 1925.

43. Feis, *Diplomacy of the Dollar,* pp. 18-20.

44. *Ibid.,* pp. 7-8. Joseph S. Tulchin, *The Aftermath of War: World War I and U.S. Policy toward Latin America* (New York: New York University Press, 1971), pp. 155-205.

45. Feis, *Diplomacy of the Dollar,* pp. 11-12.

46. Tulchin, *Aftermath of War,* pp. 155-205. Leland Harrison, "Loans" (Box 17, Harrison Papers).

47. Harrison, "Loans."

48. Young, "The Department of State and Foreign Loans"; Harrison, "Loans." See memoranda in State Department Loan File, RG 59, 823, NA.

49. Wallace McClure, "American Commercial Policy," to FSS, June 10, 1925; Leland Harrison, "Policy of U.S. Government regarding Granting of Licenses for Cables," to FSS, June 17, 1925; Paul T. Culbertson, "The Petroleum Situation," to FSS, June 13, 1925; Alanson B. Houghton, "The Rubber Situation," to FSS, March 18, 1926. Tulchin, *Aftermath of War,* pp. 118-54, 206-33

50. Tulchin, *Aftermath of War,* pp. 118-233. Feis, *Diplomacy of the Dollar,* pp. 40-60.

51. Brandes, *Herbert Hoover and Economic Diplomany, passim.* Lay, *Foreign Service of the United States, passim.*

52. Tulchin, *Aftermath of War, passim.* Lay, *Foreign Service of the United States,* pp. 254ff.

53. Institute of Government Research, *Bureau of Foreign and Domestic Commerce* (Service monograph for the United States Government; Baltimore: Johns Hopkins University Press, 1925), pp. 17-24; U.S. House, Committee on Foreign Affairs, *Hearings on H.R. 9937 and H.R. 10213, relating to the Foreign Intercourse of the United States* (67th Congress, 3rd Sess., 1922), pp. 3-19; Calvin Coolidge, *Establishing A System of Cooperation Abroad.*

54. Lay, *Foreign Service of the United States,* pp. 254-302.

55. Alanson Houghton, "Disarmament," to FSS, March 18, 1926.

56. Gibson, "Diplomacy," and his "Papers on Disarmament" (Boxes 3, 13, 14, Gibson Papers). See also Merze Tate, *The United States and Armaments* (Cambridge: Harvard University Press, 1948), Part II, pp. 63-120.

57. Glad, *Charles Evans Hughes,* pp. 136-50; Ferrell, *Peace in Their Time.*

58. Ferrell, *Peace in Their Time,* pp. 131-34, 140-65, 225-30.

Epilogue

1. E. g., Wilbur J. Carr, William Castle, Hugh Gibson, Leland Harrison.

2. E. g., Joseph C. Grew, Stanley K. Hornbeck, Nelson T. Johnson, George Messersmith, J. Pierpont Moffat, William Phillips, Sumner Welles, Hugh Wilson.

3. 282 Foreign Service officers received commissions from the State Department from 1925 until 1931. Of these, 188 (66.7%) remained in the State Department until after the Second World War; 30 (10.61%) retired from 1946 to 1949; 50 (17.%) retired from 1950 to 1954; 39 (13.38%) retired from 1955 to 1959; and 79 (28.01%) remained in the Department after 1960. (Department of State, *Biographical Register* [1926-61], *passim.* I am indebted to Louis Ortmayer for help in compiling these statistics.) Some of the more important recruits of the '20s who achieved high positions in the State Department after 1945 were Joseph Ballantine, David K. E. Bruce, Charles Bohlen, Seldin Chapin, J. Rives Childs, John Paton Davies, Eugene Dooman, Loy Henderson, George F. Kennan, Foy D. Kohler, Robert D. Murphy, Henry Willard, and Joseph C. White.

4. Robert Buell, "The Class of 1925" *American Foreign Service Journal,* XXVII, No. 12 (December, 1951), p. 26; Richard S. Patterson, "The Foreign Service: Four Decades of Development," Department of State *Newsletter,* No. 39 (July 1964), pp. 12-13.

5. John Paton Davies, Jr., *Foreign Affairs and Other Affairs* (New York: Norton, 1964), pp. 83-117; Kennan, *Memoirs,* pp. 216-502; Murphy, *Diplomat among Warriors* pp. 98-365; Henry Villard, *Affairs at State* (New York: Thomas Crowell, 1965), pp. 40-167; J. C. White, "Reminiscences," pp. 100-39.

6. James L. McCamy, *The Conduct of the New Diplomacy* (New York: Harper and Row, 1964), pp. 183-87; Kennan, *Memoirs,* pp. 254-63. Dean Acheson,

Present at the Creation: My Years at the State Department (New York: Norton, 1969), pp. 354-70.

7. Mr. X (George F. Kennan), "The Sources of Soviet Conduct," *Foreign Affairs*, XXV, No. 4 (July 1947), pp. 566-82; Kennan, *Memoirs*, pp. 254-67.

8. Paul Y. Hammond, "NSC 68: Prologue to Rearmament," in *Politics, Strategy and Defense Budgets*, Warner R. Schilling, Paul Y. Hammond, Glenn H. Snyder (New York: Columbia University Press, 1962), pp. 310-317.

9. Acheson, *Present at the Creation*, p. 347.

10. Harold K. Jacobson and Eric Stein, *Diplomats, Scientists and Politicians: The United States and the Nuclear Test Ban Negotiations* (Ann Arbor: University of Michigan Press, 1966), pp. 470-89.

11. Don Kash, *The Politics of Space Cooperation* (Lafayette, Ind.: Purdue University Press, 1967), *passim*.

12. Hooker, *Moffat Papers*, p. 90; William L. Langer and S. Everett Gleason, *Challenge to Isolation* (New York: Harper's, 1952), pp. 8-9; Robert F. Bendiner, *The Riddle of the Department of State* (New York: Farrar, Rinehart, 1943), p. 110; and his "Roosevelt's Foreign Policy," *American Foreign Service Journal*, XIII, No. 1 (January, 1936), p. 19.

13. Harold J. Stein, "The Foreign Service Act of 1946," in Harold J. Stein, ed., *Public Administration and Political Development* (New York: Harcourt, Brace and World, 1952), pp. 661-71.

14. *Ibid.*, pp. 671-737.

15. R. Joseph Monsen, Jr., and Mark W. Cannon, *The Makers of Public Policy: American Power Groups and Their Ideologies* (New York: McGraw-Hill, 1965), pp. 222-257.

16. John E. Harr, *The Professional Diplomat* (Princeton: Princeton University Press, 1969), pp. 14-40.

17. Secretary of State's Public Committee on Personnel (Wriston Committee), *Toward a Stronger Foreign Service*—a Report to the Secretary of State— (Washington: GPO, 1954), pp. 3-47.

18. From a Foreign Service of under 500 in 1929 and only 1,000 in 1940 to over 6,000 in 1960. The new agencies which had grown faster than the State Department were intelligence, foreign aid, and the specialists attached to the U.N. and the various international conferences of the post-war years. See testimony of Aaron Brown, Deputy Assistant Secretary of State for Personnel, U.S. Congress, House, Committee on Foreign Affairs, Hearings on S. 2633 and H.R. 12547, *A Bill to Amend the Foreign Service Act of 1946* (86th Congress, 3rd Sess., February 16, 1960), pp. 199-200.

19. Phillips, *Ventures in Diplomacy*, p. 36. Kennan, "Foreward" to Lewis Einstein, *A Diplomat Looks Back*, p. vi.

20. Phillips, *Ventures in Diplomacy*, p. 36.

21. Anthony Downs, *Inside Bureaucracy*, (Boston: Little, Brown, 1967), chap. III.

22. Regis Walther, *Orientations and Behavioral Style of Foreign Service Officers* (Foreign Affairs Personnel Service, No. 6; New York: Carnegie Endowment for International Peace, 1965), pp. 7-12.

23. Robert Elder, *The Policy Machine: The Department of State and American Foreign Policy* (Syracuse: Syracuse University Press, 1960); James L. McCamy, "Rebuilding the Foreign Service," *Harper's Magazine*, CCXIX (November 1959), pp. 80-89; McCamy, *Conduct of the New Diplomacy;* Zara Steiner, *Present Problems of the Foreign Service* (Princeton: Center for International Studies, 1961); Brookings Institution, *The Formulation and Administration of United States Foreign Policy*, Study No. 9, U.S. Congress, Senate, Committee on Foreign Relations, *Compilation of Studies* (Washington: U.S. Government Printing Office, 1961). The State Department sponsored Chris Argyris, *Some Causes of Organizational Ineffectiveness within the Department of State*, Center for International Research, *Occasional Papers*, No. 2 (January 1967). The Carnegie Endowment sponsored Frederick C. Mosher, et. al., *Personnel for the New Diplomacy* (New York: Carnegie Endowment for International Peace, 1962). Together, the State Department and the Carnegie Endowment sponsored the following six Foreign Affairs Personnel Studies: Arthur Jones, *The Evolution of Personnel Systems for U.S. Foreign Affairs;* Robert E. Elder, *Overseas Representation and Service for Federal Domestic Agencies;* John E. Harr, *The Development of Careers in the Foreign Service*, and his *Anatomy of the Foreign Service: A Statistical Profile;* Walther, *Orientations and Behavioral Styles of Foreign Service Officers;* Francis Fiedler and Godfrey Harris, *The Quest for Foreign Affairs Officers: Their Recruitment and Selection.* (New York: Carnegie Endowment for International Peace, 1965.) The Foreign Service Association published *Toward a Modern Diplomacy: A Report to the American Foreign Service Association* (Washington: American Foreign Service Association, 1969).

24. McCamy, *Conduct of the New Diplomacy, passim.;* Brookings Institution, *Formulation and Administration*, pp. 795-805; Steiner, *Present Problems of the Foreign Service*, pp. 1-8.

25. Walther, *Orientations and Behavioral Styles*, pp. 7-12; Steiner, *Present Problems*, pp. 24-28; U.S. Senate, Committee on Foreign Relations, *Summary of Views of Retired Foreign Service Officers, United States Foreign Policy: Compilation of Studies* (Washington: GPO, 1961), pp. 1431-43; John E. Cunningham, "Are We Administering away Our Effectiveness?" *Foreign Service Journal*, XXXVI, No. 2 (February 1959), pp. 19-21; William Y. Elliott, "Training in and for a Modern Foreign Service," *ibid.* XXXIX, No. 10 (October 1962), pp. 19-22; Norman B. Hannah, "Craftsmanship and Responsibility: A Restatement of the Generalists-Specialist Problem," *ibid.*, XXXIX, No. 4 (April 1962), pp. 21-24; Hopkins, "Executive Ability In the Foreign Service," *ibid.*, XXXIX, No. 11 (November 1962), pp. 21-24; and his "Planning for Foreign Policy Leadership, *ibid.*, XXXIX, No. 3 (March 1962), pp. 21-23; U. Alexis Johnson, "Internal Defense and the Foreign Service: Is the Service Ready for the Sixties?" *ibid.*, XXXIX, No. 7 (July 1962), pp. 20-23; George F. Kennan, "Diplomacy as a Profession," *ibid.*, XXXIX, No. 5 (May 1961), pp. 23-26; James V. Martin, Jr., "The Quiet Revolution in the Foreign Service," *ibid.*, XXXVII, No. 2 (February 1960), pp. 19-22; John Y. Millar, "The Future of the Foreign Service," *ibid.*, XXXIX, No. 2 (February 1962) pp. 21-27, James K. Penfield, "Is the Foreign Service a Profession?" *ibid.*, XXXVII, No. 3 (March 1960), pp. 21-23; his "Still Another Look at Specializa-

tion" *ibid.*, XXXIX No. 12 (December 1959), pp. 19-20; and his "Recruitment and Training," *ibid.*, XXXVII, No. 7 (July 1960), pp. 42-45.

26. Chris Argyris, *Executive Leadership* (New York: Harper, 1953); his *Personality and Organization* (New York: Harper, 1957); and his "Understanding Human Behavior in Organization," *Modern Organization Theory: A Symposium of the Foundation for Research on Human Behavior,* edited by Mason Haire (New York: John Wiley and Sons, 1959), pp. 115-54.

27. Argyris, *Some Causes of Organizational Ineffectiveness within the Department of State, passim.*

28. Gordon Tullock, *The Politics of Bureaucracy,* (Washington, Public Affairs Press, 1965), pp. 42-43.

29. Charles Frankel, *High on Foggy Bottom* (New York: Macmillan, 1968).

30. Simpson, *Anatomy of the State Department.*

31. John Franklin Campbell, *The Foreign Affairs Fudge Factory* (New York: Basic Books, 1971).

32. Brookings Institution, *Formulation and Administration,* pp. 795-936.

33. John F. Kennedy, "The Great Period of the Foreign Service," *Foreign Service Journal,* XXXIX, No. 7 (July 1962), pp. 28-29; Joseph Kraft, "The Comeback of the State Department," *Harper's Magazine* CCXIX (November 1961), pp. 43-50.

34. Oscar Morgenstern, *The Question of National Defense* (New York: Random House, 1959).

35. Oskar Morgenstern, "Brass Hats and Striped Pants," *Foreign Service Journal,* XXXVII, No. 7 (July 1960), pp. 21-24; and his "Decision Theory and the State Department," *ibid.*, XXXVII, No. 12 (December 1960), pp. 19-22.

36. Editorial, "Is Our Service Training Adequate," *Foreign Service Journal,* XXXVII, No. 7 (July 1960), p. 28; Letters to the Editor, *Foreign Service Journal,* XXXVIII, No. 3 (September 1960), pp. 52-53; No. 12 (December 1960), pp. 24-26; XXXVIII, No. 4 (April 1961), p. 56.

37. Frederick C. Mosher and John E. Harr, *Programming Systems and Foreign Affars Leadership: An Attempted Innovation* (New York: Oxford University Press, 1970). A study prepared for the inter-University Case Program.

38. *Ibid.*, pp. xvii-xix, 182ff.

39. *Ibid.*, pp. 107-17.

40. *Ibid.*, pp. 75-171, 188-242.

41. *Ibid.*, pp. 192-94; Foreign Service Association, *Toward a Modern Diplomacy, passim.*

42. U.S. Department of State, *Diplomacy for the Seventies: A Program of Management Reforms for the Department of State* (Department of State publication 8551; Washington: U.S. GPO, 1970).

43. *Ibid.*, "Summary Report," pp. 1-30; Report of Task Force VII, pp. 291-341.

44. Kennan, "Diplomacy as a Profession," pp. 23-26. The article reprinted an address Kennan made to the American Foreign Service Association on March 30, 1961.

45. Henry A. Kissinger, *A World Restored: Metternich, Castlereagh and the Problems of Peace, 1812-1822* (Boston: Houghton-Mifflin, 1957); his *Nuclear Weapons and Foreign Policy* (New York: Harper [for the Council on Foreign Relations], 1957); and his *Necessity for Choice: Prospects of American Foreign Policy* (New York: Harper, 1961). For a tendentious, lengthy, and laudatory account of Kissinger's intellectual career, see Stephen R. Graubard, *Kissinger: Portrait of a Mind* (New York: Norton, 1973). For a brief, stylish attack on Kissinger's conduct of diplomacy, see William Pfaff, "Reflections: The Statesman and the Conqueror," *The New Yorker*, June 3, 1972. The most recent laudatory account of Kissinger is that of Marvin and Bernard Kalb, *Kissinger* (Boston: Little, Brown, 1974).

46. "The Eclipse of the State Department," *Foreign Affairs*, XLIX, No. 4 (July 1971), pp. 606-08. I. M. Destler, in "The Nixon NSC: Can One Man Do?" *Foreign Policy*, No. 5 (Winter 1971-72), pp. 28-40, suggested that the National Security Council is ill-placed and insufficiently staffed to direct foreign policy. Destler believed that professional diplomats could regain a preeminent role in foreign policy through the adoption of superior techniques of modern management; he expanded his argument in *Presidents, Bureaucrats and Foreign Policy* (Princeton University Press, 1972).

Critical Bibliography

Introduction

THIS book is a study in both the administrative and the intellectual history of foreign affairs. Previous students of the Foreign Service have concentrated almost exclusively upon its bureaucratic development. The works of Warren Frederick Ilchman (*Professional Diplomacy in the United States, 1779-1939: A Study in Administrative History* [Chicago: University of Chicago Press, 1961]) and William Barnes and John H. Morgan (*The Foreign Service of the United States: Origins, Development and Functions* [Washington: Government Printing Office, 1961]) were good administrative history. They did not, however, scrutinize the political ideas of the diplomats themselves, except as they pertained to the organization of the Foreign Service. Ilchman and Barnes and Morgan either praised Foreign Service officers' beliefs as incontestably "realistic" or ignored their opinions as irrelevant to the development of the Service. A later study on professionalism and bureaucracy in the Foreign Service by Waldo Heinrichs, Jr. ("Bureaucracy and Professionalism in the Development of American Career Diplomacy," in John Braeman, Robert H. Bremner, and David Brody, eds. *Twentieth Century American Foreign Policy* [Columbus: Ohio State University Press, 1971], pp. 119-206) which superseded the works of Ilchman and Barnes and Morgan, explained more fully the Foreign Service officers' conception of their roles. Unfortunately, Heinrichs, like his predecessors, did not discuss the impact which the several attempts to reform the Foreign Service had upon foreign policy. His study surpasses the earlier works, however, in its description of a persistent tension in the officers' outlook between the high ideals of professionalism and the more mundane constraints placed upon the Foreign Service officers by their position in a large bureaucracy. Heinrichs believed that when diplomats met their highest professional ideals, their opinions on world politics were indeed more intelligent and "realistic" than those of outsiders. Yet he also noted that much of the behavior of Foreign

Service officers was determined by their position in a large, complex organization. On the other hand, Heinrichs not only at times overestimated the diplomats' success in establishing an autonomous professional discipline, but was often insufficiently critical of their assumptions with regard to world politics. Nevertheless, Heinrichs demonstrates conclusively the bureaucratic aspect of Foreign Service behavior.

Those who have studied the general course of American thought on foreign affairs have largely overlooked the contribution of professional diplomats, particularly their belief in the convergence of American selfishness and disinterest. In the two decades after the Second World War, some historians and political scientists concluded that American diplomacy in the forty years after 1898 had been conducted in a "moralistic-legalistic" fashion. Robert H. Ferrell, George F. Kennan, Hans J. Morgenthau, and Robert E. Osgood, the most prominent of the critics, called themselves "realists."[1] Their realism consisted in a belief in the contentious nature of the state system and the tragic nature of human affairs, and they consciously followed the neo-Orthodoxy of the Protestant theologian Reinhold Neibuhr, who argued that the United States, an upright and good-hearted nation, operated within an immoral system. American policy-makers, according to Neibuhr, had to shoulder global responsibilities with a tragic spirit, aware of their nation's limitations, yet confident that action on the part of America would improve the world.[2] The realists criticized the preceding practitioners

1. The "realistic" critique of United States foreign policy may be found in: Robert H. Ferrell, *American Diplomacy in the Great Depression: Hoover-Stimson Foreign Policy, 1929-1933* (New Haven: Yale University Press, 1957); George F. Kennan, *American Diplomacy, 1900-1950* (Chicago: University of Chicago Press, 1954); Hans J. Morgenthau, *In Defense of the National Interest: A Critical Evaluation of United States Foreign Policy* (New York 1951); Robert E. Osgood, *Ideals and Self-Interest in America's Foreign Relations: The Great Transformation of the Twentieth Century* (Chicago: University of Chicago Press, 1953). For an exposition of realism before the Second World War by an English academic who abhorred the utopianism he saw after 1919, see E. H. Carr, *The Twenty Years' Crisis* (London: Macmillan, 1939). For a recent and thorough critique of the "realists' " sloppy use of the concept of political power, see Charles McClelland, *Theory and the International System* (New York: Macmillan, 1965).

2. Reinhold Neibuhr, *The Children of Light and the Children of Darkness* (New York: Charles Scribner's Sons, 1944), pp. 161-83; and his *Irony of American History,* (New York: Charles Scribner's Sons, 1952), *passim.* For the debt other realist critics owed to Neibuhr's work, see Kenneth W. Thompson, *Political Realism and the Crisis of World Politics: An American Approach to Foreign Policy* (Princeton: Princeton University Press, 1960). Thompson quotes George Kennan as saying that Neibuhr was "the father of us all." See Hans Morgenthau, *Science: Servant or Master?* (New York: New American Library, 1972), dedicated to Neibuhr's memory.

of American foreign policy for their blindness to the importance of force in world politics and their sense of the United States as a redeemer nation. Such accusations, however, did not take into account the skeptical realism of earlier career diplomats, and they overlooked the moralizing tone of the realist critics' own thought. Both the career diplomats of the 1920s and the realists of the 1940s and 1950s contended that the United States operated in a competitive state system, pursuing its unselfish national interest by regulating that system. Moreover, both groups saw themselves at odds with more ''idealistic'' thinkers.

Historians have long abandoned the argument that the repudiation of the Versailles Treaty in 1920 sparked off an isolationist trend during a decade of American foreign policy.[3] William Appleman Williams, who, more than anyone else, exploded the legend of the isolationism of the twenties, was less successful in describing the various aspects of the outlook of American diplomats during those years. He not only relied too exclusively on the diplomats' notion of commercial expansion as the sum of their foreign policy, but neglected to analyze the rhetorical uses to which diplomats put the commerical argument.[4] Robert H. Ferrell, obscured even more the complexity of the professional diplomats' outlook by insisting that they underestimated the basically contentious nature of the state system.[5] For a better appreciation of the diplomatic outlook that replaced Wilson's idea of world politics and the effect of that outlook upon foreign policy, historians must needs understand the diplomatic mind. The major sources which contributed to the reconstruction of that outlook are listed in the following annotated Bibliography.

Private Papers and Correspondence

Beer, Richard Cameron. Sterling Memorial Library, Yale University, New Haven, Conn.
Some vignettes of life in an American consulate in the Caribbean and Europe.
Butler, Nicholas Murray. Butler Library, Columbia University, New York, N.Y.

3. For the view that the '20s were isolationist, see Selig Adler, *The Isolationist Impulse, Its Twentieth Century Reaction* (New York: Abelard-Schuman, 1957), pp. 112-73; Thomas A. Bailey, *Woodrow Wilson and the Great Betrayal* (New York: Macmillan, 1945), pp. 356-70; Allan M. Cranston, *The Killing of the Peace* (New York: Viking, 1945), pp. ix-x; Foster Rhea Dulles, *America's Rise to World Power, 1898-1954* (New York: Harper, 1955), pp. 108-66.
4. William A. Williams, *The Tragedy of American Diplomacy* (rev. ed., New York: Delta, 1962), pp. 106-59.
5. Ferrell, *American Diplomacy in the Great Depression,* pp. 19-21, 25.

Includes correspondence on professional diplomacy and education for the Foreign Service.

Carr, Wilbur J. Manuscript Division, Library of Congress, Washington, D.C.
An extremely important source, largely neglected by previous students of Foreign Service reform. These papers reveal the prominent role Carr played in drafting the Rogers Act, and portray a complex personality, with a keen appreciation of the needs of consuls and the meaning of professional diplomacy.

Einstein, Lewis D. Coe Library, University of Wyoming, Laramie.
An enormous collection of letters to other diplomats, especially valuable for indicating Einstein's resentment of the pretentions of American consuls.

Fletcher, Henry P. Manuscript Division, Library of Congress, Washington, D.C.
A large correspondence with diplomats and politicians on Foreign Service reform, foreign policy, and Republican politics.

Gibson, Hugh. Archives of the Hoover Institution of War, Peace and Revolution, Stanford University, Stanford, Calif.
Important correspondence of a Family man, and intriguing vignettes of the diplomats' competition with consuls.

Grew, Joseph C. Houghton Library, Harvard University, Cambridge, Mass.
An invaluable source of letters to other diplomats and a provocative diary. Also, copies of the Minutes of the Foreign Service Personnel Board from 1924 to 1927.

Harrison, Leland. Manuscript Division, Library of Congress, Washington, D.C.
Shows the web of relationships at the Family headquarters, 1718 H Street, Washington.

Hornbeck, Stanley K. Archives of the Hoover Institution of War, Peace, and Revolution, Stanford University, Stanford, Calif.
Many letters to diplomats and educators on diplomacy, Foreign Service training, and the Far East.

House, Edward M. Sterling Memorial Library, Yale University, New Haven, Conn.
Useful for understanding the attitudes of high officials in the Wilson administration toward professional diplomats.

Johnson, Nelson T. Manuscript Division, Library of Congress, Washington, D.C.
Much material on the rising morale of diplomats and the sinking spirits of consuls during the mid-twenties.

Lane, Arthur Bliss. Sterling Memorial Library. Yale University, New Haven, Conn.
Gives a vivid portrait of work in the American embassies in Mexico under Ambassador Henry Fletcher and in Poland under Minister Hugh Gibson.

Lansing, Robert E. Manuscript Division, Library of Congress, Washington, D.C.
Lansing's desk memoranda of 1919, containing many references to the need to reorganize the Department of State and the Foreign Service.

Moffat, Jay Pierrepont. Houghton Library, Harvard University, Cambridge, Mass.
Moffat's correspondence with William R. Castle, describing the attitudes of diplomats to consuls. Good portraits of Hugh Gibson, Joseph Grew, and Henry Fletcher. The diary traces Moffat's meteoric career.

Phillips, William. Houghton Library, Harvard University, Cambridge, Mass.
The diary and letters cover the whole range of questions relating to the diplomatic mind.

Polk, Frank L. Sterling Memorial Library, Yale University, New Haven, Conn.
 Helps explain the attempts to reorganize the State Department in 1919.
Shotwell, James T. Butler Library, Columbia University, New York, N.Y.
 Contains some information on the movement for Foreign Service training.

Some former historians have had access to the diary of William R. Castle, which contains descriptions of many State Department officials. The diary has now been deposited in the Houghton Library at Harvard University though it is not yet open to scholars.

Oral History

Transcripts of all of the following interviews may be found in the Oral History Collection of Butler Library at Columbia University, New York, N.Y.
Ballantine, Joseph (1961)
 Gives keen impressions of many diplomats and explains the sentiments of consuls in Japan in the twenties.
Bundy, Harvey Hollister (1960)
 Contains several impressions of William R. Castle, Wilbur J. Carr, and Henry Stimson.
Dennis, Lawrence (1966)
 Explains Dennis's difficulties with the Foreign Service Personnel Board in 1927.
Dooman, Eugene H. (1968)
 Recounts the attitudes of diplomats and consuls in Tokyo in the twenties.
Galpin, Perrin Comstack (1956)
 A reminiscence by the editor of Hugh Gibson's memoirs, including impressions of Gibson's diplomatic work.
Griscon, Lloyd Carpenter (1951)
 Very useful material on the reasons why Griscom embarked on a diplomatic career.
Johnson, Nelson Trusler (1954)
 A large (730-page) memoir of every facet of Johnson's career. Very useful in reconstructing professional attitudes of the first generation of career diplomats.
Phillips, William (1951)
 Supplements Phillips's memoir, *Ventures in Diplomacy,* and the material in his private papers. Much more acerbic than the published memoir.
Poole, DeWitt Clinton (1952)
 A full account of the career of one of the most articulate of career diplomats.
Shotwell, James T. (1965)
 Supplements Shotwell's *Autobiography,* and explains his work on the Inquiry and his attitude toward the diplomats he encountered in Paris in 1919.

Public Documents

Swiggert, Glen Levin, ed. "The Conference on Training for Foreign Service," U.S. Bureau of Education *Bulletin,* No. 37 (1917).

Contains complete transcripts of the Conference on Training for Foreign Service held in conjunction with the Second Pan-American Scientific Conference, December 31, 1915.

———— . "Practices and Objectives in Training for Foreign Service; Report on the National Conference on Foreign Service Training, Washington, December 26, 1923," U.S. Bureau of Education *Bulletin*, No. 21 (1924).

Explains the changes in Foreign Service training wrought by the First World War.

———— . "Training for Foreign Service." U.S. Bureau of Education *Bulletin,* No. 27 (1921).

A collection of course outlines on international subjects.

U.S. Bureau of Education. *Courses on International Relations in American Universities,* Commercial Education Circular, No. 7, October, 1921.

Describes the increased enrollment in international studies courses after the First World War.

U.S. *Congressional Record.* Vols. LXIV, LXV, and LXXII.

Contains the debates on the Rogers and the Moses-Linthicum Bills.

U.S. Department of State. *The American Consular Service; General Information for Applicants and Sample Entrance Examination Questions,* 1914-23.

Provides the Department's expectations of those it recruits for the consular service.

———— . *The American Diplomatic Service: General Information for Applicants and Sample Entrance Examination Questions,* 1917-23.

The Department's bulletin for aspiring diplomats.

———— . *The American Foreign Service: General Information for Applicants and Sample Entrance Examination Questions,* 1924-34.

A continuation of the two preceding series of pamphlets in the years after passage of the Rogers Act.

———— . *Biographical Register,* 1900-60.

Contains valuable biographical data on everyone who held a State Department appointment. Also useful for finding Executive or Departmental Orders and definitions of diplomatic functions.

———— . *The Department of State: Personnel and Organization.* Washington: Government Printing Office, 1922.

A popular pamphlet which reports on reforms in the personnel organization of the consular service.

———— . *Diplomacy for the Seventies: A Program of Management for the Department of State.* Department of State Publication No. 8551, 1970.

Reports from "Task Forces" of career diplomats who wanted to give more political authority to "creative" generalists. Includes the disquieting idea that "creativity" can be measured scientifically. Reiterates many of the contradictions in the diplomatic outlook of the twenties.

———— . *A Guide for Political Reporting.* Departmental General Instruction 258, April 12, 1924.

A manual of diplomatic department.

———— . *Information regarding Appointments and Promotions in the Corps of Student Interpreters of the United States in China, Japan, and Turkey,* 1911-23. Presents the requirements for admission and the career possibilities of student interpreters.

———— . *Executive Committee of the Foreign Service Personnel Board.* Departmental Order 295, June 9, 1924.
A document that emerged from the struggle between diplomats and consuls for the control of the reformed Foreign Service.

———— . *The Foreign Service School.* Departmental Order 296, June 9, 1924.
Defines the purposes of the School and the functions of the Chief Instructor.

———— . *Lectures Delivered at the Foreign Service School.* 1925-1930. State Department File E 623, RG 59. National Archives of the United States.
An invaluable source of information on the political and professional thought of Foreign Service officers in the 1920s.

———— . *Minutes of the Foreign Service Personnel Board.* 1924-1934. State Department File E 617, RG 59. National Archives of the United States.
Access to these records is controlled by the Office of the Historical Advisor, Department of State. The Department permits scholars to cite records without mentioning personalities. A copy of the Minutes from 1924 to 1927 is in the Grew Papers, Harvard University, and is open to scholars without restrictions.

———— . *Rogers Act File.* State Department File 120, No. 3, RG 59. National Archives of the United States.
All of the internal memoranda, the dispatches from abroad, and the public correspondence regarding Foreign Service reform from 1921 to 1924 have been collected in this valuable file.

———— . Argyris, Chris. *Some Causes of Organizational Ineffectiveness within the Department of State.* Center for International Research. Occasional Papers, No. 2. January 1967.
A report on the attitudes of post-World-War-II Foreign Service officers. Argyris found that morale in the Department suffers because officers believe they are supposed to appear more genial than intelligent.

———— . Division of Publications. *A Short Account of Department of State of the United States,* 1922.
A pamphlet designed to generate public support for Foreign Service reform.

———— . Legal Advisor's Office. *Consular Reorganization, 1922-1923.*
Describes the reforms in personnel organization instituted by Wilbur J. Carr and Tracy H. Lay.

———— . Office of Equal Opportunity. *A Chronology of Key Negro Appointments in the Department of State and the Foreign Service, 1869-1969.* (Mimeographed, May 1969.)
Provides essential empirical evidence on the recruitment of black Foreign Service officers.

———— . Secretary of State's Public Committee on Personnel. *Toward a Stronger Foreign Service.* A Report to the Secretary of State. Washington: Government Printing Office, 1954.

The report of the Wriston Committee recommending an amalgamation of the Foreign Service with officers stationed at the Department of State in Washington.

U.S. House of Representatives. Committee on Appropriations. *Diplomatic and Consular Appropriations Bill, Hearings for fiscal year* 1922. 67th Congress, 3rd Session, February 10, 1922.

Contains testimony on the new international role of the Foreign Service.

————— . Committee on Foreign Affairs. *For the Reorganization of the Consular Service of the United States,* Report No. 3305, to accompany H.R. 16023. 57th Congress, 2nd Session, January 21, 1903.

The favorable report on the bill for consular reorganization advocated by the National Business League.

————— . *Hearings, on H.R. 12543, for the Reorganization and Improvement of the Foreign Service of the United States.* 67th Congress, 4th Session, December 11-19, 1922.

Contains much testimony on the need for career diplomats, and reveals the intentions of the various groups interested in reform.

————— . *Hearings, on H.R. 17 and H.R. 6357, Foreign Service of the United States.* 68th Congress, 1st Session, January 14-18, 1924.

More testimony on the Rogers Bill.

————— . *Hearings, on H.R. 15857 and H.R. 15953, Further Regulating the Granting of Visas by Diplomatic and Consular Officers of the United States.* 66th Congress, 3rd Session, January 22, 24, 28, 31, 1921.

Includes testimony from John Jacob Rogers and Wilbur J. Carr, who said that consuls must be given more authority to exclude dangerous political radicals and social undesirables from the United States.

————— . *Purchase of Embassy, Legations and Consular Buildings Abroad.* Report No. 1332, to accompany H.R. 19122. 64th Congress, 2nd Session, October, 1917.

A report submitted by John Jacob Rogers suggesting that the United States augment the prestige of its Foreign Service officers by housing them properly.

————— . *Reorganization of the Foreign Service of the United States.* Report No. 1479, to accompany H.R. 13880. 67th Congress, 4th Session, January 30, 1923.

A favorable report on the Rogers Bill.

————— . *Hearings on H.R. 9937 and H.R. 10213, Relative to the Foreign Intercourse of the United States.* 67th Congress, 2nd Session, February 15-19, 1922.

Reports on relations between the consuls and the commercial attachés.

————— . Committee on Foreign Affairs, Subcommittee on State Department Organization and Foreign Operations. *Hearings on S.2633 and H.R. 12547.* A Bill to Amend the Foreign Service Act of 1946 as Amended and for Other Purposes. 86th Congress, 2nd Session, February 1, 2, 9, 16, and June 2, 1960.

Testimony on the State Department's need for area specialists in the sixties.

U.S. President, 1901-09 (Roosevelt). *Board of Examiners, Consular Service,* November 10, 1905.

The first application of the merit principle to either the diplomatic or the consular service.

———— . *Consular Service: Regulations Governing Appointments and Promotions,* June 27, 1906.

Roosevelt's second order applying the merit principle to the consular service.

———— . *Establishing a System of Cooperation Abroad.* Executive Order 3987, April 4, 1924.

Places all overseas agencies under the direction of the Department of State.

———— . 1923-29 (Coolidge). *Regulations Governing the Reorganized Foreign Service.* Executive Order 4022, June 7, 1924.

Establishes the Personnel Board and the Foreign Service School.

U.S. Senate. *Foreign Commerce of the United States: Letters from the Heads of Executive Departments.* Senate Document No. 190. 66th Congress, 2nd Session, March 6, 1919.

Reports on relations between the Commerce and State Departments.

———— . Committee on Foreign Relations. *Reorganization of the Foreign Service.* Report No. 1142, to accompany H.R. 13880. 67th Congress, 4th Session, February 28, 1923.

A favorable Senate report on the Rogers Bill.

———— . *Personnel Administration of the Reorganized Foreign Service.* Senate Report 1069. 70th Congress, 1st Session, May 3, 1928.

A report of a subcommittee of the Foreign Relations Committee chaired by Senator George Moses of New Hampshire. The report found that diplomats had profited more than consuls from the operation of the Rogers Act.

———— . *United States Foreign Policy: Compilation of Studies.* 86th Congress, 2nd Session, 1961.

Contains thirteen studies commissioned by the Committee on Foreign Relations projecting the aims, conduct, and organization of Foreign policy in the sixties.

Unpublished Dissertations

Billman, Calvin J. "Backgrounds and Policies of Selected Diplomats to Latin America, 1898-1938." Ph.D. dissertation, Tulane University, 1954.

Pedestrian biographies, culled mostly from *Who's Who,* of forty three diplomats in Latin America.

Dunning, William. "The Diplomatic Career of William H. Buckler." Master's thesis, George Washington University, 1957.

An unanalytic account of Buckler's diplomatic career in London during the First World War.

Eppinga, Richard. "Huntington Wilson and United States Foreign Policy." Ph.D. dissertation, Michigan State University, 1969.

Supplements Wilson's *Memoirs of an Ex-Diplomat,* and contains some useful material on Wilson's relations with William Phillips and Henry P. Fletcher.

Preussen, Ronald. "Toward the Threshold: John Foster Dulles, 1880-1939." Ph.D. dissertation, University of Pennsylvania, 1968.

Useful for understanding relations between John Foster and Allen Dulles.

Pugach, Noel H. "Progress, Prosperity and the Open Door: The Diplomatic Career of Paul S. Reinsch." Ph.D. dissertation, University of Wisconsin, 1967.

A very long account of Reinsch's diplomatic career. Helpful in explaining the rationality and "realism" of Reinsch's thought.

Zimmerman, Marcia L. "Lewis Einstein: Twentieth Century Diplomat and Critic of Foreign Policy." Master's thesis, University of Wyoming, 1962.
An insufficiently critical account of Einstein's thought.

Memoirs, Letters, and Diaries

Acheson, Dean G. *Present at the Creation: My Years at the State Department*. New York: W. W. Norton, 1969.
A lawyer's brief for the diplomatic outlook in the post-World-War-II period.

Beaulac, Willard L. *Career Ambassador*. New York: Macmillan, 1951.
Thin on political events but gives superb impressions of State Department life in the twenties.

Briggs, Ellis O. *Farewell to Foggy Bottom*. New York: Random House, 1965.
An indictment of the public for being insufficiently appreciative of professional Foreign Service officers.

Campbell, John Franklin. *The Foreign Affairs Fudge Factory*. New York: Basic Books, 1971.
A witty, irreverent memoir of a junior Foreign Service officer.

Childs, J. Rives. *Foreign Service Farewell: My Years in the Near East*. Charlottesville: University of Virginia Press, 1969.
A light-hearted account of Childs's early career, but grows increasingly bitter during the post-World-War-II period.

Davies, John Paton, Jr. *Foreign and Other Affairs*. New York: Norton, 1964.
Useful on the training of diplomats in the late twenties. Davies's bitterness seems more justified than that of other diplomats.

Einstein, Lewis D. *A Diplomat Looks Back*. Edited by Lawrence E. Gelfand, with a Foreword by George F. Kennan. New Haven: Yale University Press, 1968.
A delightful book, intended by its author to stand midway "between history and gossip." Einstein, and Kennan's Foreword, show how the diplomats' professional pride has abided.

Frankel, Charles. *High on Foggy Bottom*. New York: Macmillan, 1968.
A professor of philosophy recounts several stories of Foreign Service incompetence.

Galpin, Perrin C. *Hugh Gibson, 1883-1954: Extracts from His Letters and Anecdotes from His Friends*. Introduction by Herbert Hoover. New York: Belgian-American Educational Federation, 1956.
A charming volume of comments on professional diplomacy.

Grew, Joseph C. *Turbulent Era; A Diplomatic Record of Forty Years*. Edited by Walter Johnson. 2 vols. Boston: Houghton-Mifflin, 1952.
Selections from Grew's diary and letters. A rich vein that has been often mined. Much of Grew's thinking about professional diplomacy has not been collected here and must be read in Grew's papers at Harvard.

Griscom, Lloyd C. *Diplomatically Speaking*. Boston: Little, Brown, 1940.

One of the better descriptions of diplomatic life in the late nineteenth and the early twentieth centuries.

Hooker, Nancy Harvison, ed. *The Moffat Papers: Selections from the Diplomatic Journals of Jay Pierrepont Moffat.* 2 vols. Cambridge: Harvard University Press, 1956.

Hooker's biographical sketch of Moffat helps explain his reason for seeking a diplomatic post. As in Grew's *Turbulent Era,* these papers concentrate on political questions. For an understanding of Moffat's attitude toward his career, consult the Moffat collection at Harvard.

Kennan, George F. *Memoirs, 1925-1950.* Boston: Atlantic, Little, Brown, 1967.

A fascinating account of diplomatic life after the reforms of the Rogers Act. Kennan saw professional diplomats as an embattled elite, trying to survive in a world of ignoramuses in foreign affairs.

Morison, Elting E., ed. *The Letters of Theodore Roosevelt.* 8 vols. Cambridge: Harvard University Press, 1951-54.

Contains many comments on professional diplomats and career diplomacy.

Murphy, Robert D. *Diplomat among Warriors.* New York: Doubleday, 1964.

Refreshingly free of the diplomats' usual snobbery and sense of being neglected.

Patterson, Jefferson. *Diplomatic Duty and Diversion.* Cambridge: Riverside Press, 1956.

Follows the pattern of initial happiness in his career in the twenties and later disillusionment. Patterson thought the American public did not understand foreign policy and did not appreciate Foreign Service officers.

Peabody, James Bishop, ed. *The Holmes-Einstein Letters: Correspondence of Mr. Justice Holmes and Lewis Einstein, 1903-1935.* London: Macmillan, 1964.

A wide-ranging collection which reveals the breadth of Einstein's mind.

Phillips, William. *Ventures in Diplomacy.* North Beverly, Mass.: Privately printed, 1952.

Covers the personal aspects of Phillips's long diplomatic service. Phillips is not as overbearing here as in his Oral History "Reminiscences."

Shotwell, James T. *At the Paris Peace Conference.* New York: Macmillan, 1937.

Sheds light on relations between Grew, Harrison, and the specialists of the Inquiry.

Simpson, Smith. *Anatomy of the State Department.* Boston: Houghton-Mifflin, 1967.

A disillusioned diplomat criticizes the State Department for excessive snobbery.

———. *Autobiography.* Indianapolis: Bobbs-Merrill, 1961.

Explains the Wilsonian trend in international-relations thinking in the twenties.

Villard, Henry. *Affairs at State.* New York: Thomas Y. Crowell, 1965.

Nostalgia for the high *esprit* of the diplomats of the twenties.

Wilson, Hugh R. *Diplomat between Two Wars.* New York: Longmans, Green, 1941.

The second volume of Wilson's memoirs. Presents the diplomats' sense of superiority over consuls, and recounts the personnel policies of the Department after 1924.

———— . *The Education of a Diplomat*. New York: Longmans, Green, 1938.

How Wilson became a diplomat and how little he thought of consuls, politicians, and foreigners. It is very hard to like Wilson.

Reports and Pamphlets

American Foreign Service Association. *Toward a Modern Diplomacy*. A Report to the Association. Washington: American Foreign Service Association, 1968.

Asks: "Whatever happened to the Foreign Service?" Concludes that it lost its authority to technical specialists and that the Secretary of State ought pay more attention to the advice of diplomats.

Commission of Inquiry on Public Service Personnel. *Better Government Personnel*. Report of the Commission. New York: McGraw-Hill, 1935.

A report that applauds the Foreign Service for having applied the merit principle since 1919.

Conference on Training for National Service. *University Training for National Service*. Report of the Conference held at the University of Minnesota, October 1932. Minneapolis: University of Minnesota Press, 1932.

Carr and Poole spoke to this conference reiterating their views that good diplomats were generalists, not specialists.

Dubois, James T. *Pressing Needs of the Consular Service*. Pamphlet. Chicago: National Business League of America, 1905.

Part of the Business League's campaign for Consular reorganization and university Foregn Service training.

Elder, Robert E. *Overseas Representation and Service for Federal Domestic Agencies*. Foreign Affairs Personnel Studies, No. 2. New York: Carnegie Endowment for International Peace, 1965.

A report on the lasting rivalry between the State Department and other government agencies which maintain representatives abroad.

Fiedler, Frances, and Godfrey Harris. *The Quest for Foreign Affairs Officers: Their Recruitment and Selection*. Foreign Affairs Personnel Studies, No. 6. New York: Carnegie Endowment for International Peace. (Mimeographed, limited distribution.)

Describes the post-World-War-II expectations of Foreign Service recruits.

Harr, John E. *The Development of Careers in the Foreign Service*. Foreign Affairs Personnel Studies, No. 3. New York: Carnegie Endowment for International Peace, 1965.

A brief survey of the professionalization of the Foreign Service, concentrating on events since the Foreign Service Act of 1946.

Jones, Arthur J. *The Evolution of Personnel Systems for United States Foreign Affairs*. Foreign Affairs Personnel Studies, No. 1. New York: Carnegie Endowment for International Peace, 1965.

Records the many attempts since 1914 to find a "scientific" standard for selecting State Department officials. Very thin on the pre-World-War-II period.

Mosher, Frederick C., et al. *Personnel for the New Diplomacy*. A report of the Committee on Foreign Affairs Personnel of the Carnegie Endowment. New York: Carnegie Endowment for International Peace, 1965.
Describes the applauds the guild mentality of Foreign Service officers.

National Board of Trade. *The Consular Service*. Washington: National Board of Trade, 1897.
An early pamphlet explaining to businessmen the work the consular service did for them.

National Business League of America. *American Universities, American Foreign Service and an Adequate Consular Service*. 2nd amplified ed., Chicago: National Business League of America, 1909.
Contains the results of Austen Burnham's poll of university presidents. Everyone tells the League what a splendid job it was doing trying to improve the consular service.

———. *Constitution and Official Directory*. 4th-14th eds., 1900-1914. Chicago: National Business League of America, 1900-14.
Contains various resolutions passed by the League on consular reform.

———. *Pointed Paragraphs on the "Merit System" versus the "Spoils System" in regards to the American Consular Service*. Chicago: National Business League of America, 1906.
Propaganda for the consular service.

National Civil Service Reform League. *The Foreign Service: The First Year of the Harding Administration*. Report of the Committee on Foreign Service. New York: National Civil Service Reform League, 1922.
Pats the Harding administration on the back for appointing many professionals to diplomatic and consular posts.

———. *Report on the Foreign Service*. Report of the Committee on Foreign Service. New York: National Civil Service Reform League, 1919.
Indispensable for understanding the reform plans of the postwar years.

National Foreign Trade Convention. *Official Reports, 1914-1920*. New York: National Foreign Trade Convention, 1914-20.
Contains several speeches and resolutions on the need for a career Foreign Service to maintain a competitive position in world commerce.

Opportunities for Women in the Foreign Service. New York: National Federation of Womens Clubs, 1928.
An overly sanguine pamphlet about the prospects of women being admitted to the diplomatic guild.

Osborne, John Ball. *Education for the New Consular Career*. 2nd rev. ed., New York: North American Review Publishing Company, 1908.
Osborne, Chief of the State Department's Bureau of Trade Relations, puts the Department's stamp of approval on the movement for Foreign Service training.

Walther, Regis. *Orientations and Behavioral Styles of Foreign Service Officers*. Foreign Service Personnel Studies, No. 5. New York: Carnegie Endowment for International Peace, 1965.
An ambitious and not completely successful attempt to quantify the diplomatic outlook in the post-World-War-II period.

White, Andrew D. *The Diplomatic Service of the United States: With Some Hints toward Its Reform*. Hamilton Lecture, delivered at the Smithsonian Institution, Washington, D.C., June 13, 1905. *Smithsonian Miscellaneous Collections,* XLVIII, Part 2, 1906.

A recommendation for an education for diplomats that could be applied to several other careers.

White, Henry. *Diplomacy and Politics*. An address delivered before the American Historical Association, Washington, D.C., December 30, 1915. Washington: American Historical Association, 1916.

A statement of the need for professional diplomats, profoundly influenced by the course of war in Europe. Displays ambivalence toward European diplomats—liking their methods, but distrusting their aims.

Periodicals and Articles

American Consular Bulletin, 1-V, 1919-24.

The professional journal of the consular service, published from 1919 until the amalgamation of the consular and diplomatic services. Every issue contains articles on professionalism and consular attitudes. An indispensable source.

"American Diplomats," *Nation,* CXXV, No. 1 (July 6, 1927), pp. 5-6.

A liberal attack on the Foreign Service officer's insularity, which briefly dissects the contradictions in the diplomats' outlook.

American Foreign Service Journal, VI-XLIII, 1924-71.

The successor to the *American Consular Bulletin* and official organ of the American Foreign Service Association. Contains many accounts of the organization of the Foreign Service in the five years after passage of the Rogers Act.

Argyris, Chris. "Top Management Dilemma: Company Needs vs. Individual Development," *Personnel,* XXXII (1955), pp. 115-54.

An explanation of the primacy of human feelings in personnel administration.

———— . "Understanding Human Behavior in Organizations," *Modern Organizational Theory,* Mason Haire, ed. (New York: John Wiley, 1959), pp. 115-54.

Argues that knowledge of actual personal relations are more important for understanding organization than is knowledge of formal structure.

Belmont, Perry. "The First Line of National Defense," *North American Review,* CCI (June 1915), pp. 884-89.

One of the many suggestions that trained diplomatic specialists were as important as a military force in maintaining America's status as a world power.

Bendix, Reinhard. "Bureaucracy," *Encyclopedia of the Social Sciences,* Vol. II, (New York: Macmillan Co. and the Free Press, 1968), pp. 206-19.

The best introductory survey of an important subject in sociology.

———— . "Bureaucracy: The Problem and Its Setting," *American Sociological Review,* XOI (1947), pp. 493-507.

A swift review and critique of the classic works of bureaucracy theory.

Bishop, A. L. "The Recent Reforms in the Consular Service of the United States," *Yale Review,* XVI, No. 2 (May 1907), pp. 39-55.

A good guide through the tortured history of consular reform in the administration of Theodore Roosevelt.

Blau, Peter M. "Co-operation and Competition in a Bureaucracy," *American Journal of Sociology,* LIX (1954), pp. 530-35.

Explains the nonorganizational goals of members of a government office.

Bliven, Bruce. "The Diplomat as High Priest," *New Republic,* XXIX (January 4, 1922), pp. 7-9.

A liberal editor's opposition to the Rogers Act. Summarized in the five words of the title, the diplomats' conception of their role.

Borah, William E. "The Perils of Secret Treaty Making: How Conspiring Diplomacy and Public Ignorance Create War," *Forum,* LX (December 1918), pp. 657-67.

Crucial for understanding why Borah supported the Rogers reforms. He despised European diplomats for their secrecy, but believed that American Foreign Service officers should apply the knowledge of the Old and the aims of the New Diplomacy.

Bowles, Chester. "Toward a New Diplomacy," *Foreign Affairs,* XL (January 1962), pp. 244-51.

A congratulatory essay on the Kennedy administration's efforts to improve coordination of overseas activities under the control of American ambassadors.

Carr, Wilbur J. "To Bring Our Foreign Affairs up to Date," *Independent,* CV (February 26, 1921), pp. 207-30.

One of Carr's public relations efforts.

Chapin, Seldin. "The United States Foreign Service," *Fortune Magazine,* XXXIV (July 1946), pp. 191-212.

Contains worthwhile impressions on the social background of diplomats in the previous fifty years.

_____. "Training for Foreign Service," In Joseph McLean, ed., *The Public Service and University Education* (Princeton: Princeton University Press, 1949), pp. 104-20.

An unsuccessful attempt to define the relationship between technical and general knowledge in Foreign Service practice.

Craig, Gordon A. "The Professional Diplomat and His Problems, 1919-1939," *World Politics,* IV, No. 2 (January 1952), pp. 145-58.

A brilliant essay on the difficulties encountered by the dynastic diplomats of Europe when they tried to apply the methods of the Old Diplomacy in the era of public supervision of foreign affairs.

Crawford, William H. "An Interview with Charles Evans Hughes," *World's Work,* XL, No. 6 (June 1921), pp. 129-31.

The Secretary of State presents his view that modern international relations require the sure direction of career diplomats.

Dennis, Alfred L.P. "The Foreign Service of the United States," *North American Review,* CCXIX (February 1924), pp. 175-85.

One of the diplomats' attempts to generate public support for the Rogers Act.

Destler, I. M. "The Nixon NSC: Can One Man Do?" *Foreign Policy,* No. 5 (Winter 1971-72), pp. 28-40.

A brilliant, brief survey of the task expansion of the National Security Council in the Nixon administration.

Dimock, Marshall E. "Bureaucracy Self-Examined," *Public Administration Review,* IV, No. 3 (July 1944), pp. 276-89.
Describes the intellectual self-doubts often expressed by American civil servants. Useful for comparing Foreign Service officers to other government officials.

Egan, Maurice Francis. "More Business in Diplomacy," *Colliers,* LXX (February 4, 1922), pp. 22-26.
The most important of a five-part series of articles that Egan wrote for *Colliers* on the Foreign Service. Recounts the new commercial role of diplomats after the First World War. Intended to show how diplomats do not disdain trade.

Einstein, Lewis D. "American Peace Dreams," *National Review,* LXIV (January 1915), pp. 837-50.
Einstein's statement that the United States could not remain neutral in the European war. A clear violation of the professional code of obedience to the political directors of Foreign policy.

_____. "The Contraband Difficulty: An American Difficulty." Letter to the Editor, *The Times* (London), December 31, 1914.
A plea to Englishmen to understand American insistence upon neutral rights. Einstein implies that Britain needn't have worried about American hostility.

_____. "A Great Danger." Letter to the Editor, *The Spectator* (London), No. 114 (January 30, 1915), pp. 152-55.
Explains the danger if the United States were to have persisted in her neutrality.

_____. "The Origins of the War." Letter to the Editor, *The Times* (London), August 4, 1917.
On the third anniversary of the war's outbreak, Einstein claims that Germany's overbearing diplomacy was responsible for it.

_____. "The War and American National Policy." *National Review,* LXIV (November 1914), pp. 357-76.
Einstein's first criticism of President Woodrow Wilson's neutrality. In this article Einstein applies the principles he had established in *American Foreign Policy.*

_____. "The United States and Anglo-German Rivalry," *National Review,* LX (January 1913), pp. 736-50.
The article which earned Einstein his reputation as a keen prophet of international affairs. In it he predicted that the Anglo-German rivalry was likely to lead to a war in which the United States would have a vital interest.

Eisenstein, S. N. "Bureaucracy and Bureaucratization," *Current Sociology,* VII (1958), pp. 99-124.
A review of the literature of bureaucracy and a lament that formal organizations squeezed the spirit out of modern society.

Ellis, William T. "Frank Words on the 'Trained' Diplomats," *Outlook,* CXXVII (March 1921), pp. 381-89.
A sharp, unfriendly exposé of the contradictions in the diplomats' idea of technical and general knowledge.

"Foreign Service Reorganization," *Congressional Digest,* V, No. 1 (January 1924), entire issue.

Devoted to the Rogers Act, containing articles by John Jacob Rogers, Henry Cabot Lodge, J. Charles Linthicum, Tom Connally, and R. Walton Moore. Recapitulates the Congressional debate on professional diplomacy that took place in February 1923.

Form, William. "Occupations and Careers," *International Encyclopedia of the Social Sciences,* XI (New York: The Macmillan Co. and the Free Press, 1968), pp. 252-53.

Fox, William T. R. "Interwar International Relational Research: The American Experience," *World Politics,* II, No. 2 (January 1949), pp. 67-79.

A bitter, disillusioned attack by a "realist" on the "utopianism" of James T. Shotwell, James W. Garner, Manley O. Hudson, and Charles Seymour.

———— and Annette Fox. "The Teaching of International Relations in the United States," *World Politics,* XIII, No. 3 (April 1961), pp. 309-61.

Repeats the charges Fox made in his 1949 article, but shows satisfaction at the fact that the post-World-War-II teaching of international relations had been more "realistic."

Furniss, Edgar S., Jr. "The Contribution of Nicholas John Spyckman to the Study of International Politics," *World Politics,* IV, No. 3 (April 1952), pp. 382-401.

Praises the "realism" of Spyckman, while heaping scorn upon the "utopianism" of other international relations theorists in the interwar period.

Gerver, Israel, and J. Bensman. "Toward a Sociology of Expertness," *Social Forces,* XXXII (1954), pp. 226-35.

A categorization of "experts" in accordance with the functions they perform within organizations or society.

Hammond, Paul Y. "NSC-68: Prologue to Rearmament," *Politics, Strategy and Defense Budgets.* Edited by Warner Schilling, Paul Y. Hammond, and Glenn Snyder (New York: Columbia University Press, 1962), pp. 267-378.

A case study of Foreign Service officers' reluctance to make specific, detailed plans.

Harvey, George. "The Diplomats of Democracy," *North American Review,* CXCIX (February 1914), pp. 161-74.

A confused plea for trained diplomats who both followed and formed public attitudes on foreign affairs.

Heinrichs, Waldo, Jr. "Bureaucracy and Professionalism in the Development of American Career Diplomacy." In *Twentieth Century American Foreign Policy.* Edited by John Braemer, Robert H. Braemer, and David Brody (Columbus: Ohio State University Press, 1971), pp. 119-206.

A splendid administrative history that supersedes the work of Warren Ilchman. Limited to a discussion of bureaucratic development; does not treat Foreign Service officers' ideas on world politics or foreign policies.

Hickman, Martin, and Neil Hollander. "Undergraduate Origin as a Factor in Elite Recruitment and Mobility: The Foreign Service—A Case Study," *Western Political Quarterly,* XIX (June 1966), pp. 337-42.

An attempt to document quantitatively the greater success in the Foreign

Service of graduates from private eastern colleges. Concentrates on the post-World-War-II period. Confirms, however, the findings of this essay for the earlier period and the conclusions of the Foreign Affairs Personnel Studies of the Carnegie Endowment.

Hill, David Jayne. "Shall We Stabilize Our Diplomatic Service?" *Harper's,* CXXVIII (April 1914), pp. 31-36.

A professional's plea for a guaranteed career.

Hudson, Manley O. "The Liberals and the League," *Nation,* CXVI (April 4, 1923), pp. 383-85.

A Wilsonian's attack upon disillusioned liberals' repudiation of the League of Nations. Hudson also accuses professional diplomats of a destructive cynicism.

Hughes, Charles Evans. "Some Aspects of the Work of the State Department," *American Journal of International* Law, XVII, No. 3 (July 1922), pp. 348-54.

Hughes discusses the intimate connection between commerce and foreign policy and how professional diplomats best understood that connection.

————. "Some Observations on the Conduct of Our Foreign Relations," *American Journal of International Law,* XVII, No. 3 (July 1922), pp. 355-64.

Hughes's cogent argument that if the United States reduced her armed forces, she should logically augment her Foreign Service.

Janowitz, Morris, and Deil Wright. "The Prestige of Public Employment, 1929 and 1954," *Public Administration Review,* XVI, No. 1 (Winter 1956), pp. 11-14.

Detects greater public respect in the later period because public service careers became increasingly professional. Touches very briefly upon the distinction between generalism and specialization.

Kennan, George F. "The Needs of the Foreign Service." In Joseph McLean, ed., *The Public Service and University Education.* Princeton: Princeton University Press, 1949.

For Kennan the Service's greatest need was for more public deference. Attempts to explain why diplomacy is an art.

Kraft, Joseph. "The Comeback of the State Department," *Harper's Magazine,* CCXXIII (November 1961), pp. 43-50.

A quaint, hopeful account of the Kennedy administration's faith in the State Department. Nearly all of its predictions proved wrong.

Lansing, Robert E. "The Proposed Consolidation of the Diplomatic and Consular Service of the United States," *American Journal of International Law,* XVIII, No. 2 (April 1923), pp. 121-29.

Gives critical support to the Rogers Bill, but suggests that diplomats cavalierly denied the provisions of the proposed law to drafting officers in the Department of State. Lansing's views are an indication of why diplomats found him difficult to deal with.

Leacacos, John P. "The Nixon NSC: Kissinger's Apparat." *Foreign Policy,* No. 5 (Winter 1971-72), pp. 3-27.

A tabulation of the activities of the National Security Council from 1969 to 1971.

Loomis, Francis B. "The Foreign Service of the United States," *North American Review,* CLXIX (September 1899), pp. 603-09.

An impression of how the years after the Spanish-American War would demand reorganized diplomatic and consular services.

McAneny, George. "How Other Countries Do It," *Century,* LVII (February 1899), pp. 604-07.
An early report on Foreign Service reorganization in Europe, emphasizing American diplomats' sense of inferiority to their European counterparts.

McCamy, James L. "Rebuilding the Foreign Service," *Harper's Magazine,* CCXIX (November 1959), pp. 80-89.
Advocates the creation of a corps of specialists in policy-planning at every level of the Foreign Service.

McClintock, Samuel. "A Unified Foreign Service," *American Political Science Review,* XVI, No. 4 (November 1922), pp. 381-89.
McClintock, dean of a commercial college, leader of the Foreign Service training movement, and friend of Wilbur J. Carr, presents his view that commercial expansion demanded an amalgamated Foreign Service.

Maslow, Albert P. "Evaluating Training and Experience." In J. J. Donovan, ed. *Recruitment and Selection in the Public Service* (Chicago: Public Personnel Association, 1968), pp. 239-54.
Report on the persistent problem of assessing the value of technical knowledge for a civil service recruit. Maslow concludes that claims of personnel officers to scientific objectivity were unjustified.

Miller, August L., Jr. "The New State Department," *American Journal of International Law,* XXXIII, No. 3 (July 1939), pp. 500-19.
Discusses the desire of Foreign Service officers since 1924 to gain more political authority.

Moore, John Bassett. "Review of Charles C. Hyde, *International Law, Chiefly as Interpreted by the United States,*" *Columbia Law Review,* XXIII, No. 1 (January 1923), pp. 83-85.
A vehicle for Moore's view that the American understanding of international law was both "realistic" and high minded.

————. "Review of Sir Ernest Satow, *A Guide to Diplomatic Practice,*" *American Historical Review,* XXIII, No. 4 (December 1918), pp. 634-38.
Admires Satow's worldly wisdom but faults him for underestimating the democratic tendencies in American diplomatic practice.

Morrison, Donald R. "The Interview in Personnel Selection." In J. J. Donovan, ed., *Recruitment and Selection in the Public Service.* Chicago: Public Personnel Association, 1968.
A very useful review of fifty years of literature on the problem of scientific measurement of character by means of oral examinations.

Morse, Muriel, and Joseph W. Hawthorne. "Some Notes on Oral Exams," *Public Personnel Review,* VII, No. 1 (January 1946), pp. 15-18.
Confirms the State Department's practice that oral exams reflected the shared, unstated assumptions of the examiners.

Mosher, Frederick C. "Careers and Career Service in the Public Service," *Public Personnel Review,* XXIV, No. 1 (January 1963), pp. 546-71.
The chairman of the Carnegie Endowment's Committee on Foreign Affairs

Personnel presents his view that the Foreign Service exhibited formal professional characteristics in the four decades after passage of the Rogers Act.

Mosher, William E. "Public Service as a Career," *Annals of the American Academy of Political and Social Science,* CLXIX, No. 2 (April 1933), pp. 120-43.
Contains approving references to the professionalization of the Foreign Service.

Nelson, Henry Loomis. "The Need for Trained Diplomats and Consuls," *Harper's Weekly,* XLV (July 17, 1901), pp. 13-19.
Argues that the increasing complexity of commercial rivalries demanded full-time foreign affairs experts.

Norton, Henry K. "Foreign Office Organization: A Comparison of the Organization of the British, French, German, and Italian Foreign Offices with That of the Department of State of the United States of America," *Annals of the American Academy of Political and Social Sciences,* CXLIII, Supplement (May 1929), pp. i-ix, 1-86.
An extremely rich source of facts about the attitudes of consuls and diplomats toward one another in the four years after passage of the Rogers Act. The comparative material, based upon extensive interviews with European and American officials in 1928-29, indicates that the American Foreign Service was less secure professionally than its European counterparts.

Osborne, John Ball. "Trade Protection Work of the Department of State," *Pan-American Union Bulletin,* XXXIII (December 1911), pp. 1134-36.
The Chief of the State Department's Bureau of Trade Relations explains the commercial work of the Foreign Service.

Parsons, Talcott. "Professions," *International Encyclopedia of the Social Sciences,* XII (New York: The Macmillan Co. and the Free Press, 1968), pp. 536-47.
A surprisingly lucid essay on the literature of the development and function of professions and professionals.

Patterson, Richard S. "The Foreign Service: Four Decades of Development," *Department of State Newsletter,* No. 39 (July 1964), pp. 11-14.
Praises the growth of the Foreign Service's political influence.

Perkins, Dexter. "The Department of State and American Public Opinion." In *The Diplomats: 1919-1939.* Edited by Gordon A. Graig and Felix Gilbert (Princeton: Princeton University Press, 1953), pp. 282-308.
Claims that an isolationist public restrained the Department of State from pursuing a forward overseas policy.

Pfaff, William. "Reflections: The Statesman and the Conqueror," *The New Yorker,* June 3, 1972.
A pithy description of the return to the Old Diplomacy in the Nixon administration.

Phillips, William. "Cleaning Our Diplomatic House," *Forum,* LXIII (February 1920), pp. 161-57.
An important source for understanding Phillips's intentions at the end of the First World War.

Rich, H. Thomson. "Our Diplomatic Service: The Facts," *Forum,* LVI (November 1916), pp. 513-19.
Criticizes public disdain for professional diplomats.

Root, Elihu. "The Need for a Popular Understanding of International Law," *American Journal of International Law,* I, No. 1 (January 1905), pp. 5-9.
Explains what international law did for commerce and peace.

———. "A Requisite for the Succession of Popular Diplomacy," *Foreign Affairs,* I, No. 1 (September 1922), pp. 21-34.
Explains how popular diplomacy needed the skill of career diplomats to guide it.

Selznick, Phillip. "Foundations of the Theory of Organization," *American Sociological Review,* XIII (1948), pp. 25-35.
A survey of previous writings and Selznick's brilliant exposition of his ideas of cooptation and goal displacement in organizations.

Shaw, G. Howland. "The American Foreign Service," *Foreign Affairs,* XIV, No. 2 (January 1936), pp. 323-33.
A cursory history of the professionalization movement.

Simpson, R. L. "Vertical and Horizontal Communication in Formal Organizations," *Administrative Science Quarterly,* IV (1959), pp. 188-96.
Notes that members of organizations communicated laterally to each other as often as to their superiors.

Stein, Harold J. "The Foreign Service Act of 1946." In Harold J. Stein, ed., *Public Administration and Political Development* (New York: Harcourt, Brace and World, 1952), pp. 661-737.
A perceptive study of the aims of Foreign Service reformers during World War II, showing how the legislative history of the Act of 1946 resembled the lobbying for the Rogers Act.

Stowell, Ellery C. "The Ban on Alien Marriages in the Foreign Service," *American Journal of the International Law,* XXXI, No. 1 (January 1937), pp. 91-94.
The history of a minor skirmish in the struggle to make the Foreign Service reflect nationalistic attitudes.

———. "The Conference of American Teachers of International Law," *American Journal of International Law,* XIX, No. 3 (July 1925), pp. 542-47.
Records some disputes between "realists" and "utopians."

———. "Cramping Our Foreign Service," *American Journal of International Law,* XXIX, No. 2 (April 1935), pp. 314-17.
Stowell expresses his unhappiness at the fact that the Roosevelt administration did not follow the practice of the twenties of deferring to the Foreign Service.

———. "Examinations for the American Foreign Service," *American Journal of International Law,* XXIV, No. 3 (July 1930), pp. 577-81.
Reports on the quality of examinations and applicants. Vital information about women applicants and interesting on Stowell's touchiness regarding the question of women in the Foreign Service.

———. "The Foreign Service School," *American Journal of International Law,* XIXX, No. 4 (October 1925), pp. 763-68.
Reports the hopes of developing a diplomatic outlook in the new Foreign Service School.

———. "The Moses-Linthicum Act and the Foreign Service," *American Journal of International Law,* XXV, No. 3 (July 1931), pp. 515-18.

Records the consuls' satisfaction with the Act, but also criticizes the Congress for drafting the law on its own, without consulting the career men in the Department, and compares the law unfavorably to the Rogers Act.

―――. "Reforms in the State Department and Foreign Service," *American Journal of International Law,* XXII, No. 3 (July 1928), pp. 606-10.
Reports the relations between diplomats and consuls in the four years after passage of the Rogers Act.

Sweetser, Arthur. "Why the State Department Should Be Reorganized," *World's Work,* XXXIX (March 1920), pp. 511-15.
Claims that commercial rivalry and political complexity after Versailles demanded critical Foreign Service officers.

Weber, Max. "Politics as a Vocation." *From Max Weber: Essays in Sociology.* Edited by Hans Gerth and C. Wright Mills (New York: Oxford University Press, 1946), pp. 77-128.
A classic statement of Weber's distinction between men who live for and men who live off politics.

Williams, William Appleman. "Brooks Adams and American Expansion," *New England Quarterly,* XXV, No. 3 (June 1952), pp. 217-32.
An intelligent discussion of the rationality of the writing of a misunderstood publicist.

Woodward, Rear Admiral Clark H. "Relations between the Navy and the Foreign Service," *American Journal of International Law,* XXXIII, No. 2 (April 1939), pp. 283-91.
A former Minister to Nicaragua explains how the aims of military and Foreign Service officers were similar, i.e., the use of force and persuasion to maintain peace.

Secondary Sources

Adams, Brooks. *America's Economic Supremacy.* New York: Macmillan, 1900.
An expansionist's argument that influenced Foreign Service reformers.

―――. *The New Empire.* New York: Macmillan, 1902.
A more famous work by Adams on the American global role after the Spanish-American War.

Adams, Henry. *The Education of Henry Adams.* Boston: Houghton-Mifflin, 1968.
This fascinating confession contains references to professional diplomats and Adams's ideas on foreign policy.

Adler, Selig. *The Isolationist Impulse: Its Twentieth Century Manifestation.* New York: Thomas Y. Crowell, 1957.
More a political broadside than a work of history, it criticizes Americans for rejecting their global responsibilities.

Argyris, Chris. *Executive Leadership.* New York: Harper, 1953.
Argyris's first statement of the biological functions of complex organizations.

―――. *Personality and Organization.* New York: Harper, 1957.
Explains the effects on personality of working in an organization and the impact upon organizational goals of personality changes.

Bailey, Thomas A. *Woodrow Wilson and the Great Betrayal*. New York: Macmillan, 1945.
An account of the vicissitudes of the Treaty of Versailles in the United States Senate. Better on the legislative history of the Treaty's rejection than on the theories of world politics of Wilson and his opponents. Believes the repudiation of the Treaty began a decade of isolationism.

Barnard, Chester I. *The Function of the Executive*. Cambridge: Harvard University Press, 1938.
Asserts that executives succeeded when they persuaded rather than coerced their subordinates. Barnard's informal practice of leadership was often followed by members of the former diplomatic branch in their competition with the former consuls in the twenties.

Barnes, Harry Elmer. *The Genesis of the World War*. 2 vols. New York: Macmillan, 1926.
A disillusioned liberal criticizes professional diplomats of hoodwinking the public before 1914.

Barnes, William, and John H. Morgan. *The Foreign Service of the United States: Origins, Development and Functions*. Washington: Government Printing Office, 1962.
An official history written by two Foreign Service officers. The administrative history is not as penetrating as that in Ilchman's *Professional Diplomacy in the United States,* and the book lacks an analysis of the political outlook of diplomats.

Beale, Howard K. *Theodore Roosevelt and the Rise of America to World Power*. Baltimore: Johns Hopkins University Press, 1956.
An exceptionally good essay on the intellectual basis of foreign policy in the early twentieth century.

Bendiner, Robert F. *The Riddle of the Department of State*. New York: Farrar, Rinehart, 1943.
A journalist ridicules professional diplomats as "cookie pushers." Venomous.

Bingham, Walter V. *Oral Examinations in Civil Service Recruitment: With Special Reference to Experiences in Pennsylvania*. Chicago: Civil Service Assembly of the United States and Canada, 1939.
A survey of recruitment practices in the twenty years after the First World War, which denied the possibility of a scientific standard of selection.

———— and Bruce V. Moore. *How to Interview*. New York: Harper Brothers, 1931.
The first edition of a standard work in personnel administration. Discusses some of the difficulties in administering oral examinations when examiners are unsure what qualities they desire.

Blau, Peter M. *The Dynamics of Bureaucracy*. 2nd rev. ed. Chicago: University of Chicago Press, 1963.
A theoretical statement and two case studies of the informal lines of communications, friendships, antipathies, and work habits of members of bureaucracies. Very useful in explaining how informal arrangements, like the Family of diplomats, contribute to organizational success.

Blum, John Morton. *The Republican Roosevelt*. Cambridge: Harvard University Press, 1954.

A keen essay which explains some of the tensions in Roosevelt's attitudes toward world politics which resembled those of professional diplomats.

Boulding, Kenneth E. *The Organizational Revolution*. New York: Harper, 1953.
A provocative discussion of the effect upon contemporary ethics caused by the rise of complex organizations since the nineteenth century.

Brandes, Joseph. *Herbert Hoover and Economic Diplomacy: Department of Commerce Policy, 1921-1929*. Pittsburgh, University of Pittsburgh Press, 1962.
A flawed book on an extremely important subject. Contains an account of relations between the Departments of State and Commerce.

Bryce, James. *International Relations: Eight Lectures Delivered in the United States in 1921*. New York: Macmillan, 1922.
The round-table discussions Bryce led at the Williamstown Institute. Praises professional diplomats and doubts the possibilities of popular direction of foreign affairs.

Buffington, Arthur H. *The Institute of Politics: Its First Decade*. Williamstown, Mass.: Institute of Politics, 1931.
The President of Williams College explains how the first ten years of the Williamstown Institute had helped provide the public with a deeper awareness of American world obligations.

Buhite, Russell D. *Nelson T. Johnson and American Policy toward China, 1925-1941*. East Lansing: Michigan State University Press, 1968.
A straightforward political biography of a diplomat who played a minor role in the professionalization of the Service, but was instrumental in setting U.S. policy toward China.

Carr, Edward Hallett. *The Twenty Years' Crisis: An Introduction to the Study of International Relations*. London: Macmillan, 1939.
An early, brilliant, yet flawed, exposition of the "realist" viewpoint on world politics.

Carr-Saunders, A. W., and P. M. Wilson. *The Professions*. Oxford: Oxford University Press, 1933.
An excellent introduction to the various definitions of professionalism.

Cattell, Raymond B. *The Description and Measurement of Personality*. New York: World Book Co., 1957.
A psychology text which casts doubt upon the use of interviews to measure personality "scientifically."

Childs, J. Rives. *The American Foreign Service*. New York: Henry Holt, 1948.
A diplomat discusses the form of the Service, paying special attention to the reforms of 1946. The material on the earlier period comes primarily from Tracy H. Lay's *The Foreign Service of the United States*.

Coolidge, Archibald Carey. *The United States as a World Power*. New York: Macmillan, 1910.
Professor Coolidge's statement on American global interests and the need for a new Foreign Service. An important source of the diplomatic outlook.

Coolidge, Harold J., and Robert H. Lord. *Archibald Carey Coolidge: Life and Letters*. Boston: Houghton-Mifflin, 1932.
A dull biography, but very interesting letters.

Crane, Katherine E. *Mr. Carr of State: Forty-seven Years in the Department of State*. New York: St. Martin's Press, 1961.

An unanalytical biography of an exceptionally important leader of Foreign Service reformers. Carr's complex personality, political beliefs, and theories of professionalism deserve more serious attention than Crane gives them.

Cranston, Allan M. *The Killing of Peace*. New York: Viking, 1945.

Ostensibly an historical account of the Senate's refusal to ratify the Versailles Treaty in 1919, but actually a political pamphlet designed to generate support for the United Nations in 1945.

Croly, Herbert. *The Promise of American Life*. New York: Macmillan, 1909.

A progressive plea for the simultaneous reform of internal and foreign policies. The forward foreign policy Croly advocates resembles that of the Foreign Service reformers. Croly, however, did not mention professional diplomacy.

Curti, Merle, and Vernon Carstenson. *The University of Wisconsin: A History, 1848-1925*. 2 vols. Madison: University of Wisconsin Press, 1949.

Good institutional history, which discusses the "Wisconsin idea" of graduate education.

Dallek, Robert. *Democrat and Diplomat: The Life of William E. Dodd*. New York: Oxford University Press, 1969.

A good biography, which concentrates on Dodd's ambassadorship to Germany from 1933 to 1938, but which also contains some information on Dodd's Wilsonianism in the 1920s.

Dalton, Melville. *Men Who Manage: Fusion of Feeling and Theory in Administration*. New York: Wiley and Sons, 1959.

An excellent case study of the effects of informal behavior patterns and personality in a business organization.

Dodd, William E. *Woodrow Wilson and His Work*. Garden City, New York: Doubleday, Page, 1921.

The credo of a Wilsonian.

Downs, Anthony. *Inside Bureaucracy*. Boston: Little, Brown, 1967.

A political economist presents several hundred provocative general hypotheses about complex organizations.

Dulles, Foster Rhea. *America's Rise to World Power, 1898-1954*. New York: Harper and Row, 1954.

A popular diplomatic history which reveals more about the politics of the 1950s than about the foreign policy of earlier years.

Einstein, Lewis. *American Foreign Policy by a Diplomatist*. Boston and New York: Houghton-Mifflin, 1909.

Einstein's important statement on the relations between professional diplomacy and a forward-looking foreign policy.

————. *A Prophecy of the War*. Foreword by Theodore Roosevelt. New York: Columbia University Press, 1917.

A collection of Einstein's journalism of the years 1913-16, which describes the increasing European rivalry and America's stake in the war.

Ellis, L. Ethan. *Frank B. Kellogg and American Foreign Policy*. New Brunswick: Rutgers University Press, 1961.

A cursory survey of Kellogg's tenure as Secretary of State, containing a few references to the Foreign Service in the post-Rogers-Act years.

Etzioni, Amitai. *Modern Organizations*. Foundations of Modern Sociology Series. Englewood Ciiffs, N.J.: Prentice-Hall, 1964.
A fine introduction to the theory of bureaucracy from Max Weber to the 1960s.

Ferrell, Robert H. *Depression Diplomacy: Hoover-Stimson Foreign Policy, 1929-1933*. New Haven: Yale University Press, 1957.
An intelligent but misleading account of American foreign policy in the twenties, written from a "realistic" point of view.

————. *Peace in the Time*. New Haven: Yale University Press, 1952.
A realist's brutal attack on the Kellogg-Briand Pact. Ferrell finds the professional diplomats' resistance to the pact the single redeeming episode in an otherwise foolish exercise.

Forcey, Charles. *The Crossroads of Liberalism: Croly, Lippmann, Weyl and the Progressive Era*. New York: Oxford University Press, 1961.
A brilliant discussion of the tensions in progressive social thought. Useful in placing the intellectual inconsistencies of the diplomatic mind in proper perspective.

Foster, John W. *The Practice of Diplomacy as Illustrated in the Foreign Relations of the United States*. Boston: Houghton-Mifflin, 1906.
A former Secretary of State discusses the democratic principles which distinguished American professional diplomacy from that of Europeans.

Fowler, W. B. *Anglo-American Relations, 1917-1918: The Role of Sir William Wiseman*. Princeton: Princeton University Press, 1969.
An intriguing account of the use of special agents in wartime, revealing the small part the State Department played in the diplomacy of the First World War.

Frankel, L. K., and A. Fleisher. *The Human Factor in Industry*. New York: Macmillan, 1920.
A guide for personnel officers which discusses the use of interviews in hiring. Influenced State Department practice.

Garner, James W. *International Law and the World War*. 2 vols. New York: Longmans, Green, 1920.
A Wilsonian idealist recounts with regret how the First World War had damaged the fabric of the law of nations.

Gelfand, Lawrence F. *The Inquiry: American Preparations for Peace, 1917-1919*. New Haven: Yale University Press, 1963.
A lengthy history of the research organization which provoked much jealousy on the part of professional diplomats.

Glad, Betty. *Charles Evans Hughes and the Illusions of Innocence: A Study in American Diplomacy*. Urbana: University of Illinois Press, 1966.
A psychological explanation of Hughes's behavior, which argues cogently that his advocacy of Foreign Service reform was rooted in his meliorative view of world politics.

Haber, Samuel. *Efficiency and Uplift: Scientific Management in the Progressive Era, 1890-1920*. Chicago: University of Chicago Press, 1964.
A shrewd discussion of the progressive desire to apply social science to social problems.

Harr, John E. *The Professional Diplomat*. Princeton: Princeton University Press, 1969.
A penetrating analysis of the attitudes of American professional diplomats in the 1960s. Fine bibliography on professional diplomacy.

Hartz, Louis. *The Liberal Tradition in America: An Interpretation of American Political Thought since the Revolution*. New York: Harcourt, Brace, 1955.
An enlightening introduction to the theory of American exceptionalism which inspired diplomats.

Heinrichs, Waldo H., Jr. *American Ambassador: Joseph C. Grew and the Development of the United States Diplomatic Corps*. Boston: Little, Brown, 1966.
An excellent biography of a career diplomat, which places Grew's career in the context of the professionalization of the Foreign Service. The book is slightly marred by the author's great admiration for his subject, a difficulty common to many biographers.

Hendrick, Burton J. *The Life and Letters of Walter Hines Page*. 3 vols. Garden City, N.Y. Doubleday, Page, 1922-25.
Three ponderous volumes which contain some information on relations between Ambassador Page and his professional staff.

Hofstadter, Richard. *The Age of Reform*. New York: Vintage Press, 1955.
A provocative essay, containing an account of the anxieties of professionals in the forty years after the Civil War.

Hoxie, R. Gordon, et al. *A History of the Faculty of Political Science of Columbia University*. New York: Columbia University Press, 1955.
Recounts the history of the Yale-Columbia program in Foreign Service subjects.

Hulen, Bertram. *Inside the Department of State*. New York: McGraw-Hill, 1939.
Supposedly an exposé by a journalist, but it would not seem that Hulen got past the outer lobby.

Ilchman, Warren Frederick. *Professional Diplomacy in the United States, 1779-1939: A Study in Administrative History*. Chicago: University of Chicago Press, 1961.
Proved an indispensable source for this essay. Ilchman compiled an excellent statistical profile of the Foreign Service from 1900-30. His account is distorted by his commitment to the "realistic" criticism of Robert Osgood, which prevented him from analyzing the political outlook of diplomats.

Institute for Government Research. *The Bureau of Foreign and Domestic Commerce* (Service Monograph of the United States Government, No. 29). Baltimore: Johns Hopkins University Press, 1924.
Discusses relations between the State and Commerce Departments.

Jacobson, Harold K., and Eric Stein. *Diplomats, Scientists and Politicians: The United States and the Nuclear Test Ban Negotiations*. Ann Arbor: University of Michigan Press, 1966.
A case study of the contending views of international relations, science, and the negotiations of the several groups who made up the American teams of negotiators for the Moscow Treaty of 1963. Indicates that Foreign Service officers doubted the competence of scientists or politicians to conduct negotiations.

James, Henry. *Nathaniel Hawthorne*. London: Macmillan, 1879.
    James's essay on American culture, written two years after he had moved to
    London to live. Contains a reference to America's lack of a diplomatic service
    as contributing to the innocence of Americans.
Jones, Chester Lloyd. *The Consular Service of the United States*. New York:
    Macmillan, 1906.
    A former consul and future University of Wisconsin colleague of Stanley K.
    Hornbeck expresses the need for consular reform.
Jordan, David Starr. *Imperial Democracy*. New York: Macmillan, 1899.
    The President of Stanford University describes the dangers inherent in overseas
    expansion. The books of Coolidge and Reinsch were designed, in part, as a
    response to Jordan.
Kash, Don. *The Politics of Space Cooperation*. South Bend, Ind.: Purdue University
    Press, 1967.
    A brief account of the bureaucratic rivalries (in which Foreign Service officers
    played a prominent role) over American policy toward international coopera-
    tion in outer space.
Kennan, George F. *American Diplomacy, 1900-1950*. Chicago: University of
    Chicago Press, 1951.
    A diplomat's criticism of the legalism and moralism of amateur foreign-policy
    directors.
———— . *Realities of American Foreign Policy*. Princeton: Princeton University
    Press, 1954.
    A "realist's" statement of foreign policy objectives for the fifties.
Kirk, Grayson L. *The Study of International Relations in the United States*. New
    York: The Council on Foreign Relations, 1948.
    A "realist's" criticism of international-relations courses before the Second
    World War.
Laird, Donald. *The Psychology of Selecting Men*. New York: McGraw-Hill, 1925.
    Discusses oral examinations as a method of finding congenial men.
Lay, Tracy Hollingsworth. *The Foreign Service of the United States*. New York:
    Prentice-Hall, 1925.
    An invaluable, popular exposition of the consular point of view.
Levin, N. Gordon, Jr. *Woodrow Wilson and World Politics: The American Response
    to War and Revolution*. New York: Oxford University Press, 1967.
    A provocative application of Louis Hartz's theory of American exceptionalism
    to foreign policy analysis.
Link, H. C. *Employment Psychology*. New York: Macmillan, 1919.
    One of Wilbur Carr's sources for developing a "scientific" scheme of person-
    nel selection in the twenties.
McCamy, James L. *The Administration of American Foreign Affairs*. New York:
    Alfred A. Knopf, 1952.
    Suggests that world responsibilities demanded a complex State Department
    organization.
———— . *he Conduct of the New Diplomacy*. New York: Harper and Row, 1964.

Tries to define the generalism of American diplomats.

Mahan, Alfred Thayer. *The Influence of Sea Power upon History*. Boston: Little, Brown, 1890.

Geopolitics, which profoundly influenced the thinking of Coolidge, Einstein, and other professional diplomats.

————— . *The Interest of America in International Conditions*. Boston: Little, Brown, 1910.

Mahan's journalism in the previous decade.

————— . *The Interest of America in Sea Power: Past and Present*. Boston: Little, Brown, 1898.

Mahan's call for a forward-looking foreign policy in the twentieth century.

————— . *The Problem of Asia and Its Effect upon International Policies*. Boston: Little, Brown, 1900.

Several articles which demanded American participation in the colonial rivalry in East Asia.

Maslow, Albert P. *Oral Tests: A Survey of Current Practices*. Chicago: Civil Service Assembly of the United States and Canada, 1952.

A pessimistic survey of the accuracy of oral examinations.

Mathews, John Mabry. *The Conduct of American Foreign Relations*. New York: Century, 1922.

Suggests that professional diplomats be given more political authority. Often recommended by lecturers at the Foreign Service School.

Maxwell, Robert S. *LaFollette and the Rise of the Progressives in Wisconsin*, Madison: State Historical Society of Wisconsin, 1956.

Very informative on the attempts of University of Wisconsin professors, including Paul S. Reinsch, to enter the political arena.

Merton, Robert K., et al. *A Reader in Bureaucracy*. Glencoe, Illinois: The Free Press, 1952.

Contains over twenty selections from classic studies of bureaucracies. A good place to start exploring this rich literature.

Monson, R. Joseph, Jr., and Mark W. Cannon. *The Makers of Public Policy: American Power Groups and Their Ideologies*. New York: McGraw-Hill, 1965.

Contains a shrewd discussion of the self-doubts of American diplomats.

Moon, Parker T., ed. *A Syllabus on International Relations*. New York: Columbia University Press, 1925.

A very useful list of the books a "utopian" professor thought most valuable for the study of international relations.

Moore, Bruce V., ed. *The Personnel Interview: A Bibliography*. New York: Personnel Research Federation, 1928.

An extensive list of the literature on an important aspect of recruitment practices in the twenties.

Moore, John Bassett. *The Collected Papers of John Bassett Moore*. 6 vols. Edited by Edward M. Borchard. New Haven: Yale University Press, 1945.

A fine collection of Moore's essays and reviews, in which he explains his theories of international law and diplomacy.

———— . *International Law and Some Current Illusions*. New York: Macmillan, 1923.

Presents Moore's attack upon postwar "utopians" and disillusioned liberals.

———— . *The Principles of American Diplomacy*. New York: Harper and Brothers, 1918.

Expresses the commercial and democratic "realism" of American foreign policy.

Morgenthau, Hans J. *In Defense of the National Interest: A Critical Examination of United States Foreign Policy*. New York: Alfred A. Knopf, 1951.

A leading "realist" critic condemns the twentieth-century practice of American foreign policy.

Mosher, Frederick, and John E. Harr. *Programming Systems and Foreign Affairs Leadership: An Attempted innovation*. A Study Prepared for the Inter-University Case Program. New York: Oxford University Press, 1970.

Two of the leaders of the abortive attempts in the middle sixties to introduce a new budgeting system in the State Department narrate the history of the reform, tell why it failed, and present hopes for future State Department reform

Mosher, William E., and J. Donald Kingsley. *Public Personnel Administration*. New York: Harper Brothers, 1936.

Refers approvingly to the professionalization of the Foreign Service.

Mowrer, Paul Scott. *Our Foreign Affairs*. New York: Dutton, 1924.

A former Wilsonian journalist attacks amateur practitioners of foreign policy and approves of professional diplomats.

Nevins, Allan. *Henry White: Thirty Years of American Diplomacy*. New York: Harper and Brothers, 1930.

A good biography, very useful for reconstructing the quality of life in an American embassy.

Nicolson, Harold. *Diplomacy*. 3rd rev. ed. New York: Oxford University Press, 1963.

An English politician, writer, and former diplomat explains the vital role Old Diplomats played in the twentieth-century era of the New Diplomacy.

Niebuhr, Reinhold. *The Children of Light and the Children of Darkness*. New York: Charles Scribner's Sons, 1944.

A neo-orthodox expression of the tragic nature of human affairs and world politics. Profoundly influenced "realist" critics of foreign policy.

———— . *The Irony of American History*. New York: Charles Scribner's Sons, 1952.

Niebuhr recommends an active, "realistic" policy of confrontation with the Soviet Union in the 1950s.

Noble, David W. *The Progressive Mind, 1900-1917*. Chicago: Rand-McNally, 1970.

A good introduction to the domestic and international thought of progressives.

Oakeshott, Michael. *Rationalism in Politics*. London: Metheum, 1962.

A conservative English philosopher discusses the relations between technical and general knowledge in politics and reaches conclusions very similar to those of American Foreign Service officers.

Osgood, Robert E. *Ideals and Self-Interest in America's Foreign Relations: The Great Transformation of the Twentieth Century*. Chicago: University of Chicago Press, 1953.

An important "realistic" essay which criticizes American diplomats for neglecting the importance of power in international relations. Suggests that a "realist" has to amalgamate power and morality, but does not suggest how. Relies, in the end, on the grace of God.

Ordway, Samuel H., Jr. *Oral Tests in Public Personnel Selection*. Chicago: Civil Service Assembly of the United States and Canada, 1943.

Suggests that the shared assumptions of examiners were the most important determinants of success on oral examinations.

Perkins, Dexter. *Charles Evans Hughes and American Democratic Statesmanship*. Boston: Little, Brown, 1956.

Overestimates Hughes's responsibility for the Rogers Act.

Petrov, Vladimir. *A Study in Diplomacy: The Story of Arthur Bliss Lane*. Chicago: Henry Regnery, 1971.

A good biography by a writer sympathetic to Lane's conservative politics. Petrov is often able to criticize his subject's style if not his actions.

Poole, DeWitt Clinton. *The Conduct of Foreign Relations under Modern Democratic Conditions*. New Haven: Yale University Press, 1924.

Poole's lectures to the Williamstown Institute, which deny that the New Diplomacy would replace the Old Diplomats.

Pusey, Merlo J. *Charles Evans Hughes*. 2 vols. New York: Macmillan, 1951.

An unanalytic biography which gives Hughes too much credit for initiating the movement for Foreign Service reform.

Reinsch, Paul S. *American Legislatures and Legislative Methods*. New York: Century, 1907.

Presents Reinsch's faith in administrators and distrust of politicians.

———. *Colonial Administration*. New York: Macmillan, 1905.

Reinsch discusses the possibilities of trained overseas agents contributing to international harmony.

———. *Colonial Government: An Introduction to the Study of Colonial Institutions*. New York: Macmillan, 1902.

Explains the dangers and the hopes of the great power scramble for overseas possessions.

———. *Secret Diplomacy: How Far Can It Be Eliminated?* New York: Harcourt, Brace, 1922.

Reinsch's survey of postwar diplomatic practice, which concludes that trained experts were needed, whatever form negotiations took.

———. *World Politics at the End of the Nineteenth Century: As Influenced by the Oriental Situation*. New York: Macmillan, 1922.

Reinsch's doctoral dissertation, which brilliantly analyzes the implications of commercial rivalry in the Far East.

Republican National Committee. *Republican Campaign Textbook, 1920*. Washington: Republican National Committee, 1920.

Contains Lewis Einstein's attack on the Wilson administration for crippling the Foreign Service.

Satow, Sir Ernest. *A Guide to Diplomatic Practice*. 2 vols. London and New York: Longmans, Green, 1917.
  A standard manual of English practice which American diplomats greatly admired and simultaneously distrusted.
Schlesinger, Arthur M., Jr. *The Vital Center*. 2nd rev. ed. Boston: Houghton-Mifflin, 1962.
  A ''realist's'' plea for liberal politics in the post-World-War-II period, including the greater use of professional diplomats.
Schuyler, Eugene. *American Diplomacy and the Furtherance of Commerce*. New York: Charles Scribner's Sons, 1886.
  An early plea for a reformed consular service, often referred to at the Foreign Service School.
Seymour, Charles. *The Diplomatic Background of the World War*. New Haven: Yale University Press, 1919.
  A Wilsonian reviews the duplicity of dynastic diplomats.
_____. *Woodrow Wilson and the World War: A Chronicle of Our Own Times*. New Haven: Yale University Press, 1921.
  A sincere tribute to Wilson's high-mindedness and his intelligent exercise of diplomacy.
Stearns, Harold. *Liberalism in America: Its Origins, Its Temporary Collapse, Its Future*. New York: Boni & Liverwright, 1919.
  A liberal recounts his disillusionment with his support of the war and curses all professional diplomats.
Steiner, Zara S. *Present Problems of the Foreign Service*. Princeton: Center for International Studies, 1961.
  A student of the Foreign Service criticizes its members for snobbishly dismissing the need for technical training and technical experience in an era that demanded more skills than the political reporters of the old Foreign Service possessed.
Stewart, Frank M. *History of the National Civil Service Reform League*. Austin: University of Texas Press, 1929.
  A straightforward account of civil service reform from the Civil War to the 1920s.
Stowell, Ellery C. *International Law: A Restatement of Principles in Conformity with Actual Practice*. New York: Henry Holt, 1931.
  Represents two decades of Stowell's ''realistic'' approach to the law of nations and world politics.
Stuart, Graham H. *The Department of State*. New York: Appleton-Century, 1948.
  A diplomat's popular account of the development of his profession.
Symons, Farrel, ed. *Courses on International Affairs in American Colleges, 1930-1931*. Introduction by James T. Shotwell. Boston: World Peace Federation, 1931.
  Discusses international-relations courses as a means of eliminating irrational conflicts among states.
Trask, David F. *The United States in the Supreme War Council: American War Aims*

and Inter-Allied Strategy, 1917-1919. Middletown, Conn.: Wesleyan University Press, 1961.

A valuable monograph on an aspect of wartime diplomacy which reveals the subordinate role of the Department of State.

Tulchin, Joseph S. *The Aftermath of War: World War I and U.S. Policy toward Latin America*. New York: New York University Press, 1971.

A very useful discussion of the central role the Family of diplomats played in setting a commercial-strategic policy toward Latin America.

Tullock, Gordon. *The Politics of Bureaucracy*. Washington: Public Affairs Press, 1965.

A former diplomat, turned political scientist, expounds a witty and often penetrating theory of bureaucratic behavior. Many of the remarkably funny examples in the book came from Tullock's experience inside the Department of State.

Van Dyne, Frederick C. *Our Foreign Service: The "ABC" of American Diplomacy*. Rochester, N.Y.: The Lawyer's Co-operative Publishing Co., 1909.

A handbook for aspiring diplomats and consuls, especially illuminating in its derogatory comments about "Female Diplomatists."

Ware, Edith E., ed. *The Study of International Relations in the United States*. New York: Columbia University Press, 1934.

Reviews the growing "realism" of international studies since the twenties.

Webster, Sir Charles. *The Art and Practice of Diplomacy*. London: Chatto & Windus, 1961.

A British diplomatic historian expresses the need for serene generalists as diplomats.

White, Leonard D. *Introduction to the Study of Public Administration*. New York: Macmillan, 1926.

Refers to the Foreign Service as an emerging profession.

Williams, William Appleman. *The Roots of the Modern American Empire: A Study in the Growth and Shaping of Consciousness in a Marketplace Society*. New York: Random House, 1969.

A strong case for the "revisionist" notion that the desire to expand overseas commerce has dominated American thought since the eighteenth century.

_____. *The Tragedy of American Diplomacy*. 2nd rev. ed. New York: Delta Books, 1962.

An important book in post-World-War-II diplomatic history. Denies that the diplomats of the twenties were "isolationists," but underestimates the complexity of their thought.

Wilmerding, Lucius, Jr. *An Analysis of the Problem of Government Personnel*. New York: McGraw-Hill, 1935.

The Secretary of the Commission on Government Personnel reports how the Foreign Service had developed differently from any other government bureau.

Wilson, Hugh R. *Diplomacy as a Career*. Cambridge: Riverside Press, 1941.

Wilson's address to the students of Milton Academy, explaining that diplomacy could be learned through experience but could never be taught.

Index